Quality of governments, governance, civil societ[y] … critical role.

Countries and governments that did not focus on … results. Nations with weak leaders, ineffective civil … apathetic societies failed to rise to the occasion. USA lost its … longer seen as a world leader. Some nations passed with flying colours, some failed badly, and some are still finding their way. In this book, Devadas Krishnadas studies many countries and analysed the good and the bad of each. This is a useful reference for all to learn lessons for future incidences of similar disruptions, particularly being prepared for Disease X.

Based on extensive studies and analysis, Devadas has suggested a masterplan – a playbook of sorts – and recommendations that governments, societies, and all people should study carefully if we want to emerge stronger from not only COVID-19, but any future pandemic we will face. It is critical that all sectors of society and nations learn and be prepared for the new normal the world will see soon – a very different world that will shape how future generations live and govern the world.

Prof Inderjit Singh Dhaliwal
Entrepreneur and former Member of Parliament, Singapore (1996 to 2015)

In this Age of Uncertainty, nation states need to be very aware of the fast changing environment in order to prepare the required capacity in a timely manner to prevent and/or lessen the effects of these high impact driving forces, trends and events – especially with the example of a 'black swan' type of event like the COVID-19 pandemic, which is upon us and with no end in sight. Governments need to understand the future scenarios of new normals that will happen after COVID-19 and plan accordingly. This book is very relevant, providing information, insights and analysis about the challenges that are facing us today and will do in the future. Devadas suggests future scenarios, which can be the basis for understanding and for planning at global, regional and national levels. I would recommend that all analysts and strategists, as well as planners and CEOs, read this book.

General Jerdwut Kraprayoon
Special Advisor, Royal Thai Armed Forces;
Advisor to Senate Committee on Military and National Security

This book further cements Devadas Krishnadas's position as one of Singapore's most insightful business owners and public intellectuals. He captures very clearly the enormity of the economic, political and societal challenges faced by all countries as they respond to the pandemic's onslaught on public health and on their economies. He demonstrates how effective, selfless leadership at all levels providing clear, timely communication makes all the difference. He argues convincingly that our planet and species need the glue of multilateralism to make our interconnected and interdependent world function optimally and ensure its and our survival. Devadas's analysis makes for compelling and instructive reading because it is always insightful.

Victor Mills
Chief Executive, Singapore International Chamber of Commerce

This is an important and timely book. It lucidly makes the critical point that variance in the quality of governance explains the wide difference in COVID-19 outcomes evident around the world. The author has not pulled his sparkling intellectual punches on the challenges leaders everywhere now face in trying to address the institutional weaknesses exposed by the pandemic. Its consequences will be with us for decades to come, so the author's clear and practical guidance for surviving the crisis is a must-read for policymakers everywhere.

Max Everest-Phillips
Former Director of the UNDP's Global Centre for Public Service Excellence, Singapore

This book personifies Devadas Krishnadas – a man who is not only an intellectual heavyweight but someone who has also built a successful global business from the sweat of his brow. He is an authentic voice that will add to the conversation we need to have as a global community facing increasingly global challenges. *Confronting COVID-19* is a guidebook which gives anyone in a leadership position – or anyone aspiring to be in leadership – the tools to come out on top in what is the most systemic threat to the world since the Great Depression. A must-read.

Gerard L Pennefather
Chairman, Huntington Partners LLP

Devadas Krishnadas has – in his characteristic style – pointed out how COVID-19 has and still is affecting all segments of societies and economies across borders. This is by far one of the best attempts at making sense of the world in the aftermath of the pandemic. It is a meaningful read – not just for policymakers and corporate strategists – but for anyone seeking to understand and position themselves to cope with the changes that lie ahead.

Lee Kok Fatt
Chairman, Chandler Institute of Governance

COVID-19 is an unprecedented pandemic of the modern world, with repercussions affecting every country in unforeseen ways. This book, which is well-researched, well-written and easily understood, gives a comprehensive and in-depth analysis of the effects of the pandemic, as well as an honest review of the response by individuals, societies and governments. Readers are made aware of the broader consequences of the pandemic, which, as individuals, we are unable to fathom due to our limited exposure. Policymakers, key opinion leaders, economists, entrepreneurs and even students will benefit from the insights promulgated. As the COVID-19 situation is constantly evolving, the contents of the book will provide us a framework to build on so that global societies will come together in a concerted effort to aid all those affected, so that none are left behind.

Dr Steve Yang
Consultant Respiratory Physician and Intensivist, The Respiratory Practice, Singapore

Confronting COVID-19 takes a serious, systematic look beyond the political and personalities to the governance issues that will determine the effectiveness of the response to COVID-19, and the new future beyond. Devadas Krishnadas brings a unique and valuable perspective to bear, from his decades as a top public policy professional and strategist. With chapters considering macro- and micro-issues. as well as policy challenges and solutions, this book makes an important contribution to the discussion, and should be considered a 'must-read' for leaders across the public and private sectors.

Ian Herbison
Co-founder and Group CEO, Speyside Group

A highly relevant, timely, fact-filled work of great depth and scope about the worst pandemic in living memory. Carefully researched and filled with informative graphics and case studies, nothing is sugar-coated. As always, Devadas is willing to propose recommendations at global, regional, and national levels along with some ambitious "future-moves" focused on "structural changes that will permanently alter geopolitics, societal norms, international relations and the need for new mindsets." Required reading for all concerned citizens, leaders, and decision makers.

Bob Gattie
Advisory Board Member and Mentor

An impressively comprehensive and intelligent snapshot of how governments are coping with their biggest challenge of recent times, by one of the sharpest observers of global trends.

Prof Geoff Mulgan
Professor of Collective Intelligence, Public Policy and Social Innovation,
University College London; former CEO of Nesta and
former Director of UK Government Strategy Unit

This is a highly recommended read for students, policymakers, and anyone interested in the impact of infectious diseases on society, politics, and economies. Devadas Krishnadas has cleverly organised the discussion into bite-sized segments, allowing readers to easily navigate to sections of their specific interest. As an economist, I went straight to the parts on economic policy and the author's global growth forecast model. I believe that long after COVID-19 finally leaves us, and when leaders sit down to prepare for future pandemics, they should start by reading *Confronting COVID-19: A Strategic Playbook for Leaders and Decision Makers.*

Francis Tan
Investment Strategist, UOB Private Bank

Devadas Krishnadas has the rare courage that comes from deep thinking, experience and intuition. The rigour of the analysis in this essential book is stunning, but that's not the endgame. Devadas connects all the dots and designs a new framework for a new post-Covid world, equipping businesses and policymakers with a reliable compass. But more than anything else, this book is a call to leadership – as real as it gets.

Andrea Isaia
Global Talent Manager of a Multinational Chemical Group

A true Singaporean, Devadas Krishnadas is a pragmatist. This book does away with the ubiquity and imprecision that has plagued the concept of governance and offers a utilitarian framework to resolve one of the world's most potent 'wicked problems' – COVID-19.

Greg Lopez
Murdoch University Executive Education Centre, Perth

This book is short enough to be digestible but huge in its scope and depth of analysis into the COVID-19 crisis. It offers a worldwide panoramic view of the situation with pre-COVID-19 context, current situational analysis and sober forward projections. At the same time, the author provides a mass of microscopic insights into the particular pandemic experiences of nations and regions. The book offers plain language, clear logic and a wealth of data, supported by easily assimilated graphics.

Krishnadas arrives at some sobering conclusions, presented as three scenarios. He gives a cautiously optimistic most-likely outcome, predicated on the need for nations and individuals to return to collaboration across borders for the sake of the future world.

I found the book not just a worthy "strategic playbook for leaders and decision makers" – as its subtitle claims – but also a valuable potential source of opinions and data, which can be accessed at any desired level by influencers, policymakers and, indeed, by any serious commentator on world affairs.

Iain Martin
Board Chair, C-Suite Advisor, and Author on Global Leadership
www.ijmartin.com

Devadas Krishnadas' insightful *Confronting COVID-19* is an important contribution to the study of the public policy response to the public health emergency. The comparative approach adopted recognises the contexts, capabilities, and constraints unique to each jurisdiction in tackling COVID-19, which has unleashed tremendous and unprecedented economic, political, and social challenges.

There may perhaps not be a single playbook in dealing with pandemics but *Confronting COVID-19* demonstrates the imperative of a coherent strategy that embraces a multi-stakeholder approach at the domestic and international level. It will add to the body of expert knowledge that is so vital if we are not to waste the COVID-19 crisis.

This timely work can help us be better prepared for "Disease X", a serious international epidemic caused by a currently unknown pathogen. COVID-19 may well be the "dress rehearsal" for Disease X. There is no time to waste, as Devadas Krishnadas emphasises.

Early cross-cutting whole-of-society preparedness is our insurance and assurance that we not only come out better but also emphasises the urgent need to remake the world to be more resilient, collaborative, and one that recognises the humanistic ethos and endeavour that must be at the heart of humanity's response to the ravages of a deadly crisis.

Eugene Tan
Associate Professor of Law, Singapore Management University

Devadas Krishnadas

CONFRONTING COVID-19

A Strategic Playbook for Leaders and Decision Makers

Marshall Cavendish Editions

Published in 2020 by Marshall Cavendish Editions
An imprint of Marshall Cavendish International

A member of the
Times Publishing Group

Other Marshall Cavendish Offices:
Marshall Cavendish Corporation, 800 Westchester Ave, Suite N-641, Rye Brook, NY 10573, USA • Marshall Cavendish International (Thailand) Co Ltd, 253 Asoke, 16th Floor, Sukhumvit 21 Road, Klongtoey Nua, Wattana, Bangkok 10110, Thailand • Marshall Cavendish (Malaysia) Sdn Bhd, Times Subang, Lot 46, Subang Hi-Tech Industrial Park, Batu Tiga, 40000 Shah Alam, Selangor Darul Ehsan, Malaysia

National Library Board Singapore Cataloguing-in-Publication Data

Name(s): Krishnadas, Devadas.
Title: Confronting COVID-19 : a strategic playbook for leaders and decision makers / Devadas Krishnadas.
Description: Singapore : Marshall Cavendish Editions, 2020.
Identifier(s): OCN 1198018763 | ISBN 978-981-49-2828-1 (paperback)
Subject(s): LCSH: COVID-19 (Disease)--Government policy. | COVID-19 (Disease)--Prevention. | COVID-19 (Disease)--Epidemiology. | Epidemics --Government policy. | Epidemics--Prevention.
Classification: DDC 614.592--dc23

Printed in Singapore

To my dear friends, Mr and Mrs Victor Mills – "KBO"

Let us not be blind to our differences – but let us also direct attention to our common interests and to the means by which those differences can be resolved. And if we cannot end now our differences, at least we can help make the world safe for diversity. For, in the final analysis, our most basic common link is that we all inhabit this small planet. We all breathe the same air. We all cherish our children's future. And we are all mortal.

President John F. Kennedy
Commencement Address at American University, Washington DC (10 June 1963)

CONTENTS

FOREWORD

During US President Richard Nixon's path-breaking visit to the People's Republic of China in 1972, his principal host, Premier Zhou Enlai, was asked about the influence of the French Revolution. He famously replied: "Too early to say." Only decades later did we learn from interpreters on the scene that Zhou's tentative assessment was *not* about July 1789 and the demise of an *Ancien Régime* personified by Louis XVI. He was almost certainly thinking instead about May 1968 and the series of student revolts, strikes, civil unrest, and political paralysis leading to the demise of *le Général* and, perhaps, his Fifth Republic. Humorous wit about settled events in the distant past turned out to humble wisdom about events in the recent past still unfolding in the present.

Zhou's comment could easily apply to Devadas Krishnadas and his new book, *Confronting COVID-19*. In it, Krishnadas assesses the "history" of the COVID-19 pandemic less than a year after its emergence in Wuhan, China; fewer than seven months after it prompted national lockdowns across the globe; only four weeks before US voters judge the (in)effectiveness of policy responses to it in a presidential election; and only-God-knows how long before safe and effective therapeutics and vaccines arrive in force to mitigate its lethal impact.

There is so much that may be too early to say about this pandemic, its immediate impact on global public health, and its deeper economic, political, and social implications. In that context, it may seem audaciously premature to propose concrete near- and longer-term policy prescriptions for individual countries and international institutions connecting them. The academic in me would voice caution about whether even to hazard such a narrative let alone propose policies for shifting that narrative's future course.

Luckily, Krishnadas, is *not* listening to the same voice. Leaders in business, government, and civil society need accurate information, evidence-based advice, and practical guidance in real time to confront a clear and present danger that we do not and cannot understand comprehensively today. *Confronting COVID-19* does just that. The data explaining current pandemic trends are recent, reliable, replicable. The advice is grounded in commentary from acknowledged experts and in cleverly-presented descriptive statistics often conveying non-intuitive near-term trends. The policy guidance reflects a discernible theoretical logic attractive to academics and a practical "feel" attractive to politicians and their constituents. For business executives, government ministers and international organisation leaders, ambiguity and uncertainty in strategic decision-making are ineluctable. They go with the job. Krishnadas's book makes that job so much easier in the case of COVID-19 and its multi-dimensional implications.

Let me give you two examples from two experts profiled in the book. One is obvious. Any narrative about the emergence and spread of COVID-19 will feature the World Health Organization's Director General Tedros Adhanom Ghebreyesus. If there is one indispensable player in the public health response to this pandemic, he is it. In the past year, Ghebreyesus has been best positioned to inform, activate, and orchestrate collective international responses ranging from health inspections, to testing, implementation of different mitigating behaviors like social distancing, and coordination of national research efforts to develop and diffuse therapeutics and vaccines.

The narrative in *Confronting COVID-19* provides an even-handed judgment of Ghebreyesus's performance to date. He merits commendation for enlisting Japan, Germany, Norway, and several other wealthy industrialised countries in the COVID-19 Vaccine Global Access Facility (COVAX) – an initiative to pool resources in vaccine development. He also merits criticism for failing to enlist other countries like China and Russia. Indeed, Ghebreyesus let himself become an election-year punching bag for a Trump Administration looking to blame rather than befriend international organisations. Krishnadas conveys the facts, renders judgments, and points out lessons for leaders and decision makers.

Another name in *Confronting COVID-19* is less obvious, but still worth close study. Eric Rosengren is an accomplished financial economist and President of the US Federal Reserve Bank in Boston. Rosengren's academic and policy credentials position him as an opinion leader about how the US should sequence public health and economic policy responses to the pandemic. His opinion makes causal sense. The current downturn in economic growth and employment follows from a public health crisis, not vice versa. Investing in public health today – ventilators, personal protective equipment, Internet access, mandates to wash hands, wear masks, keep social distance – increase rather than undermine economic growth and employment tomorrow.

It is hard for many outside the US to understand why such reasoning would be controversial, why such policies would attract opposition. But walk a mile in Rosengren's shoes – he competes for media attention with others seeking to shift responsibility (and blame) for a botched US federal government public health response to state and local government politicians. Washington's illogical response to Rosengren's logic has included billions of US dollars in tax cuts and trillions of US dollars in subsidised grants and loans to individuals and businesses.

For this opposition, massive economic stimulus somehow leads to public health progress. It doesn't. And most of Rosengren's opponents know it. They are just trying to temporarily mislead American voters on their way to the voting booth. The ploy seems destined for failure. Massive economic stimulus cannot even improve public health precautions in the White House where President Trump has recently been laid low by the virus. We need more voices like Rosengren's. *Confronting COVID-19* explains why for leaders and decision makers around the world.

There are so many incisive points in this book. Let me note one here about the importance of public governance. I define the term as how a polity assures members of fair return on whatever they contribute:

how a mayor assures adequate public safety, education, transportation to local taxpayers; how an industry regulator assures an adequate return on investment to a telecommunications enterprise providing universal service to remote, rural regions of the country; how a health minister assures timely reimbursement to hospitals treating COVID-19 patients out of a job and the health insurance that job used to provide. For Krishnadas, public governance quality is the single most important factor explaining variation in country performance since viral infections fanned out from China in early 2020. It is the single most important factor to invest in and strengthen as we learn how to control and, in due course, suppress and eradicate the virus in 2021-2022.

Governance knows no single political system. It does not intrinsically favor more electorally-competitive democracies like the UK or Spain over more authoritarian systems with one dominant party like Russia of China. It does not intrinsically favor centralised unitary systems such as in France or Japan over federal systems such as in Germany or Canada. And it does not intrinsically favour great wealth and technology as in the US. Public governance can flourish or founder in any of these contexts. Krishnadas tells us how not to flounder and, perhaps, how to flourish in a world with COVID-19. Leaders should take note.

As I conclude this foreword, I cannot resist responding to Krishnadas's prediction of an end to US economic and political leadership globally:

> "[I]n the post-Covid world, nations will no longer look towards the United States for leadership, reversing a dynamic that has been in place for more than a century. Indeed, they are likely to consider the United States as a threat, or at least a risk, they have to consider when deciding how best to respond to any regional or global threat of any nature."

Heady stuff. And not without some substantial justification given Trump Administration policies critical of most international alliances, most institutions, and well, most nations. But remember that all important factor, public governance. It explains differences in country performance in the current COVID-19 pandemic. It also explains how countries alter efforts when performance is poor. In just a few weeks, Americans will have an opportunity to change politicians and policies responsible for that poor performance. If current polls are any indication, then the US may soon be positioned to change the negative view so many other nations currently have. The US may soon be positioned to retake the leadership role it has played for nearly a century. The US may soon be positioned to use that leadership to champion more political and economic openness within other countries, more mutual assistance financially and otherwise between countries.

Will that happen? As Zhou said in 1972, it is too early to say. Ask me again in a few months. Meanwhile, enjoy reading this terrific book.

Paul M. Vaaler
Professor and John and Bruce Mooty Chair in Law & Business,
Law School & Carlson School of Management,
University of Minnesota

October 2020

PREFACE

Dear Reader,

The objective of this book is to frame an understanding of COVID-19 at the global, regional and local levels. Taking an evidence-based approach to the analysis, I identify insights and make actionable recommendations relevant to a wide number of people, particularly leaders and decision-makers operating within the political and public sectors, corporate entities, community organisations, international organisations and Non-Governmental Organisations (NGOs).

COVID-19 is the most challenging crisis the world has faced for almost a century. This is for a range of reasons:

First, it is a global pandemic, not a localised one, so no one individual or country is immune from the impacts of the virus.

Second, policy responses and public infrastructure and readiness are very uneven from country to country. This is further complicated by the fact that neither are these two things correlated. In other words, countries with reasonably developed public infrastructure can have belated, uneven, and misguided policy responses.

Third, to contain the spread of the virus, international travel has dramatically reduced. While this has created serious operational and financial consequences for the aviation industry, there will be long-tail ripple effects through the supply chain, and secondary effects on hospitality and the food and beverage sectors in most countries. It also limits the crossflow of human capital to take up opportunities cross-nationally, which makes it difficult to ascertain the long-tail effects on economic performance.

Fourth, the pandemic is having a severe general economic impact, with rising levels of unemployment and underemployment, and falling levels of investment. This 'scissors' phenomenon is likely to be sustained throughout the remainder of 2020 and well into 2021. Again, there will be long-tail effects but, importantly, they will also have social and political consequences. Consumption will fall, thus depressing final demand, which will impact supplying and entrepot economies, as well as air, sea and land transport sectors.

Fifth, the economic impacts will translate into financial stress, both in international capital markets and trade credit, making the financial stability of banks and the financial institutions more vulnerable to non-performing loans. Financing fiscal policy interventions will also add to public debt in many countries, several of which already have debt overhangs. Again, this will have long-tail effects.

Sixth, there will be a combination of sustained uncertainty and the prospect of transformative opportunities in how people work and firms organise themselves is likely to accelerate the adoption of artificial intelligence and digitalisation. This may lead to labour substitution, inadvertently creating employment displacement that could become structural and create higher barriers of entry into the workforce.

Seventh, a global leadership vacuum created by an "America First" United States and its active attempts to undermine international organisations – most notably the World Health Organization (WHO) – will frustrate and complicate the inter-government coordination necessary to best manage the multi-dimensional challenges. This, paralleled by the protectionism and anti-China doctrine adopted by the administration of President Donald Trump, creates greater uncertainty as it leads to a "decoupling" between the world's two largest economies.

The COVID-19 story is a fast-moving goal post that veers off in multiple directions. This is not helped by unpredictable political developments such as the imminent 2020 US Presidential Election. Nevertheless, this book highlights positive developments and important lessons which should be noted.

COVID-19 is the first – but unlikely to be the last – pandemic of the 21st century. Learning and adapting from its lessons will be critical for countries and their economies to be better prepared for future challenges. Perhaps the most important insight within these pages is the importance of the role of governance – its quality and its definition. 'Governance', by right, should be limited to governments, but I take a broader interpretation to include expert communities, the private sector, local, regional, and international NGOs, and community-based action groups.

*

The book has been organised into four sections, comprising nine meaningfully interlinked parts.

Section I frames the COVID-19 pandemic by categorically identifying variables and factors central to understanding how COVID-19 has panned out. In this important first step, the central vector of governance will be delineated, which will crucially guide subsequent in-depth analysis.

Section II follows with an examination of the pandemic in the realms of politics, public health and economics, using both cutting-edge qualitative and quantitative analysis.

Section III then performs in-depth country case studies, while also forecasting the future of global growth, and delineating possible futures for the world. Recommendations are also given, based on the best scientific evidence and on all the foregoing rigorous, fact-based analysis of the coronavirus pandemic.

Finally, **Section IV** looks beyond the immediate imperatives and impacts of the ongoing pandemic to the 'post-Covid' world and posits what major structural changes will define it permanently.

Further explanation of each section is provided in the Summary.

*

It will take many hands to bring the pandemic under control and time will be needed to recover public health, trade, economic growth and public trust in governments.

Given that this book goes beyond rigorous analyses and projections to the provision of actionable recommendations, this book will prove useful to leaders and decision-makers in:

- Government: from the Cabinet down through practically every public agency
- International organisations: such as the WHO, International Monetary Fund (IMF) and World Bank
- International aid organisations, such as the Red Cross and Médecins Sans Frontières
- NGOs
- Multinational corporations
- Insurance sectors and public health consortiums, such as COVAX

Ultimately, this is a book for both general readers and policymakers. It is not concerned with theories but with hard truths.

As the reader will see, the central truth this book reveals is that the quality of governance – at the local, national, international and global levels – is the primary independent variable that determines success or failure when confronting existential challenges.

And in the case of a pandemic where success or failure is measured in terms of the number of people left dead, jobs lost, businesses destroyed and futures compromised – quality of governance has never been more crucial.

I hope this book helps to not only promote good governance but nudges governments towards a more collective, collaborative and cooperative world. If it can shift policymakers even an inch in that direction it has more than succeeded.

Devadas Krishnadas
Singapore, October 2020

SUMMARY

In 2020, the COVID-19 pandemic has disrupted life as we know it. It has closed national borders, overwhelmed healthcare systems, shrunk economies, and created significant hardships for many people around the world. Yet these disruptions are also forcing us to re-examine assumptions about what our political, social, and economic compacts can look like.

How can we ensure that the world we reconstruct in the wake of the devastation wrought by the virus is one that is stronger, better, and more sustainable?

This book looks at just that, by examining:

(i) how the pandemic has disrupted the world, politically, economically and in other ways;

(ii) how various countries such as the United States, China, Sweden, Singapore and New Zealand have responded to the crisis; and

(iii) what policies will, on the evidence, help build a better world.

*

While comparisons have been made with the 2003 SARS (Severe Acute Respiratory Syndrome) epidemic, there are noticeable differences.

First, unlike SARS, COVID-19 is capable of spreading through asymptomatic individuals, and the inability for countries to control the outbreak has resulted in the most extreme of measures, including placing 20 percent of the world's population on lockdown as well as ravaging entire sectors such as tourism, airline and retail.

Second, America under the Donald Trump administration is hostile to internationalism and is failing to provide leadership and cooperation in the global effort to control the pandemic effectively.

Third, China, the original epicentre of the outbreak, now contributes 16.3 percent of global economic output, which is quadruple the amount –

about 4 percent – of what it was during the SARS epidemic.

Due to the impact on entire populations, the economic impact of COVID-19 is expected to be severe and sustained for a multi-year period. The World Bank predicts that the share of countries experiencing contractions in GDP per capita will reach the highest level since 1870.[1] The IMF forecasts a 4.9 percent contraction in global GDP in 2020 as productivity and supply chains continue to suffer losses.[2]

A protracted recession in the global economy is expected, as the economic fallout of the pandemic and its recovery process prolong diminished economic activity and leads to a compounding of issues in other areas.

Increased unemployment and the psychological impact of weathering the pandemic will affect societal cohesion and breed anxieties, while the increased dependence on technology-based solutions to problems arising from the pandemic has exposed populations to risks of cybersecurity breaches and privacy violation.

Prior global underperformance in imposing environmental laws and safeguards will suffer further setbacks in the face of the coronavirus pandemic, manifested in a reduction in climate investment and possible withdrawals from previous commitments.

Overall, as the pandemic progresses, countries will see significant shifts to their political, economic, societal, technological and environmental landscapes. These will evolve in novel ways and exacerbate associated risks.

However, the severity of impacts will vary by country and region, depending on the initial conditions of public health, quality of governance, and the rapidity and comprehensiveness of each country's precautionary responses to COVID-19.

*

This book culminates with three key takeaways, which constitute core questions for policymakers at the state level and where multilateral unity is concerned:

Governance matters

At the core, this book demonstrates that governance is the foundational constituent that feeds into both successes and failures of the global response to the coronavirus pandemic. COVID-19 has exposed two key levels of flaws in governance: a) the existence of foundational, structural weaknesses within governmental systems; and b) the inability to react with immediacy and efficacy in the face of an emergency.

Navigating heightened demand for public health resources and contending with strained economies requires not only robust and transparent public systems but leadership that is advanced with accountability and resilience.

In larger countries, government at the state and local levels are crucial to decision-making and implementation, whereas in the international sphere, non-state leaders – most notably the international organisations – are central to global cooperation.

Global cooperation

Existing international institutions lack the mandate to act decisively in global health crises and are undermined internal governance issues.

The impact of COVID-19 means multilateralism has become especially crucial in a world that currently lacks leadership, and should compel states to cooperate regionally and globally with urgency. This will be crucial to mitigate the ripple effects of global repercussions and to recover as a collective.

This book highlights innovative measures and platforms for international coordination in the coronavirus pandemic that stand in contrast to episodes like the H1N1 or H5N1 influenza pandemics. In particular, I address the rejuvenated role of non-state entities that have devised methods to collaborate with governments and fill the gaps in country-led leadership at the international scale.

Guided action

The pandemic has situated the world in a period of uncertainty, in which developments in the areas of public health, economy and social life are both accelerated and highly complex.

Responding to COVID-19 has made it necessary for governments to work iteratively, seek improvement in actions in the domestic sphere and look outward to learn from experiences of other countries and the wider global scientific community.

Action should be guided and pragmatic to create new solutions and emerge stronger at the eventual easing of the pandemic, not merely return to the status quo before the crisis.

*

This book has been organised into nine main parts:

Part A begins with an outline of the method for which subsequent analysis is framed, based on the core independent variable of governance and key pre-determined elements and critical uncertainties that explain the variation in the way countries respond at the national and international levels.

Parts B and C provide core evidence on the effects of COVID-19 on politics and economic policy. This will demonstrate the areas that require attention given the repercussions that the pandemic has brought.

Part D presents analysis of the prevalence of COVID-19 cases, healthcare resource capability and governmental effectiveness. This statistical analysis offers perspective on country responses to the pandemic, grouped by regions, to gain insight on regional similarities and differences in suppressing the pandemic.

Part E continues the analysis by examining country case studies, and highlighting variations in response effectiveness and subsequent severity of COVID-19 outbreaks. The seven countries selected display unique characteristics in experiences with COVID-19, and offer lessons for the world going forward.

In **Part F**, I forecast the long-term economic consequences of COVID-19. My forecast is on the pessimistic side, informed as it is by a cautious projection of when a vaccine will become available, and by an understanding that COVID-19 can potentially ignite further crises on the political, geopolitical, economic, financial and social fronts.

Part G examines the response of the international community as a whole, by mapping out three core scenarios to global order. The degree of international cooperation – on top of individual countries' quality of governance and the interaction between elements of pre-determinants and critical uncertainties – will produce distinct scenarios at the global level.

Then, in **Part H,** recommendations for actionable steps guided by evidence will be provided. At the global, regional and local levels, general and specific courses of action are detailed to provide a plan for combatting COVID-19 as circumstances continue to evolve.

Finally, in **Part I**, I look at the world as we can expect to be after the storm passes, and the pandemic is finally controlled – the challenges that remain, and the opportunities that must be seized.

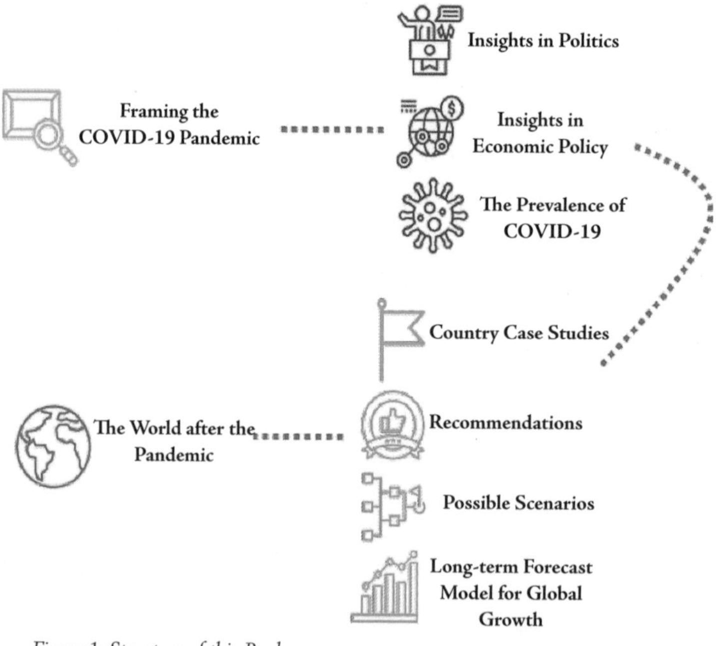

Figure 1: Structure of this Book

This is the sixth time a global health emergency has been declared under the International Health Regulations, but it is easily the most severe. COVID-19 has changed our world. It has brought people, communities and nations together, and driven them apart.

But although our world has changed, the fundamental pillars of the response have not: political leadership, and informing, engaging and listening to communities. And nor have the basic measures needed to suppress transmission and save lives: find, isolate, test and care for cases; and trace and quarantine their contacts.

Keep your distance from others, clean your hands, avoid crowded and enclosed areas, and wear a mask where recommended.

Where these measures are followed, cases go down. Where they're not, cases go up. Countries and communities that have followed this advice carefully and consistently have done well, either in preventing large-scale outbreaks – like Cambodia, New Zealand, Rwanda, Thailand, Vietnam, and islands in the Pacific and Caribbean – or in bringing large outbreaks under control – like Canada, China, Germany and the Republic of Korea.

The bottom line is that one of the most fundamental ingredients for stopping this virus is determination, and the willingness to make hard choices to keep ourselves and each other safe.

Dr Tedros Adhanom Ghebreyesus
Director General of the WHO
27th July 2020

SECTION I:
INTRODUCTION

This book begins with an outline of key variables that determine national, regional and global outcomes in the battle against COVID-19. Understanding how countries, wider regional spheres and the world have responded to the crisis first requires defining the parameters on which responses have been based. By analysing the diverse country cases and taking a broad examination of COVID-19, this section covers my diagnosis of the situation at hand, distilled into key driving factors, pre-determinants and elements of uncertainty.

Part A: Framing the COVID-19 Pandemic

Framing the method by which we understand COVID-19 is essential to the progress of this book. Factors are organised according to the key independent variable of governance and supporting elements of pre-determinants and critical uncertainties. On examination of country case studies and predicted scenarios of international order, I find that variation across cases and scenarios are a result of the interaction between pre-determinants, critical uncertainties and governance effectiveness.

- Based on the experiences of countries handling the pandemic; robust, accountable and adaptable governance constitutes the primary deciding factor for success or failure.
- A multitude of pre-determinant and critical uncertainty factors affect outcomes in a public health emergency. This book has distilled factors that are highly instrumental in the case of COVID-19, and which form the basis for country-level disparity in outcomes that are further demonstrated in Part E.
- As a public health crisis perpetuating economic, social and technological ramifications, the path to recovery should be grounded by a plan to strengthen healthcare. A dual-pillar path to tackle the immediate public health requirements of population testing and vaccine development will concentrate the efforts of countries, regions and the world towards a common aim.

QUALITY OF GOVERNANCE IS KEY

Originating from Wuhan, China, in December 2019, the COVID-19 pandemic refers to the highly virulent and deadly Severe Acute Respiratory Syndrome Coronavirus 2 (SARS-CoV-2) and has – as of the end of September 2020 – infected at least 33 million people[3] and killed more than 1 million individuals.[4] On average, one person dies every 15 seconds as a result of the pandemic,[5] and the World Health Organization (WHO) has warned that total deaths might rise to 2 million before the pandemic is finally brought under control.

This book examines the successes and failures of governance in the face of COVID-19. "Governance", in my interpretation, meaning a combination of political leadership, civil society and state institutions, which together determine the outcomes of a country's reaction to the coronavirus pandemic.

It would be a mistake to attribute the divergence witnessed in country-level responses merely to the quality of incumbent leaders alone, just as it would be equally short-sighted to regard the development of a vaccine as the end-point to the pandemic.

Moving forward, even if there exists intensive multilateral cooperation and a widely-available and effective vaccine materialises, weak governance can and will nullify these positive factors.

Where governance is weak, a country's handling of the pandemic is likely to remain vastly inadequate even in the face of external factors that act to bolster the efficacy of its response.

It is the quality of governance that I am interested in as the independent variable in this assessment. Quality of governance has two aspects: (1) the quality of government leaders, policies and institutions themselves; but also (2) broader quality of civil society, and the ability and willingness of citizens, businesses, academics and non-governmental organisations to contribute and make a difference.

Quality of Government Leaders, Policies and Institutions

As this book will show, effective leadership, evidence-based policies and well-designed institutions that facilitate a speedy and coordinated response as all crucial in combating the pandemic and its consequences.

Where there has been a failure in leadership, and a failure to adopt evidence-based policies, however, the results can be catastrophic.

In this respect, the fact that certain countries have been gone for a "herd immunity" approach provides an illustrative case study. Under such an approach, the government intentionally allows a large number of healthy people to contract and recover from the virus.

With the antibodies their immune systems would have produced, these individuals will then be immune to further infections, and this will protect more vulnerable individuals such as the elderly or those with pre-existing medical conditions.

The temptation to adopt such a strategy is obvious – it would, in theory, allow the pandemic to be curtailed without lockdowns or much economic pain. Such an approach, however, is extremely dangerous.

For one, it will require an immense death toll – given that around 60 percent to 80 percent of the population would need to have the necessary antibodies for herd immunity to be achieved,[6] and given that COVID-19's infection fatality ratio is around 0.5 percent to 1 percent.[7]

The result of the world adopting a herd immunity strategy would be anything from around 23 million to 62 million people – a truly immense death toll, *even under the best-case scenario*. And indeed, in countries like Sweden where herd immunity has been attempted, the death toll per capita has been far higher than in neighbours.

Secondly, the strategy may not even be guaranteed to work; in Sweden, less than 10 percent of Swedes carrying antibodies – a population immunity ratio that falls far short of what is required to sustain herd immunity[0].

As the executive director of WHO's Health Emergencies Program Mike Ryan has warned, "I think what we can say with certainty is, right now, as a planet, as a global population, we are nowhere close to the levels of immunity required to stop this disease transmitting. And we need to focus on what we can actually do now to suppress transmission and not live in the hope of herd immunity being our salvation. Right now, that is not a solution."

Thirdly, even healthy people who will go on to recover from the virus can experience severe symptoms such as seizures for the duration of the infection.[9] Recovery can also be accompanied by long-term organ damage.

A study from Germany showed that 78 of 100 mostly young and previously healthy patients who recovered from COVID-19 nonetheless had heart abnormalities afterwards.[10] In China, a study of more than 400 patients in Wuhan found that 20 percent of patients had heart damage during hospitalization.[11]

Given the severe economic and social impacts of imposing 'lock downs' and costs and institutional strain on public health systems of mass testing It is understandable why countries are tempted to attempt herd immunity.

This is where good governance becomes more vital than ever – policymakers must avoid motivated reasoning and instead pay attention to the evidence if they are to guide the world out of its current crisis.

Quality of Civil Society

However, *governance* is not the same as *government*, and civil society too plays an important role in formulating and executing the necessary strategies and steps needed to bring the world out of its current crisis.

Naturally, academics and experts play a vital role in producing research to inform effective, evidence-based policymaking in the first place.

They also serve as critical, outsider voices to keep government policymakers honest; indeed, it was external scientists and doctors that first raised the alarm against attempts in Sweden and the UK to go for herd immunity as a strategy.

Citizens more broadly, meanwhile, also play a vital role, as their cooperation is needed in putting into action the policies – such as social distancing – that are costly and inconvenient but ultimately necessary for fighting the pandemic.

In the United States, where there is a long-standing distrust of government, it has been difficult to get the populace at large to conform to shelter-in-place orders or mask wearing.

In contrast, and as other analysts like Andrew Sheng and Xiao Geng have noted, East Asia has kept infections and deaths under control, because a cooperative society aided the government in carrying the out the necessary public health policies: *"In every case, the government intervened early, devised comprehensive rules and guidance, and provided the resources needed to apply relevant measures. And in every case, society was receptive to government intervention aimed at advancing the common good."*

Quality of Governance is Critical

Ultimately, it is competence in leadership, public trust and confidence in government, as well as the robustness of policy, effective communication both within an administration and between leaders and citizens, which will form the basis for an evidence-based approach to mount a successful response to COVID-19.

Managing COVID-19 in any country is not centrally a clinical challenge; it is a test of governance. And governance not only in the present day but historically, as public health infrastructure and capacity, effective public administration, public finance adequacy and an educated population are the result of generations of good governance. Yet the good work of generations can be ruined by poor governance in a much shorter period.

Good governance is not only about good government, but when leadership in the civic and economic sectors work together in concert rather than in contention with each other. Vaccine or no vaccine, the quality of governance is the difference between life and death for many in every population.

Devadas Krishnadas

There is a role for Singapore that I see accentuated in the post-COVID world, because trust and reliability, as attributes of a regional or global headquarter location, are going to be fundamental.

Tharman Shanmugaratnam
Senior Minister of Singapore

PRE-DETERMINANTS

Pre-determinant variables are fixed and predictable factors in a situation of uncertainty such as COVID-19, which contribute to variances in country responses. Key pre-determinants such as (i) country demography, size and location, (ii) existing status of political and public health systems, and (iii) the extent of private sector mobilisation will be evaluated here.

Demography, Size and Location

COVID-19 has called for containment measures of quarantine, border lockdown and social distancing, all of which are generally simpler to implement and enforce in countries of smaller size.

Demography is instrumental in the spread of the virus and, ultimately, death rates. Italy with a large vulnerable elderly population, coupled with the norm of inter-generational interaction and co-residence, has seen remarkably high mortality rates in older age groups, despite the country's well-performing health and wealth status. Countries effecting response protocols should factor into account broader variables that interact with population demographics, such as variations in socio-economic status, race and ethnicity, and urban-rural divide.

Existing State of Political and Public Health Systems

COVID-19 has exposed the need for a swift and decisive government response, yet the efficacy of reaction is contingent on the existing and rooted states of political and health systems, not merely on the quality of leadership to navigate a country through the pandemic.

Generally, countries of weak democracy challenged by populist movements and societal divide, where poor health provision and implementation of containment measures are further impeded by diffused federal systems, are deeply challenged to mount a successful COVID-19 response.

Extent of Private Sector Mobilisation

Support derived from private sector players contribute critically to the COVID-19 situation both within countries and on the international sphere, as governments are fundamentally limited to contend with far-ranging effects of economic and social fall-out, independent of other partnerships.

Foundations of public-private coordination ideally should aim to support multilateral agreements such as the United Nations Sustainable Development Goals.

Domestically, a favourable environment of public-private synergy means that private hospitals, healthcare providers and firms can be mobilised at short notice to improve policy capacity which would be critical as a 'surge factor' to boost capacity and expertise to scale responses adequately to cope with a pandemic.

Figure 2: United Nations Sustainable Development Goals (Source: United Nations)

CRITICAL UNCERTAINTIES

Critical uncertainties are defined as issues whose impacts or outcomes are unclear and dependent on evolving international and domestic circumstances. The critical uncertainties in this context are identified as (i) the progress in vaccine development, (ii) any occurrence of political elections and the state of national leadership, and (iii) the state of international cooperation.

Vaccine Development and Distribution

In line with predictions by Gavi, the Vaccine Alliance, and governments across the world in consultation with scientific communities, I assume that a vaccine will meet the expectations of being available in the next 12 to 18 months.

While breakthrough advancements in human trials show potential – including Oxford University's AstraZeneca and the work of American biotechnology company Moderna – the expedited vaccine development process and subsequent possible difficulties in the global distribution process continue to shroud the goal of a licensed and efficacious vaccine. Even in this promising example, in September 2020, testing was halted due to a patient in the study falling seriously ill. This illustrates the risk in accelerating drug development.

And we need to be fair about this, because this is a global good. Vaccines for this pandemic are not for the wealthy, they are not for the poor, they are for everybody.

Dr Mike Ryan
Executive Director of the WHO's Health Emergencies Programme
22nd July 2020

Elections and Political Leadership

Holding elections during the coronavirus pandemic can entail a change in political leadership. Questioning leadership legitimacy when countries are urgently battling the virus coronavirus can also pose a direct risk to public health safety through gatherings during campaigning and rallies. Yet, the success or failure in handling the crisis can determine the political futures of national leaders.

For example, in the US, polls unsurprisingly reveal the coronavirus pandemic as one of the nation's most prominent problems. President Trump's botched handling of the situation and aversion to talking about the subject is driving further voter disapproval.

The pandemic has placed the imminent elections in uncharted waters and a possible second wave of the pandemic could even hit close to the scheduled November 2020 election. The pandemic interferes with President Trump's re-election plans, and the resulting outcome of the election will further cause shifts in the US pandemic response.

In contrast, New Zealand has a different story to tell. Support for Prime Minister Jacinda Ardern's Labour Party rose to 56.5 percent in May 2020, up by a remarkable 16.5 percent since January 2020.[1]

The main opposition, the National Party, polled at a mere 25.1 percent popularity in July, while the governing coalition partners, New Zealand First and the Green Party, also polled poorly, indicating a possibility of ejection from Parliament at the next elections.[2] Prime Minister Ardern's direction in responding and coping with the pandemic has received widespread admiration, and this success arguably contributes to positive voter sentiment on Ardern's leadership.

> *To me, leadership is not about being the loudest in the room.*
>
> **Jacinda Ardern**
> *Prime Minister of New Zealand*

International and Regional Cooperation

The coronavirus pandemic is global, and transmission of the virus is not limited to geographical boundaries. Achieving common success in containing COVID-19 will depend on the progress of large-scale integration and cooperative effort, at the country-level as well as regionally and internationally. Independent initiatives will also be needed to bolster these efforts.

The first line of response to the pandemic requires intensified global coordination in focusing scientific research on COVID-19 itself, surveillance on trends of its transmission, and ensuring the supply of protective equipment.

As every nation works towards improving the pandemic situation, the support for collective economic recovery and social policy adjustments will also depend on the extent to which there is access to shared expertise, alignment of goals, and financing at international and regional levels – especially to vulnerable countries.

Innovation in International Cooperation – Gavi and COVAX

A notable example of an innovative method of international cooperation is that of Gavi and COVAX, in the sphere of vaccine development and distribution.

Gavi, in partnership with the WHO, the Bill & Melinda Gates Foundation, and other international organisations, launched COVAX – the COVID-19 Vaccine Global Access Facility – to pool resources among different countries, non-profits and organisations to forward vaccine development.

The inclusion of sovereign governments in the agreement to support Gavi's mission to fund and distribute vaccines in lower- and middle-income countries represents a meaningful forward step in world partnership.

COVAX is championed by Singapore and Switzerland, forming a Friends of the Facility group to promote the multilateral approach, joined by The United Kingdom, Iceland, Japan, Norway, South Korea, the European Union, and New Zealand and others.

(Source: Foreign Policy)

Based on the quality of governance as the key driving force, the identified pre-determinants and critical uncertainties, Figures 3 and 4 show matrices containing variables of i) quality of governance and development level of the public health system, and ii) speed of government's response to COVID-19 and structure of government, respectively. Of interest here would be how these variables impact the severity of the COVID-19 outbreak across the different countries shown overleaf.

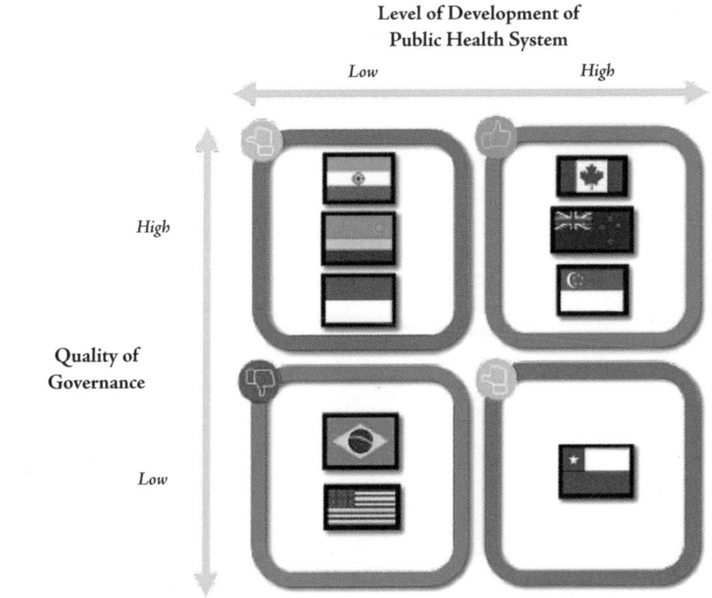

Figure 3: National Resilience Matrix on Quality of Governance and Level of Development of Public Health System (Source: Future-Moves Group)

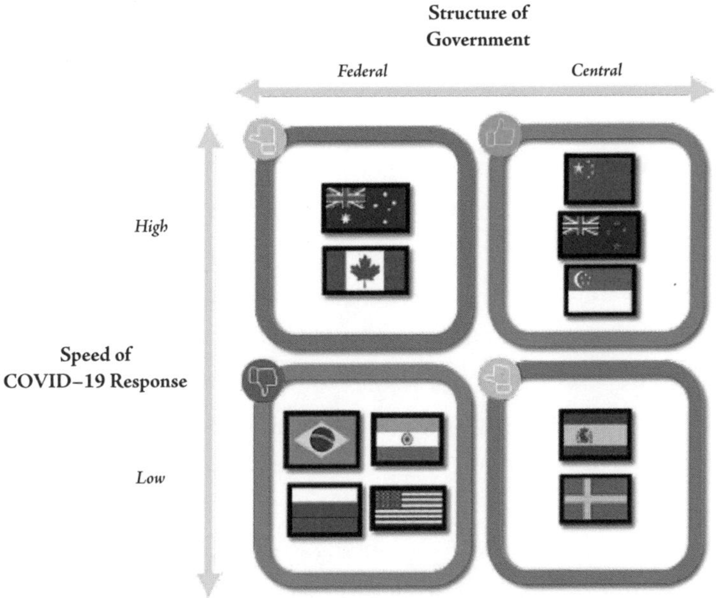

Figure 4: National Coordination Matrix on Speed of COVID-19 Response and Structure of Government (Source: Future-Moves Group)

DUAL-PATH RECOVERY

This book argues that a two-pronged approach of comprehensive testing – supported by widespread test kit distribution – and the development of a viable vaccine that is globally-accessible, are goals to be pursued in tandem. Mutation of the coronavirus and a persistent increase of COVID-19 cases are adding on to the urgency of public health recovery, alongside the challenges of economic and social recovery.

The Wave Phenomena

The wave phenomena of COVID-19 – where evolving circumstances, most notably the mutation in a viral strain of SARS-CoV-2 and new surges in confirmed cases – perpetuate new issues for the ongoing containment and mitigation efforts.

Policymakers and the international community need to be attentive to these new developments, accelerate existing measures and prepare with a longer-term view.

In recent study developments, researchers have found evidence of a viral mutation of SARS-CoV-2, known as D614G – colloquially known thereafter as COVID-G.

Before March, more than 90 percent of viral samples taken from patients in Wuhan, China, were tested and found to be of the D variation.

As the epicentre of the outbreak spread to Europe and the United States, global sampling between April and mid-May 2020 revealed that 78 percent of samples were of the mutated G variant.

And while it is most commonly found in the United States and Europe, COVID-G's presence in Asia has been increasing since March 2020, including in Singapore, Malaysia and Indonesia.

The emergence and spread of COVID-G is significant, for its D614G mutation relates to the spike protein in the SARS-CoV-2 virus, and spike proteins determine the ability of the virus to enter human cells.

There is reason to think that the mutation is consequential and that COVID-G is more infectious than its COVID-D counterpart. Three lines of evidence support this hypothesis: (i) laboratory experiments, (ii) clinical examinations and (iii) statistical studies.

Laboratory tests by Dr Betty Korber and her team at Los Alamos National Laboratory, which exposed non-human cell cultures to artificially-engineered pseudoviruses with either the G or D variant of the coronavirus spike protein, show that the G variant replicates and infects at a higher rate compared to the D variant.[14]

Viral loads from G variants were between 2.6 to 9.3 times greater than the viral loads for the D variant. This finding is corroborated by research from Dr Zhang Lizhou and his team at the Scripps Research Institute, which found that the G variant is about 10 times more infectious.[15] Separate research by Dr Zharko Daniloski and his team at the New York Genome Center, which tested the actual coronavirus variants on human lung cells, provide further confirmation, with COVID-G infecting up to 8 times more cells than COVID-D under otherwise identical conditions.[16]

Beyond laboratory tests, clinical evidence from the Los Alamos tests show that patients with COVID-G have higher levels of viral nucleic acid in the upper respiratory tract, suggesting higher viral loads and an increased probability of the infected individual spreading the virus to others.

Additionally, statistical analysis from Los Alamos shows increasing COVID-G frequency within populations where both the G and D variants were co-circulating, suggesting that the former is being positively selected for, and is capable of more rapid replication and infection.

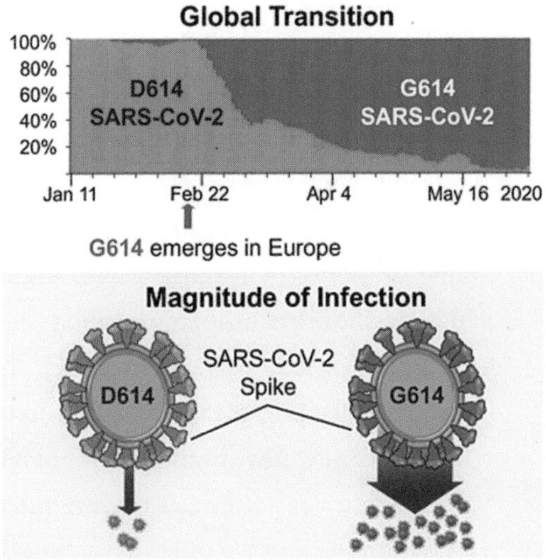

Figure 5: Global Prevalence and Magnitude of Infection for COVID-D and COVID-G (Source: Korber et al 2020)

It is important to note, however, that other scientists dispute the notion that COVID-G is necessarily more infectious.

For one, transmissibility is not just a function of how effective a virus is at entering a cell and replicating, but also of other factors such as how efficiently the virus leaves the body and how stable it is in outside environments before it latches onto a new host.[17]

Moreover, as Grubaugh, Hanage and Rasmussen point out, whether a viral strain becomes established in a region depends not just on transmission itself, but also on the number of times the strain is introduced.

Given that COVID-G became the dominant global variant at a time when COVID-D introductions from China were declining and COVID-G introductions from Europe were climbing, it could be pure luck, rather than evolutionary fitness that explains the G variant's greater spread.[18]

More generally, while laboratory and clinical data suggest that the G mutation changes the virus phenotype, the impact on the mutation on transmission, disease as well as the development of a vaccine and therapeutic treatment are unknown.[19]

The virus has mutated at a slow pace and new mutation copies remain similar to the initial sequence, prompting the likelihood that current vaccines in the development process remain efficacious.[20]

Crucially, the mutation has not altered the virus's response to antibodies from patients who had the D variant – suggesting that vaccines developed based on COVID-D will also retain effectiveness against COVID-G.[21]

Moreover, while there has been concern that levels of anti-COVID antibodies in survivors are low after a few months such that, as when Dr Wayne Marasco from Harvard Medical School says, "It's uncertain how long immunity will remain after successful vaccination", scientists have also clarified that dropping antibody counts are not abnormal.

In the ordinary course of events after a successful immune response and the receding of an infection, antibodies will decrease in number; this does not mean waning immunity, as the memory B cells that first produced those antibodies remain, standing ready to produce new batches of antibodies when required.[22]

Regardless, people and leaders are naturally worried about the mutation, and some officials, such as the Malaysian Health Ministry's director-general, Noor Hisham Abdullah, have sought to warn the broader public in their country of the COVID-G mutation and the possibility that it is 10 times more infectious.

Beyond raising alarm bells, however, this mutation shows the need for sustained and intensive scientific research to accompany the accelerated pace for vaccine development and other treatment avenues for COVID-19. COVID-19 will remain a protracted and constantly-changing situation, so countries should be careful not to be too quick to lower their guard.

> *The virus is evolving and is changing. And we don't yet know what the consequences of those changes are.*

Jonathan Stoye
Virologist at the Francis Crick Institute in London, England
7th May 2020

According to a widely-cited article in *The Lancet*,[23] a second peak could be expected in August 2020 if social distancing measures were lifted prematurely. This is due to an incubation period where patients are asymptomatic.

Using an age-adjusted, susceptible-exposed-infected-removed (SEIR) model, the study showed tangible benefits of prolonging social distancing measures to reduce the median number of infections, using Wuhan as an example.

A resurgence of cases has been observed around the globe, from the United States to Europe to Japan. In Spain, a second wave hit in mid-2020, after a loosening of precautionary measures.

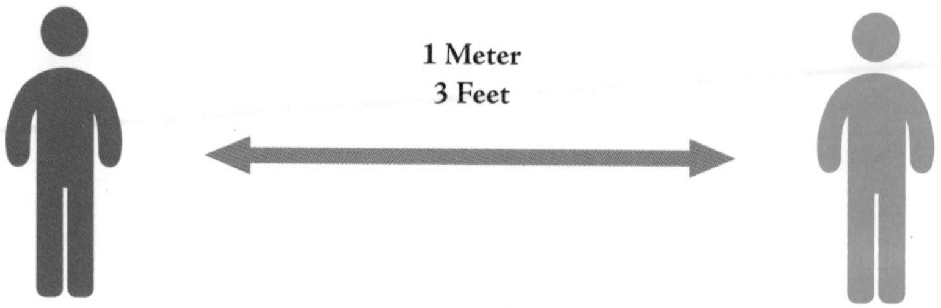

By relaxing social distancing measures one month later – in April 2020 instead of March – the study concluded that the proportion of cases averted was significantly higher, and this had the biggest impact on the very young and very old (see figure 6).

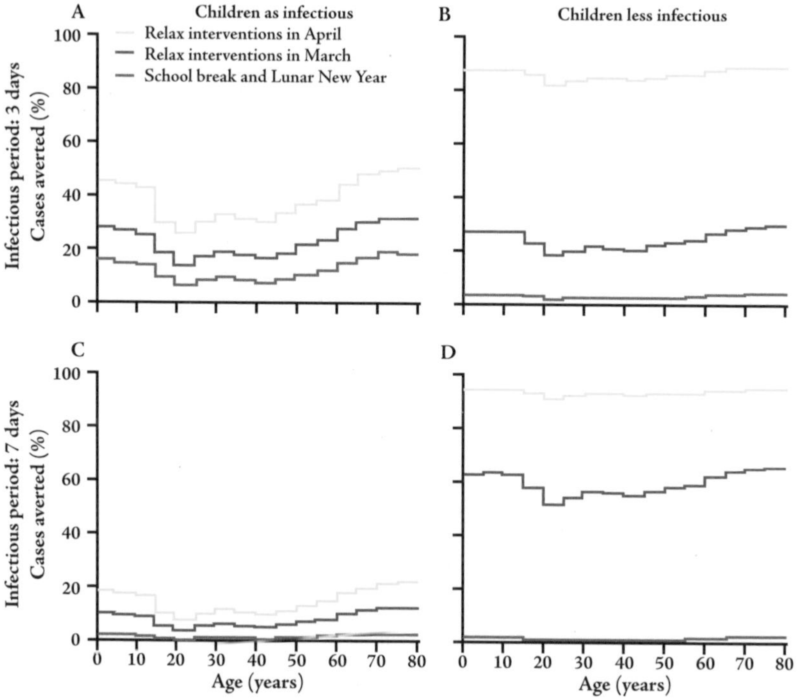

Figure 6: Effect on Cases Averted by Prolonging Social Distancing Measures (Source: The Lancet)

Additional waves may not necessarily resemble the earlier waves; for example, the WHO has expressed concern that the epidemic is changing, and that as of August 2020 the spread of the virus is being driven by people in their 20s to 40s.

This has implications, as the WHO's Regional Director for the Western Pacific explained: "Many [of these young people] are unaware they're infected— [they have] very mild symptoms or none at all. This can result in them unknowingly passing on the virus to others. This increases the risk of spillovers to the most vulnerable: the elderly, the sick, people in long-term care, people who live in densely-populated urban areas and under-served rural areas."

This necessitates a sustainable response that minimises social and economic disruptions. This might include earlier targeted responses to outbreaks, improved health systems or "new normal" habits that fight the spread of the virus without being too onerous.

In the West, where social distancing measures were taken at a later stage of the pandemic spread, it is likely to see a higher, but earlier, peak of infections.

Therefore, the economic costs of social distancing must be delicately balanced with the likelihood of a second wave, resulting from a premature relaxation of safe management interventions.

Recovery Trajectory

Given this 'Wave Phenomena', the trajectory of recovery from the COVID-19 pandemic will hinge upon immediate: i) development of an efficient and affordable global distribution system of coronavirus testing kits, and ii) development of a vaccine that is effective and affordable to be administered in all countries.

Comprehensive Testing and Test Kit Distribution

Widespread diagnostic testing that detects the presence of the coronavirus provides vital information on the evolution of the pandemic within countries.

Such tests also allow for global intelligence gathering on the overall development of the virus situation, and are useful epidemiological tools that help to estimate the prevalence of asymptomatic cases. Testing and identification of cases serve to stem transmission and detect viral outbreak hotspots at critical junctures.

A combination of active measures consisting of rapid diagnostic testing, tracing of close contacts and strict isolation or treatment of affected individuals have been applied in countries that have managed to contain COVID-19.

Countries such as South Korea and Taiwan have managed to roll out rapid testing capacity to a larger proportion of their population compared to elsewhere in the world.

This is stark contrast to countries like the US, where long, winding queues for coronavirus tests around city blocks remained the status quo in July 2020, thus providing evidence of a flawed system of testing many months after the COVID-19 situation arose.

In September 2020, the journalist Bob Woodward revealed that in interviews with President Donald Trump conducted in early February 2020, Trump said, "This is deadly stuff," but later the same month Trump publicly decried that the pandemic was the Democrats "new hoax". He admitted to Mr Woodward in an interview on 19 March 2020, when it was becoming increasingly clear that the pandemic-related infections in the United States were accelerating, that "I wanted to always play it down. I still like playing it down, because I don't want to create a panic."

President Trump also actively frustrated or sidelined government public health experts who contradicted his public statements and promises including his advocacy of the prophylactic effects of the anti-malarial drug, publicly declaring in July 2020 that "I happen to believe in hydroxychloroquine... I used it. Many, many people agree with me," even as his own health authorities were warning the public not to follow his example and explicitly withdrawing federal permission for hospitals to prescribe the drug for treatment of COVID-19.

Reserves of test kits are stretched as the outbreak accelerates in the

US, with a five-fold increase in testing numbers from April to June 2020. Similarly, other materials required for testing – such as nasopharyngeal swabs and collection containers – face a supply shortfall. This was also evident, especially in the early stages, of the outbreak in Italy, Spain and Canada, which have faced delayed testing procedures.

Ensuring ample global production of diagnostic kits and related instruments to address high testing demand for countries encountering massive outbreaks is an important aim. During the early stages of the pandemic – in March and April 2020 especially – countries limited exports of test kit supplies and logistical bottlenecks impeded distribution to countries that were in dire need of kits.

Research continues on improving point-of-care tests to yield reliable results in under an hour, and on-the-spot-results tests are also in the works. For example, Abbott Labs has developed a rapid antigen test, which can ostensibly detect a COVID-19 infection in a quarter of an hour.

However, while current evidence suggest that the Abbott Labs test produces results that tracks the gold standard PCR test's own for about 97-98 percent of the time, such findings are very preliminary, and based on a small sample size.[24] Moreover, while the Abbott Labs test has obtained approval from the US Food and Drug Administration (FDA), the FDA has also been under severe political pressure from the Trump administration.

Given the agency's previous approval of COVID-19 treatment methods despite the lack of evidence on efficacy, there is reason to doubt whether the Abbott Labs test are as effective as their approved status would otherwise suggest.

Meanwhile, other tactics, including pooled testing or drive-through testing sites, have also been presented as alternatives. Together, all this demonstrates that open global supply chains of testing instruments continue to be vital in equalising access to kits.

It's going to be one big wave. It's going to go up and down a bit… the best thing is to flatten it and turn it into just something that is lapping at your feet. But at the moment, first, second, third wave, these things don't really make sense and we're not really defining it that way.

Now we do everything we can to encourage all countries to test, because testing is absolutely essential. You don't know where your outbreak is if you're not testing people. And we also encourage all countries to make access to testing wide and available.

Dr Margaret Harris
WHO
28th July 2020

Progress in Vaccine Development and Access

Government-level public health responses and the development of a viable vaccine that is accessible and affordable are crucial elements to combat COVID-19. National governance needs to be comprehensive and scientifically-grounded, and an efficacious licensed vaccine – globally available within 12 to 18 months – will drastically impact the trajectory of recovery.

Without a widely available vaccine, containment measures of border control, testing and lockdowns have to be sustained for a longer period. Furthermore, case prevalence and fatality rates will rise in numerous countries, with severe outbreaks in the hardest-hit ones. Figure 7 shows a risk matrix comparing the development level of public health systems and vaccine development.

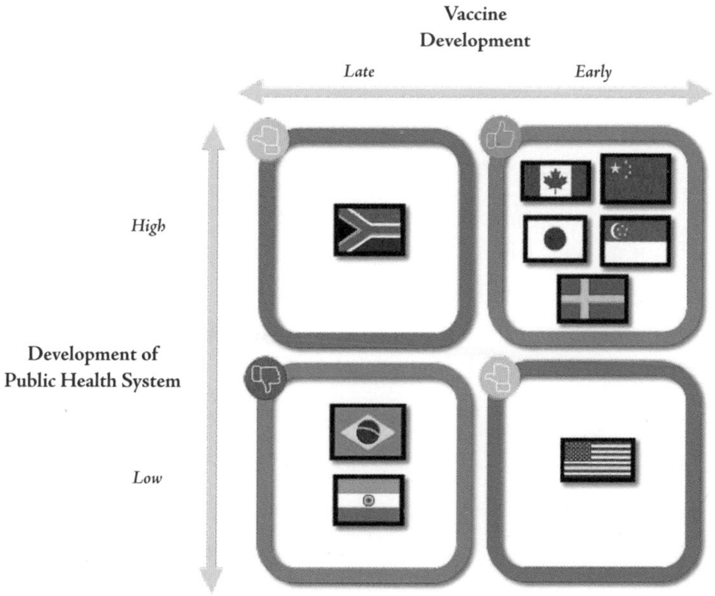

Figure 7: Matrix on COVID-19 Public Health Response and Vaccine Availability (Source: Future-Moves Group)

Under normal circumstances, vaccine development takes an average of eight to 15 years from conception in the laboratory to a commercially-available product. This certainly defies the urgent need for a safe and globally available vaccine to control and prevent the massive spread of COVID-19.

Previous vaccine development programmes provide little reason for optimism. The outbreaks of SARS and Zika ended before vaccine development could be completed, leaving manufacturers contending with losses and subsequently delaying other vaccine programmes. Despite dismal past records, the pursuit of developing a viable vaccine must persist.

US-based Moderna Inc., one of the first developers to begin trials in humans, has announced that its COVID-19 vaccine produced antibodies to the coronavirus in all patients tested in an initial safety trial.

The stimulation of antibodies capable of neutralising the coronavirus represents an important early-stage result in testing, although it does not prove that the vaccine will be effective. With these encouraging initial results, the company has begun conducting its large-scale Phase 3 clinical trials with the help of thousands of volunteers.

The University of Oxford and pharmaceutical company AstraZeneca's coronavirus vaccine has also shown promising results in early-phase human testing, with increasing levels of both protective neutralising antibodies and immune T-cells targeting the virus and prompting no serious side effects. This has allowed the company to similarly move on to the large-scale Phase 3 trials, where the vaccine will be tested on 30,000 health adults.

In June 2020, AstraZeneca reached a US $750 million agreement with CEPI and Gavi to support the manufacturing, procurement and distribution of 300 million doses of the potentially developed vaccine, with delivery starting by the end of 2020. A licensing agreement was also reached with the Serum Institute of India (SII) to supply one billion doses to low- and middle-income countries.

As of 9th September 2020, there were more than 100 vaccines in development, with most being in pre-clinical trials (i.e. animal testing).

24 were in Phase 1 safety trials, where the vaccine is given to a small number of people to test safety and dosage and to confirm that the vaccine has the intended effect of stimulating the immune system.

14 were in Phase 2 expanded trials, where the vaccine is given to hundreds of people of different demographic groups, such as the young and the elderly, to check for differential effects and to further test for safety and immune system stimulation efficacy.

9 were in Phase 3 efficacy trials, where the vaccine is given to thousands of people, and where researchers will have to wait to see how many among the vaccinated become infected relative to a control group who received a placebo. As of the time of writing, no vaccine has proven itself at the Phase 3 level or been approved for full use.

Inequitable access to vaccines and incoordination in development processes has proven to be a trait of the global public health order. For example, Indonesia, during the 2007 H5N1 spread, refused to provide viral samples to WHO, claiming that the benefits of research would not be equally shared. In 2009, developed countries placed large advanced orders for the H1N1 vaccine, buying up all the pharmaceutical companies could manufacture, and later that same year, a WHO-led intergovernmental meeting failed to agree on benefit sharing.

This time around, governments need to advance progress in multilateral coordination at international and regional levels to ensure that well-off countries do not monopolise the supply of vaccines when production begins. When the development process does begin, it is critical that knowledge is shared and not withheld.

As we move forward in this difficult time, our lives, our health systems and approaches to stopping transmission must continue to adapt and evolve, along with the epidemic. At least until a vaccine or very effective treatment is found, this process will need to become our "new normal.

Dr Takeshi Kasai
Regional Director for the Western Pacific of the WHO
21st April 2020

Recommendations on Vaccine Development at National Level

1. Diversify vaccine development channels

Countries need to support and fund a variety of vaccine development programmes, given the expedited timeline of research on a viable vaccine to combat COVID-19.

While vaccines are in development globally, countries should internally widen research effort, in tandem with advancements by the global scientific community, to bolster domestic public health capability and contribute to the wider international effort.

Singapore represents an example in this aspect. Researchers from Singapore's Agency for Science, Technology and Research (A*STAR) are in joint partnership with overseas counterparts such as Japanese Chugai Pharmabody Research in developing an antibody that targets the coronavirus.

2. Commit to Gavi's COVAX facility

Gavi's COVAX facility and the COVAX Advanced Market Commitment (AMC) seeks to accelerate vaccine development and production, and thereafter ensure fair access to all countries. As a centralised global initiative, governments should be compelled to join existing COVAX countries to reinforce support for vaccine development at the international level, for mutual benefit and inclusivity.

3. Domestic self-reliance

While global research and development in vaccines are underway with more than 100 candidates in pre-clinical trials, countries with the necessary capabilities should continue to pursue domestic testing and development efforts.

The Chinese government, for instance, is backing several internal coronavirus vaccine projects to raise the prospect that it could vaccinate its people first with the potential vaccine.

Given the rapid development of the pandemic, countries should rely on both the global coordinated effort and their internal capacities towards vaccine development situation.

4. Partner with pharmaceutical companies

Partnerships between government agencies and pharmaceutical companies to create a robust and conducive vaccine development ecosystem could speed things up.

This is especially important in commencing clinical trials and raising funds on the condition of having less bureaucratic barriers in the process.

The US government's "Operation Warp Speed" (OWS), is a plan to develop a vaccine in record time. It intensifies partnership between the federal government and pharmaceutical companies to test, manufacture and distribute a vaccine by early next year.

Under OWS, the US has invested nearly US$4 billion in pharmaceutical firms pursuing vaccines, and OWS leaders can consolidate progress and protocols in a central system with players in the pharmaceutical industry.

This nationwide, consolidated private-public partnership in the US represents a positive example where governance and the pharmaceutical sector is highly inter-related in the vaccine development process.

5. Ensure internal supply, distribution and costing

Countries will need to ensure stable, sufficient supply and distribution of vaccines, widespread accessibility and affordability to its people. Internal supplies and distribution channels for a potential vaccine need to be secured at an early stage for plans to be executed effectively when available.

In the United States for instance, a group of independent scientists and ethicists have been tasked to develop guidelines to determine the priority groups that a developed vaccine should target and a framework for its distribution.

On costing and affordability, governments will need to forecast the potential expense of a developed vaccine. The risky and high cost of investments in research and development, and manufacturing capabilities given the prevalence of COVID-19, can potentially mean that vaccines are pricier than those developed in normal circumstances.

Governments need to immediately ramp up the understanding of such procurement mechanisms, vaccine market dynamics and the complex elements of vaccine pricing – including multi-year contracts or product bundling – to prepare for the eventual distribution of an effective vaccine.

SECTION II:
EVIDENCE

From the earlier framed understanding of COVID-19, with governance as the central vector, the following section provides statistical and qualitative analysis of the pandemic by mapping information and evidence of its effects on politics, economic policy and public health. Readers will be guided to understand how the presented evidence-based approach allows for an enhanced understanding of various country reactions to COVID-19.

Part B: Insights in Politics

Part B explores general insights and changes in politics brought about by COVID-19. The pandemic is set to worsen political instability globally, call into question the organisation of urban life, and have ripple effects on the broad state of public health.

- Factors of government leadership, the organisation of cities and society, and healthcare provision are affected both adversely and positively to varying degrees by COVID-19.
- While adverse negative impacts of the virus exist, these flaws also demonstrate areas with potential for remedy. The status quo organisation of politics, social life and healthcare systems needs to be assessed, and lessons gained from experience with COVID-19 should offer future direction for improvements.
- The overall management of this global pandemic crisis requires taking seriously how elements of politics and public health intersect and interact, from the national to the international sphere.

APPROACHES TO POLITICS

The pandemic looks likely to cause political instability throughout the globe, especially in countries without robust democratic institutions, countries with greater levels of poverty and weaker health systems, and countries saddled with significant debt burdens. In general, the economic damage from the pandemic is likely to harm the political fortunes of incumbent governments. This section will also show how the pandemic manifests in divergent ways in different countries.

Intensification of the US-China Rivalry

One trend pre-dating the pandemic is the escalating US-China geopolitical rivalry, which itself derives from mutual concerns about security.

First, as China rises to rival the United States in economic and military strength, the two have become each other's greatest potential security threat. The steps each country takes to secure themselves – such as through military expansion or the soliciting of new allies – only creates further mistrust and induces the other to escalate with similar measures.

Second, the two countries have incompatible geopolitical strategies. China is seeking to push the United States military forces out of Asia-Pacific to assure its security. Having a hegemonic position in Asia will better allow China to project power into the Eastern Pacific and Western Hemisphere, and there is no doubt that the United States will seek to resist this.

In this respect, the pandemic will act not as a hinge point in history but a point of acceleration. While the pandemic itself is unlikely to precipitate any material shifts in the balance of power, as the US still retains significant advantages in military strength, soft power and its alliance with Asia-Pacific nations fearful of China's rise, relations have soured over the coronavirus.

The Trump administration blames China for originating the pandemic, while China has engaged in aggressive "wolf warrior" diplomacy that seeks to counter criticisms of itself; all of which leads to worsening ties and intensifying geopolitical rivalry.

The outcome of the 2020 US Presidential Election will not materially affect the intensification of the US-China geopolitical rivalry, as the coronavirus – along with other outstanding issues like China's growing military might – has caused a bipartisan hardening of American opposition towards China.

The 2020 US Presidential Election itself will likely feature politicians competing to be the most hawkish on China. Should the Democratic Party's nominee Joe Biden win the election, he can be expected to take a hard stand against China, albeit much less so than the posture adopted by President Trump. He is likely to rebuild alliances and relationships and pursue a multilateral approach to 'contain' China.

The Testing and Failing of Hard-Right Political Populism

While the pandemic has sparked fears of the strengthening of xenophobic nationalism, the far-right political movements that captured political office or surged in popularity throughout the democratic world in the latter half of the 2010s seem likely to be hurt politically by the pandemic – a reversal from their earlier successes.

Despite the existence of a 'rally-around-the-flag' effect, where the public moves to support incumbent governments in times of war or the wake of a significant national crisis, these hard-right governments in democratic countries have seen their general popularity suffer to different degrees.

This is true for incumbents, most notably, President Donald Trump and President Jair Bolsonaro of Brazil are seeing polling declines due to concerns over their inept handling of the coronavirus. Trump in particular is facing growing disapproval of his handling of the crisis. His response has been to wreak further havoc by politicizing the pandemic. Even simple practical measures, universally accepted and promoted by the epidemiological experts, are now politically polarized.

For instance, mask wearers are considered Democrats while Republicans champion personal rights and show resistance to mask wearing. Many of Trump's supporters refer to the pandemic as a 'plandemic' implying that the Democratic party is exploiting the pandemic by exaggerating its seriousness thereby damaging the economy and infringing individual rights, for political gain.

In the United Kingdom, Prime Minister Boris Johnson, a populist politician whose association with facts has always been cursory and opportunistic, is facing growing public criticism of his government's handling of the crisis. He had initially proposed that the most expedient solution was to allow the virus to spread unchecked to reach 'herd immunity', only to hastily withdraw this proposal when confronted by a mass revolt by the scientific community who warned this would result in between 250,000 and 500,000 deaths. Richard Horton, editor of the medical journal *The Lancet,* warned that the U.K. was "playing roulette with the public."

The common thread between right-wing populist leaders is an uninformed and anti-scientific approach, leading to incompetent management of the pandemic crisis and political opportunism rather than serious policy responses.

In Asia, largely, there have been relatively successful interventions and containment of the virus due to prompt action, except for Japan, which was slow to initiate adequate measures. India is an outlier with a very delayed, uneven and chaotic policy response.

Within ASEAN, the Philippines' President Rodrigo Duterte's failure to take the pandemic seriously in its earlier stages has led to the country seeing a record number of cases arise, while Myanmar has not been reporting trustworthy figures.

Simultaneously, opposition far-right parties in Europe have not done any much better, often due to their unpopular actions in downplaying the risks of the pandemic and in opposing lockdown measures. The Alternative for Germany (AfD), Spain's Vox, Italy's League, the Swedish Democrats, and the Netherlands's Forum for Democracy all have seen declines in popularity.

Divergent Approaches to Governance

"Antagonistic" Approach in the United States

In a global pandemic, the world will look to national and intergovernmental efforts for leadership.

Traditionally, the United States has been a global leader in public health. It is a core WHO partner in the eradication of major diseases, especially those affecting third-world countries, such as Polio, Ebola, and Zika. It has also been WHO's top donor, at least until President Donald Trump terminated American funding to the organisation in 2020 over the organisation's perceived deference to China.

Of a piece with his generally antagonistic and incompetent approach, Trump has also consistently downplayed the threat of the coronavirus and has consistently failed to take the necessary measures to control the spread of the virus and limit fatalities.

Though the Trump administration began in late January 2020 to bar foreign nationals who had recently travelled to China, it did not impose a mandatory quarantine on all returning Americans.

At the same time, the Trump administration botched the rollout of its prototype testing kits, failed to set up and execute a national contact tracing strategy, and, crucially, pushed for the lifting of lockdowns even before the virus spread was under control.

Trump has also rejected the use of the Defense Production Act to compel the production and distribution of necessary medical equipment like ventilators and face masks, and has, counterproductively, attempted to force private companies such as 3M to export masks from its Singaporean hub – meant for Asian consumption – back to the United States.

Simultaneously, President Trump has – without evidence – pushed the use of anti-malarial drug hydroxychloroquine as an effective treatment for COVID-19, even though there is evidence that this drug is in fact associated with increased risk of death in coronavirus patients.[25]

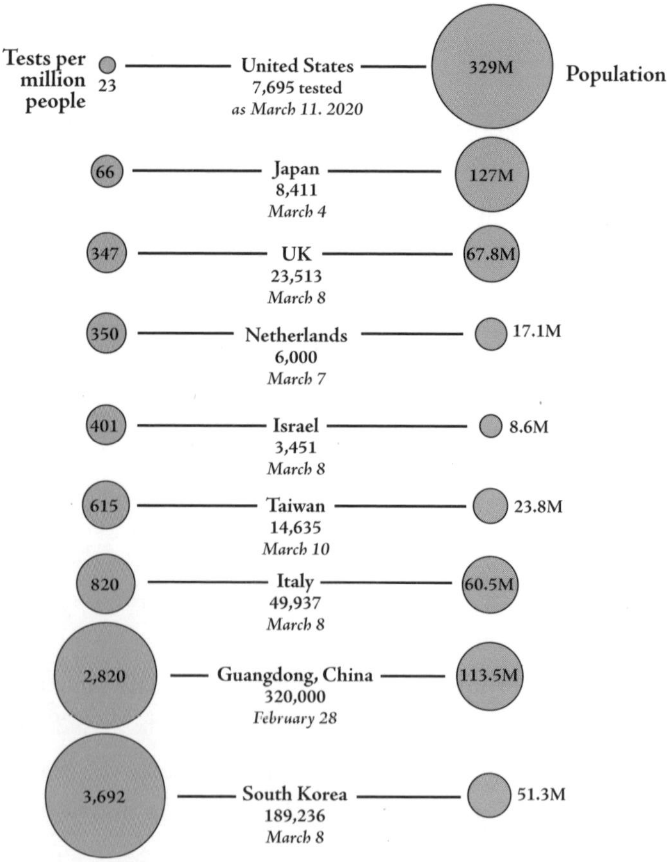

Figure 8: Early COVID-19 Testing per capita (Source: COVID Tracking Project)

"Trust-Centred" Approach in Sweden

Unlike most other countries, Sweden has adopted a trust-centred approach by not imposing lockdowns. Non-essential businesses have remained open. Sweden has implemented typical social distancing guidelines seen in other countries, but these have remained voluntary and not mandatory.

The country's Chief Epidemiologist, Anders Tegnell, believes that the relatively lax measures will serve Sweden better in the long run compared with traditional lockdown approaches.

To date, Sweden faces a death rate, relative to its population, that is about five to six times higher than that of its Scandinavian neighbours.[26] However, the calculation of a case fatality rate in Sweden would likely be unreliable if asymptomatic cases are allowed to roam freely in society with minimal enforceable restrictions.

Sweden's formula for handling the pandemic is testament to its trust in public institutions. Prime Minister Stefan Lofven's approval rating has leapt from 27 percent in March 2020 and the start of the coronavirus outbreak to 46 percent in April 2020.

> *People have learnt how to relate to the disease, to keep distance. We have become better at protecting the risk groups.*
>
> **Karin Tegmark-Wisell**
> *Head of Microbiology, Swedish Public Health Agency*
> *17th July 2020*

"Evidence-Based" Approach in Singapore

Singapore has adopted a piecemeal, stepwise approach in its handling of the pandemic. Beginning in February 2020, Singapore began COVID-19 response measures by conducting active contact tracing and in March 2020, Singapore Government Technology Agency (GovTech) launched the app TraceTogether to boost contact tracing efforts.

Singapore began by restricting all travel from Mainland China in the early days of the pandemic. It then shifted its attention to countries outside China that saw a spike in cases, including South Korea, Iran and northern Italy.

As the global situation deteriorated, Singapore proceeded to extend travel restrictions to the whole of ASEAN, and by mid-March, strongly encouraged deferring all travel until further notice, while Singaporeans returning from abroad were placed on a 14-day mandatory Stay Home Notice (SHN).

In an attempt to curb the spread of unlinked and asymptomatic cases, Singapore imposed a four-week long "circuit breaker" from 7 April 2020 to 4 May 2020. This required non-essential businesses and schools to shut their premises, to the extent that only about 20 percent of Singapore's workforce – working in essential services such as healthcare, and food and beverage – continued to commute to work.

On 2 May 2020, the multi-ministerial taskforce for the coronavirus epidemic announced a gradual easing of circuit breaker measures, starting with some relaxation of the strictest circuit breaker measures introduced on 21 April 2020.

That said, even Singapore has struggled to stick to an evidence-based approach, not least because the science itself is not necessarily settled, and new evidence has emerged over time (e.g. on the coronavirus being capable of airborne transmission) that forces changes to policy accordingly.

The nature of the pandemic requires speedy response from the government. In the process of providing that speedy response, things can go wrong.

Edward Olowo-Okere
Global Director, Governance,
World Bank Group

ORGANISATION OF CITIES

The pandemic has exposed flaws in the organisation of urban life and has also highlighted the disparities that exist between regions within countries.

The Vulnerability of Cities

An immediate consequence of the pandemic is the direct impact on huge metropolitan areas. A concentration in talent, such as the abundance of artists and musicians in New York City, for example, will now become a huge vulnerability. Besides, the gig economy has never been tested in a pandemic, and gig workers tend to be concentrated in areas with high urban density.

Even if cities have proven historically to be resilient to shock – as when Japanese cities rapidly recovered after World War II to pre-war population trend lines – the rise of working-from-home and telecommuting may bring about the long-term decline in the importance of cities and cause their reorganisation. Workers may choose to move to less expensive suburbs and companies could permanently adopt remote working not only as a sustained business continuity plan but also as a financial cost-saving measure.

Meanwhile, decentralised countries, both in terms of population and economic activity, such as Germany and the United States, might be able to come out of the crisis relatively stronger than countries that are highly centralised.

In China, one of the major expected outcomes of the pandemic is the decentralisation of urban clusters and central cities with the rise of satellite towns, which will reduce the infrastructural pressure on the core cities.

Uneven Effects Within Larger Countries

The effects of the pandemic will inevitably reach smaller towns and rural areas too, which do not have sufficient public health infrastructure nor resources to deal with the pandemic like the larger cities do. The places with the most unmanageable outbreaks in the US and Italy are not in the cities, but in the suburbs.

Over time, the pandemic will initiate a correction mechanism where suburban areas will scramble to catch up in terms of the allocation of health resources and availability of testing kits.

The pandemic is expected to disproportionately affect cities with a high urban density and/or poor public healthcare systems. London, New York City and Madrid are examples of cities becoming national epicentres in the coronavirus pandemic. This is evidence of population concentration becoming a vulnerability.

Concerning employment in cities, the pandemic looks likely to disincentivise working and living in big cities. In Canada, for example, close to half of the new jobs created in April and May 2020 were located outside of the nine main metropolitan areas. These patterns can be attributed to the barriers social distancing creates within crowded cities and the stark shortage of international travellers, which impacts metropolitan cities more than in less populated areas of the country. Within larger countries, governments will likely have to contend with changes to employment and living patterns as COVID-19 continues to trigger a re-evaluation of the benefits of city life.

	Population (millions)	No. of Cases	No. of Deaths	Infection Rate (%)	Death Rate (%)
London	8.9	5,957 [27]	590 [28]	0.07	9.90
Whole of UK	66	22,141	1,408	0.03	6.36
New York City	8.6	43,139	914	0.50	2.12
Whole of US	327	164,620	3,170	0.05	1.92
Madrid	6.5	27,509	3,603	0.42	13.10
Whole of Spain	47	85,195	7,340	0.18	8.62

Figure 9: National and Urban Area Comparison across the UK, US and Spain (Data: European Centre for Disease Prevention and Control; accurate as of 31 March 2020)

HEALTHCARE PROVISION

The coronavirus pandemic calls for a rethink on the provision of public health services and public perceptions on healthcare. On a positive note, COVID-19 has accelerated the revision of certain deficiencies in current systems of healthcare, and global scientific research looks set to benefit in the wake of the pandemic.

Beyond the direct deaths from the COVID-19 virus, the pandemic has numerous adverse consequences for public and global health.[29]

First, the coronavirus has led to routine vaccinations not being carried out. In the developed world, lockdowns and fear of the virus prevent parents from bringing their children to the doctor. In the developing world, mass immunisation drives have been suspended, given that the inoculation of infants and children in communal places poses far too great a risk of spreading COVID-19. With vaccines having saved at least 10 million lives between 2010 and 2015,[30] any significant drop off in vaccination rates could lead to a rise in the number of deaths.

Second, the pandemic has more broadly deterred people from visiting the doctor, even when suffering from significant and possibly life-threatening issues like stroke or heart attacks.

To the extent that testing and treatment of diseases like HIV and other sexually transmitted diseases (STDs) fall, serious health complications for existing sufferers as well as increased spread to previously uninfected individuals will result.

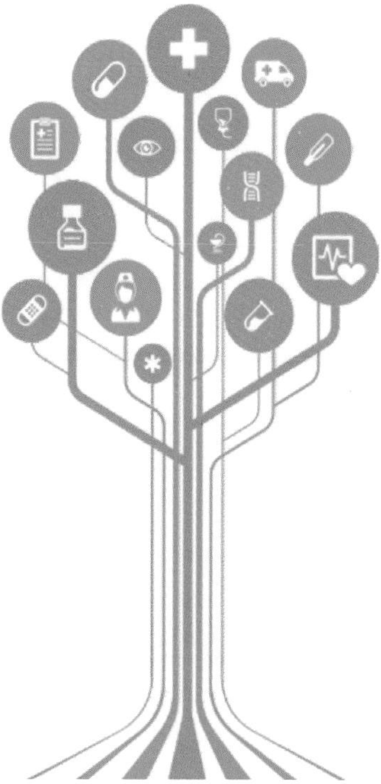

Third, elective surgeries, even for crucial procedures like cancer treatment and organ transplants, are being delayed, therefore risking the lives of individuals who require such treatment.

Fourth, the pandemic can potentially cause a second-order wave of deaths from hunger and malnutrition. Aside from disrupting the global food supply, the pandemic also undermines distribution networks.

The World Food Programme (WFP) feeds nearly 100 million people, including about 30 million living in war zones, and it is estimated that 300,000 people a day could starve to death if WFP operations are disrupted, as a result of funding cuts or border closures.

Fifth, pre-COVID-19 trends concerning the misuse of antibiotics have been accelerated by the virus itself, thus worsening the problem of antibiotic-resistant bacteria strands. COVID-19 is unaffected by antibiotics, but antibiotics are still being given to the infected by doctors to protect against secondary bacterial infections, and many people are also self-medicating with antibiotics in a misguided attempt at prophylaxis.

Such overuse of antibiotics is deadly, for it fosters the development of antibiotic-resistant bacterial strains, which kill one person every 15 minutes within the United States alone.[31]

Internationally, multidrug-resistant tuberculosis (MDR-TB) killed 240,000 people in 2016,[32] with its even deadlier variant of extremely drug-resistant tuberculosis (XDR-TB) making up half a million cases worldwide.[33]

The challenge of antibiotic resistance could become an enormous force of additional sickness and death across our health system as the toll of coronavirus pneumonia stretches critical care units beyond their capacity.

Dr Julie Gerberding
Executive Vice President and Chief Patient Officer of Merck & Co., Inc.
23rd March 2020

Sixth, the push for a COVID-19 vaccine has led to the diversion of resources away from other clinical trials, and hence the stalling of research for other illnesses. This means an additional, substantial delay to an already protracted process of getting new life-saving drugs to market and the deaths of individuals who urgently need these drugs to survive.

Seventh, the lockdowns have caused a spike in domestic abuse cases, as victims are forced to spend extended periods together with their abusers. From China to America, and from Berlin to Bratislava, reports of domestic abuse have increased significantly during the imposition of lockdowns.

Eighth, the pandemic can potentially widen healthcare disparity across countries of different income levels. As figure 10 shows, significant disparity exists with respect to health sector preparedness across advanced economies, emerging markets and developing economies and low-income countries.

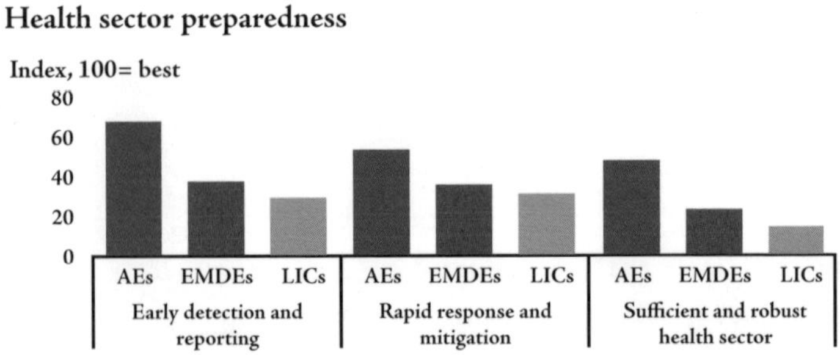

Figure 10: Health Sector Preparedness Comparison (Source: World Bank)

Part C: Insights in Economic Policy

This part explores the economic consequences brought about by COVID-19, and how policymakers can respond via fiscal and monetary means.

- The pandemic has brought both a supply and demand shock to the economy, resulting in severe recession and financial instability. The long-term structure of the economy is altered, as daily lives and work habits change with increased telecommuting practices and use of technology, but it also brings about deepening inequality and a technological oligopoly.
- To deal with the immediate economic impact of the pandemic, fiscal policymakers need to engage in expansionary fiscal policy.
- Meanwhile, monetary policymakers might need to engage in more experimental interventions such as quantitative easing and helicopter money, given interest rates are already low or near the Zero Lower Bound in many advanced economies.

"*We have to think not only about where we are now, but where we're going in the future. You have to play a longer game, not to think about just the immediate. And that's really complicated because this is unpredictable. We have never had a pandemic operate on the world economy like this.*"

Martin Wolf, CBE,
Chief Economics Commentator,
Financial Times

CHANGES IN ECONOMIC ACTIVITY

The pandemic has not only induced a severe global recession and concurrent financial instability, but it also affects the long-term trajectory of economies, as telecommuting becomes more common, the dominance of the current oligopoly of 'Big Tech' strengthens, automation is increasingly widespread, and economic inequality deepens.

Pandemic-Induced Recession

The COVID-19 pandemic has brought a significant supply shock, with lockdowns shutting down various sectors such as restaurants, retail, tourism and aviation, and the supply of related goods and services. Similarly, it has also led to accompanying demand shock, with increased unemployment reducing consumption and a bleak economic outlook depressing business investment, which will measurably contract GDP.

This is perhaps not surprising; historically, pandemics have led to initial GDP contractions of between -8 and -1 percent – and that is without factoring in the effects of the unprecedented large-scale lockdowns used for the COVID-19 pandemic.[34]

In terms of the channels through which pandemics have affected economic outcomes in the past, there are not just the demand channels –

i.e. fear and uncertainty reducing consumption – but also supply channels – i.e. death shrinking the labour force and illness reducing labour hours.

With respect to the latter, the present COVID-19 pandemic has to date differed from historical pandemics, where the supply disruption comes primarily from the prophylactic lockdowns – and not from the catastrophic collapse of the labour force due to widespread death. But in select economies with large populations, poor public health infrastructure and poor governance, this could change. As of early September 2020, the United States recorded 6.25 million cases, India 4.2 million cases and Brazil, 4.12 million cases.

The fatality rates vary across these countries given their different states of public health infrastructure, but in all three cases the fatality rates are much higher as a ratio of infections than those of better governed countries such as Singapore and New Zealand, where early and aggressive intervention has been matched by a history of long term investments in public health infrastructure.

In the United States as of early September 2020 the number of fatalities stood at 190,000, in India 72,000 and in Brazil 127,000. In all three cases the fatality ratio is climbing, not declining, and in the cases of both India and Brazil it is doing so at an accelerating pace. There is also doubt as to whether the reporting by both India and Brazil fully reflect their COVID-19 conditions given the large populations, land mass and rural concentrations.

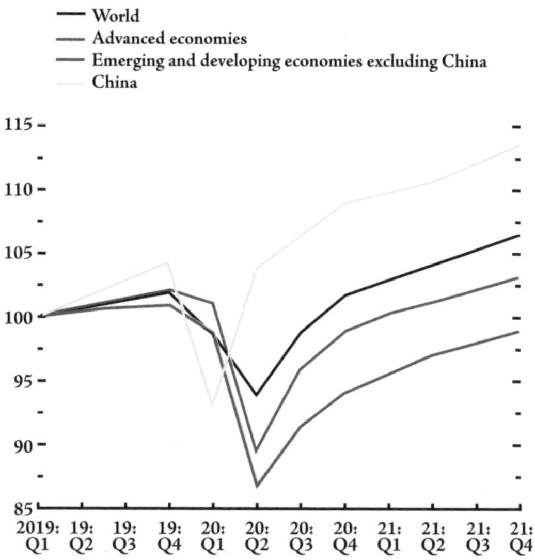

Figure 11: Projected Fall in Global GDP and Subsequent Recovery (Source: IMF)

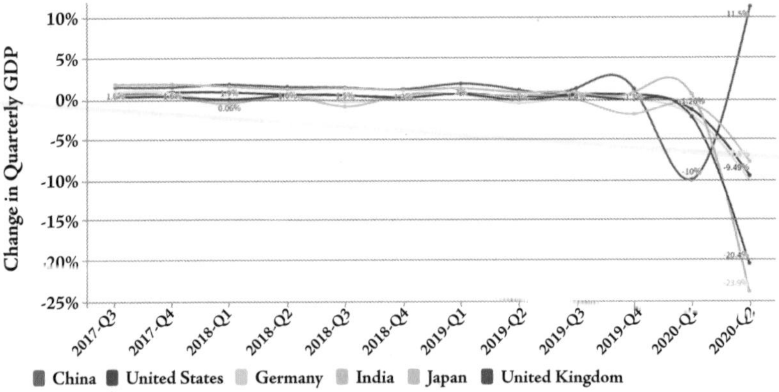

Figure 12: Quarterly GDP Growth over Time in Selected Countries (Atlantic Council)

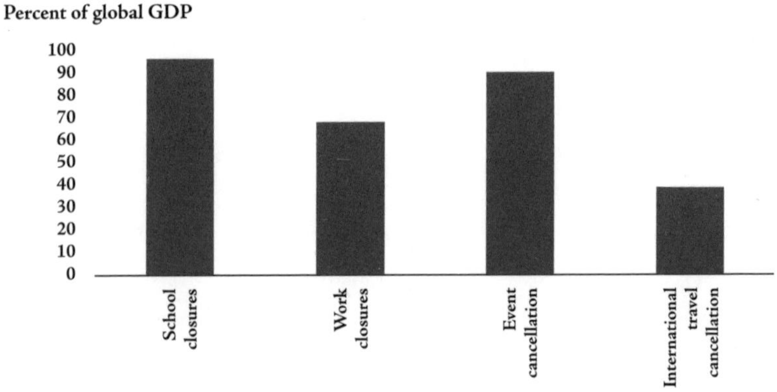

Figure 13: Extent of Pandemic's Economic Consequences, as Indicated by the Share of Global GDP Represented by Countries with Lockdowns Imposed

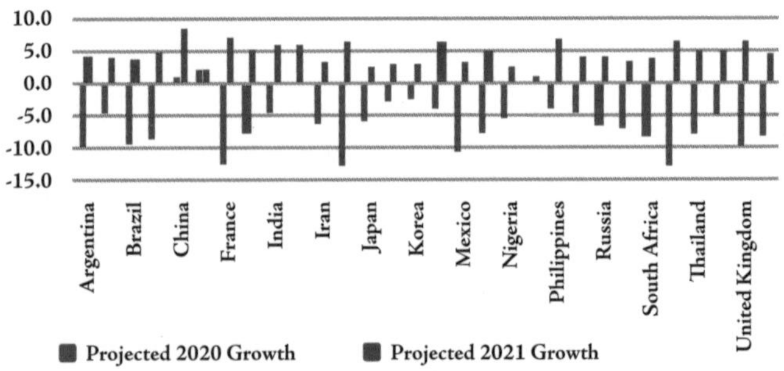

Figure 14: Consequences of COVID-19 for GDP Growth in 2020 & 2021 (Source: Future-Moves Group; data from IMF)

Sub-Saharan Africa is projected to perform better economically, relative to both the OECD and the middle-income countries. One reason for this is that, despite poorer health systems, these countries have systematic advantages.

These advantages include, for example, younger populations, lower urbanisation and poorer roads impeding mobility. Paired with relatively robust early action, such as shutting down airports and closing schools, it helped contain the spread of the virus, thereby also mitigating the economic damage.

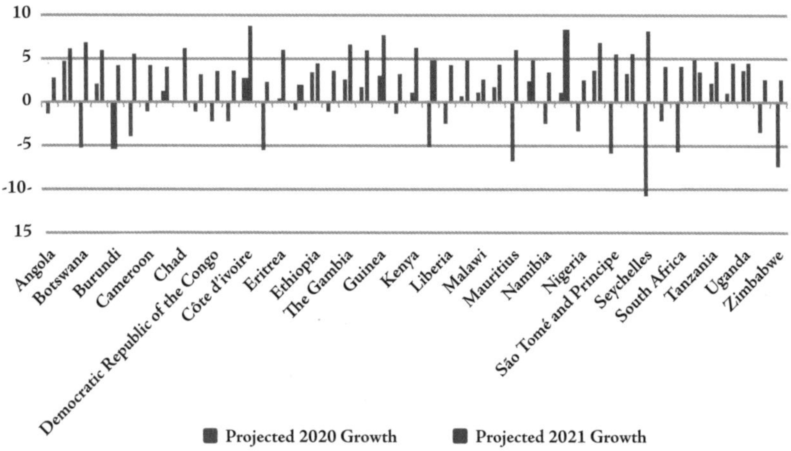

Figure 15: Consequences of COVID-19 for GDP Growth in 2020 and 2021 in Sub-Saharan Africa (Source: IMF)

Within the advanced economies, performance can also differ (see figure 16). The United Kingdom is set to be among the hardest hit as a result of its delaying the imposition of a lockdown and allowing the virus to spread out of control, which eventually necessitated an even more protracted lockdown period.

This similar fate might well befall the United States, wherein lax public health measures early in the pandemic allowed for temporarily higher economic output, only for a far more severe contraction to ensue later.

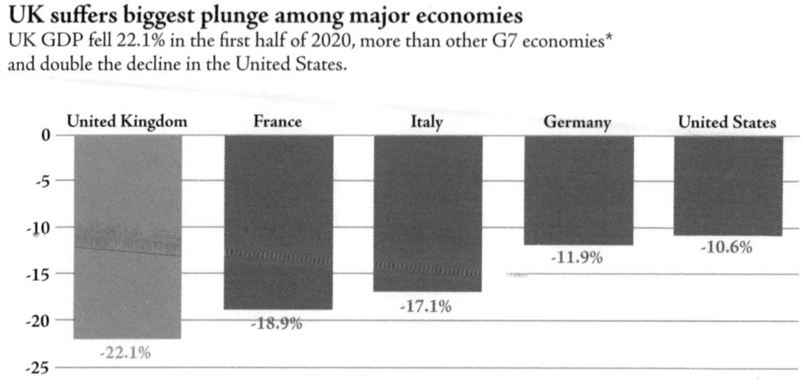

Figure 16: Comparative Economic Performance of Advanced Western Economies (Source: CNN)

In Asia, too, economic contractions have taken hold, and unemployment has risen.

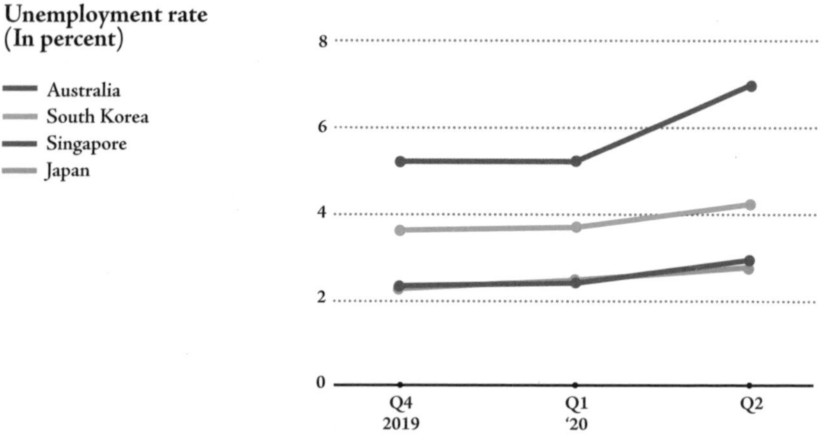

Figure 17: Unemployment Rate in Selected Asian Countries (Source: OECD & Singstat)

Some politicians and government leaders believe that there is a trade-off between the health of the economy and the health of the population, since controlling the pandemic through strict public health measures would cause deep contractions. However, this is a misunderstanding. Without getting the virus under control, aggregate demand will not rebound, since people will not resume daily life, consumers will not return to their ordinary consumption patterns (e.g. dining out) and firms will not have the confidence to invest. Meanwhile, the failure to control the virus only necessitates more draconian lockdowns in the future, lengthening the supply shock of restaurants, schools and workplaces being closed.

Limited or inconsistent efforts by states to control the virus based on public health guidance are not only placing citizens at unnecessary risk of severe illness and possible death – but are also likely to prolong the economic downturn.

Eric S. Rosengren
13th President of the Federal Reserve Bank of Boston

The International Monetary Fund's Assessment of the Economic Situation: Main Takeaways

The economic consequences of COVID-19 have been more severe than initially anticipated.

- Even as the pandemic has levelled off in some countries, it has taken a turn for the worse in others.
- The downturn is deep but globally synchronised.
- Unlike in most recessions, consumption has not proven stable, but rather has dropped. Similarly, the services sector has not, as is usual in recessions, been relatively resilient – for obvious reasons relating to social distancing measures.
- Mobility between and within countries remains limited.
- The labour market has seen a severe decline in activity.
- Global trade has contracted.
- Inflation is weaker, with declines in aggregate demand more than offsetting any cost-push pressure from supply interruptions.

Policy countermeasures by governments and central banks have helped limit the extent of economic damage.

- Governments have employed ambitious programmes, such as assistance to workers on temporary furlough. Such fiscal measures amount to $1 trillion globally.
- Central banks have taken swift and sometimes novel actions: for example, engaging in quantitative easing for the first time, or significantly increasing the scale of asset purchases to increase liquidity and also ensure the availability of cheap credit.
- The oil market has stabilized… somewhat. West Texas futures, for instance, has risen from its unprecedented negative prices in April to a more stable range.
- The US dollar has depreciated, while other countries' currencies have strengthened, including the Australian Dollar, the Norwegian Krone, the Indonesian Rupiah, Mexican Pesos, the Russian Ruble and the South African Rand. This indicates a reversal of the initial "flight-to-safety" sentiment by investors.

Overall, IMF projects a deep global downturn in 2020, before a slower turnaround in 2021, as the following extract from their *June 2020 World Economic Outlook* makes clear:

"Global growth is projected at -4.9 percent in 2020, 1.9 percentage points below the April 2020 WEO forecast. Consumption growth, in particular, has been downgraded for most economies, reflecting the larger-than-anticipated disruption to domestic activity.

The projections of weaker private consumption reflect a combination of a large adverse aggregate demand shock from social distancing and lockdowns, as well as a rise in precautionary savings.

Moreover, investment is expected to be subdued as firms defer capital expenditures amid high uncertainty. Policy support partially offsets the deterioration in private domestic demand.

In the baseline, global activity is expected to trough in the second quarter of 2020, recovering thereafter. In 2021 growth is projected to strengthen to 5.4 percent, 0.4 percentage point lower than the April forecast.

Consumption is projected to strengthen gradually next year, and investment is also expected to firm up, but to remain subdued. Global GDP for the year 2021 as a whole is forecast to just exceed its 2019 level."

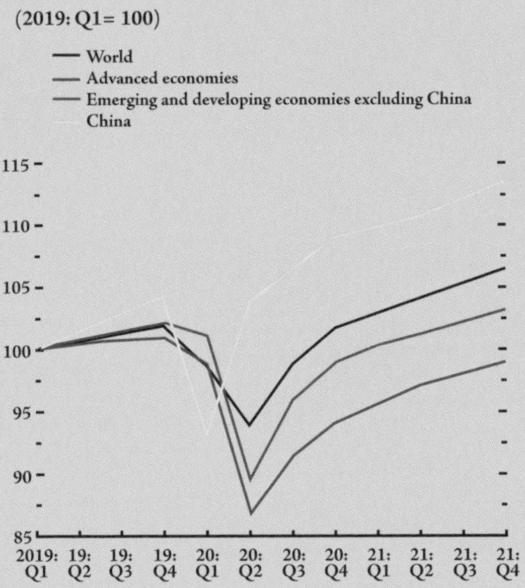

Figure 18: Quarterly World GDP 2019 forecasted to 2021 (Source: IMF)

Financial Instability

The financial outlook for the world is grim but is improving in some aspects.[36]

On the downside:

- Entering the crisis, household debt had been increasing, and aggregate corporate debt was standing at historically high levels. With the ongoing pandemic-induced recession and the negative impact on consumers' income streams and businesses' revenue streams, debt burdens might become unmanageable. Indeed, there has already been the highest pace of corporate bond defaults since the global financial crisis, even as borrowing by non-financial firms has continued to surge.
- Increased insolvencies will stress the banking sector, despite banks having higher liquidity and capital buffers as a result of Basel III and the reforms undertaken after the global financial crisis.
- Non-bank financial companies and markets will also be vulnerable in the event of a broad wave of insolvencies.
- Some developing and emerging market economies are also facing high external financing requirements, with existing debt facing high-interest rates when being rolled over.
- Even in the advanced OECD nations, public debt is high and will rise further, if a second wave of infections occurs (see figure 19).
- There has been a developing disconnect between financial markets and the real economy, where developments in the former do not track occurrences in the latter – a fact that could threaten the recovery should investor appetite for risk fall.

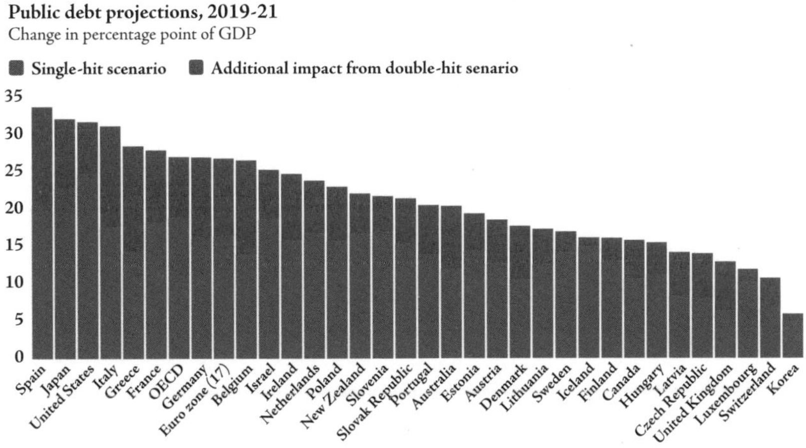

Figure 19: OECD Public Debt Projections (Source: OECD)

On the upside:

- Risk Asset prices have rebounded after the sharp fall earlier in 2020, even as benchmark interest rates have fallen – easing the general financial situation.
- Central banks have taken strong action to address market problems, which has strengthened market sentiments.

However, these upside observations come with notable and non-trivial caveats.

First, Risk Asset prices can invert easily and do not represent structural stability in capital markets. Indeed, they can be interpreted as embodying a 'Minsky Moment' – where most capital, including stimulus monies, is primarily directed toward speculative short term bets, rather than on long term returns based on productive investments such as infrastructure for transport, public security, education and health. A longer-term approach would lift general welfare and help countries recover more strongly and emerge from the pandemic with greater resiliency.

Second, central bank action carries with it the danger of capital market distortion through excess liquidity and also reduces the propensity of households and individuals to save, which stores up problems in the longer-term. Zero-bound interest rates, taken together with sustained negative global growth conditions, could result in a general deflationary scenario, which could presage the morphing of a synchronised recession into a synchronised depression.

Transition to Telecommuting

The pandemic has led to the call for companies to allow employees to work-from-home and provide even greater flexibility in working arrangements. The demand for productivity tools, such as video conferencing, work collaboration and communications software, has surged since the outbreak of COVID-19.

Several technology companies have benefitted from the work-from-home phenomenon. For instance, Zoom, a video conferencing solution provider, managed to achieve 151 percent year-on-year growth in its number of active users in March 2020.[37]

Microsoft's Teams workplace chat and collaboration tool also experienced a 38 percent surge in the number of daily active users between 11th March and 18th March 2020.[38]

Fulfilling lifestyle needs at home is another key driver in the COVID-19 economy. Certain countries, such as China, France, New Zealand, Italy, and Malaysia, have implemented mass-scale restrictive quarantines that limit leisure and business activities. In the most extreme cases, businesses were even ordered to shut down or could not operate because of a lack of manpower.

This has resulted in a large stay-at-home population whose daily necessities and entertainment needs must be fulfilled at home, prompting a surge in demand for goods and services to be delivered to homes.

Under such circumstances, companies that operate in industries such as digital payment, e-commerce, home entertainment services, and food and grocery delivery, are likely to benefit from increased demand.

For instance, Peloton, a provider of home-use cycles and treadmills with subscriptions to online classes, saw its app downloaded five times more in March 2020 compared to February 2020.[39]

The food delivery service providers in Singapore, such as Deliveroo and GrabFood, also experienced a 20 percent increase in deliveries during the outbreak.[40]

In the next few years, the effects of COVID-19 economy may linger and continue to be a significant driver that reshapes work patterns and consumption behaviour.

It has been observed that the workers whose jobs more suited to work-from-home, as well as workers who are deemed essential, have been less affected by the lockdown-induced recession, relative to workers in roles requiring social interaction, such as in restaurants and retail.

However, this pattern is not unique to this recession, which I will call the 'Great Lockdown'. During the Global Financial Crisis, tele-workable jobs were also more secure, suggesting that it is not just compatibility with social distancing, but also greater education and skill – as is typical for jobs like consulting, law and finance – that makes such tele-workable occupations more secure.

Unemployment and teleworking
Unemployment has increased less for teleworkable occupations during both the Global Financial Crisis and current pandemic-related recession.
(Change in unemployment rate, %)

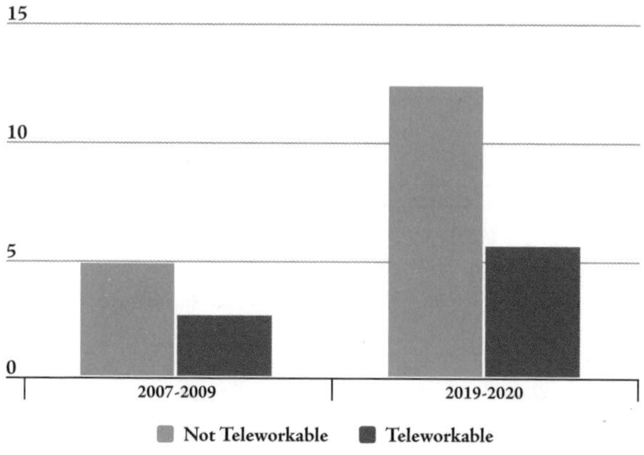

Sources: U.S. Current Population Survey, and IMF staff calculations.

Figure 20: Global Private Equity and Venture Capital Fintech Deals (Source: Preqin)

In general, it has always been the case that the low-skilled, the low-income and young have been harmed most during recessions.

One difference between the Great Lockdown and previous recessions lies in women being more severely affected. This arises from the fact that women are more likely to work in sectors and occupations affected by the lockdown, such as services, as well as from the reality that women are subject to unequal childcare burdens.

Affirmation of the Technology Oligopoly

The COVID-19 pandemic has created transitory but unidirectional shifts that have disrupted the market equilibrium. The result of this is the creation of unilateral advantages among companies which are positioned to benefit from the COVID-19 economy, either by nature or design.

Big Tech players are most likely to benefit and to further entrench their competitive advantage because of the following four factors: (i) strategic advantage; (ii) strong cash reserves; (iii) diminishing competition; and (iv) lower financing and valuation for technology startups.

Figure 21: The Technology Oligopoly (Source: Future-Moves Group)

Strategic Advantage

Big Tech: Big Tech is strategically positioned to benefit from the COVID-19 economy. The pandemic will likely accelerate the adoption of technologies such as work collaboration tools, digital payment and e-commerce. In addition to the convenience value that they bring, they help to minimise in-person contact and therefore infection risks.

Many of their products and services have also become a household essential to serve the needs of work-from-home and stay-at-home individuals.

E-commerce and Delivery Services: Delivery and online commerce services are among the sectors that have benefitted the most from the pandemic. In the United States, e-commerce sales are estimated to be approximately US$700 billion in 2020 – a US$100 billion increase from 2019.[41]

Amazon has experienced increased demand on its e-commerce platform for essential items, and while the company has committed to increasing its capacity for delivery and pick-up options, many household items listed on its platform are still running out of stock.

Streaming service companies are another group of key beneficiaries. Netflix saw a significant spike in daily active users, causing outages across Europe and the US.

Due to the increased usage, Netflix even had to lower its streaming quality to balance its data consumption and reduce the load on internet service providers.

Social Media Platforms: Social media giants have also benefitted from increased usage. For example, Alphabet's YouTube saw a 500 percent increase in views on 15 March 2020, compared to its daily average in pre-COVID-19 times.[42]

The net effect on the revenue of social media companies is uncertain because most of them make money from advertisers, who could be restricting their advertisement spending in the current situation.

Nevertheless, a dramatic increase in usage allows social media companies to hoard more consumer data, which could benefit the platforms in the longer term.

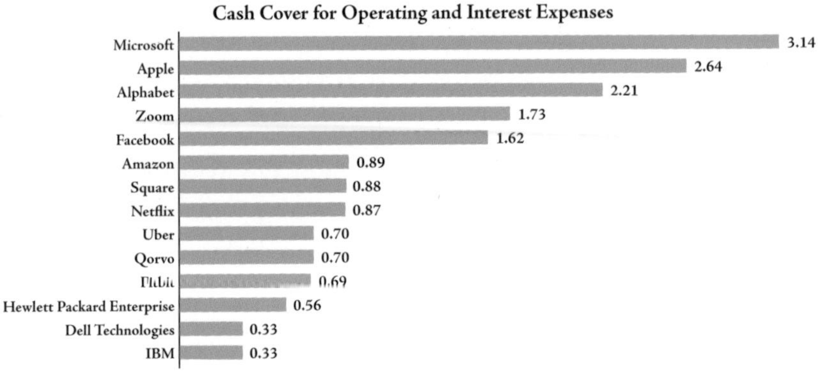

Figure 22: Cash Cover (cash plus short-term securities) to Operating and Interest Expenses Ratio Among Selected Technology Companies (Source: Future-Moves Group; data from Yahoo Finance, Company Annual Reports)

Strong Cash Reserves

Due to their dominance in the past decade, Big Tech has been sitting on a huge cash pile that provides them with a significant war chest to withstand disruptions.

Figure 22 shows the ratio of cash and short-term investments to operating and interest expenses. The higher the ratio, the greater the company's ability to maintain its operations and fulfil debt obligation.

Microsoft, Apple and Alphabet stand out from the rest. Figure 22 suggests that these three companies can fund more than two years' worth of their operating and interest expenses by using only their cash reserves.

Coupled with strong operating cash flow and additional room for debt financing, Big Tech players are well-positioned to outperform and outlast smaller competitors who might not be able to survive the longer-term impact of COVID-19.

Diminishing Competition

Consumers: The COVID-19 pandemic forces consumers to perform transactions and fulfil their needs on digital platforms, which has put brick-and-mortar businesses at a very disadvantaged position. As a result, Big Tech players have benefitted significantly from diminished competition from the traditional rivals.

Retail Industry: Retail and entertainment stores, such as grocery shops, casinos and cinemas, have suffered significantly due to declined patronage and in some cases, forced closure.

This creates significant opportunities for e-commerce players such as Alibaba and Amazon; and online streaming and entertainment companies, such as Sony, Netflix and Tencent, to step in and fill the void.

Tenants: Offices and hotels are also key losers, particularly those that bank on flexible solutions. Already suffering from cash flow and profitability issues, WeWork's business model of signing long-term leases and renting out short-term spaces is especially flawed in the current economic situation.

Without the support of long-term tenancy agreements, many co-working spaces are already facing a steep drop in occupancy. The rising awareness and acceptance for remote working could continue to gain momentum after the pandemic ends, casting further gloom on the potential future of co-working spaces.

Lower Financing and Valuation for Technology Startups

COVID-19 will also bring financial shocks that would weaken the financing pipelines for start-ups and smaller technology companies, possibly leading to intensified consolidation in the technology industry.

Even during the pandemic, investors will be seen changing their investment lenses and demanding startups to demonstrate a path to profitability.

For instance, Sequoia Capital, one of the most established venture capital firms globally, called in early March 2020 for its portfolio companies to conduct a reality check by revisiting sales forecasts, conserving cash and reducing costs, among other suggestions.

While the impact of the pandemic could be uneven for various technology startups and unicorns, business viability and valuations across all companies are likely to be challenged.

Private equity and venture capital financing showed signs of fading in 2019. Deal value and deal counts declined substantially, with many

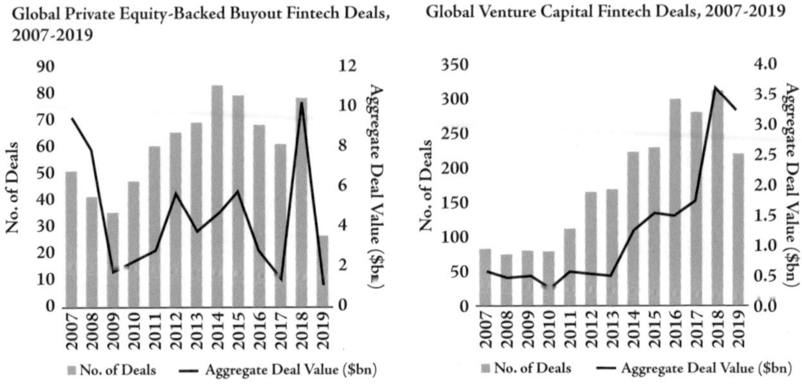

Figure 23: Unemployment Index for Select Countries (Source: IMF)

investment managers pointing out that market conditions were tough and valuations were inflated.

In a post-COVID-19 world, lofty valuations that were commonly seen in the last decade will be challenged and in the worst scenario, even the established unicorns might come to the edge of failure because of a cash crunch.

This makes for ideal conditions for consolidation in the technology industry. With significant cash reserves, Big Tech will stand to benefit from the low valuations and will be able to accelerate their investments if they want to.

After the pandemic, the likelihood of a Big Tech oligopoly, or even monopoly, in various industries is high. Under this scenario, they would dominate not only in terms of market power, but also in data advantage, innovation and talent pool.

Increased Automation

Given the reality of social distancing, companies have been using – and will increasingly use – robots and artificial intelligence to carry out tasks, where previously they would have relied on human employees.

This is the case with traditional blue-collar service jobs like food or package delivery. In Beijing, robots in apartment blocks are capable

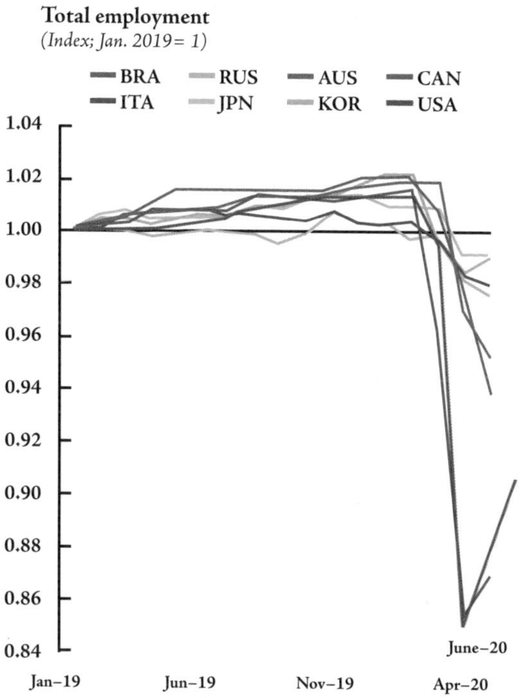

Figure 24: Unemployment Index for Select Countries (Source: IMF)

of riding elevators and navigating corridors to deliver items to a customer's door.

Robots are already being developed and deployed to do everything from floor cleaning to temperature taking; from salad making to corridor patrolling and industrial manufacturing. When mated with machine learning capabilities, the need for human supervision will diminish and eventually cease.

White-collar jobs are not exempt from this push towards automation either, even in jobs like finance and law. Algorithms can do the jobs of execution traders in finance, for example, or prepare complex legal documents upon a client answering a set questionnaire. AI chatbots, meanwhile, can take calls and respond to queries, backed as they are by natural-language algorithms.

Within the transport industry, demand for self-driving cars will grow, given the need to transport people and deliver goods while avoiding physical contact between humans. Currently, the technology is not fully mature, with various challenges still extant – interpreting and reacting to the hand gestures of human drivers, for example. However, development and testing are ongoing, and the mature version of the technology can be expected to take to the roads within the decade.

All these trends towards automation raise the spectre of structural unemployment or "technological" unemployment, and a greater risk of job insecurity.

While retraining workers into new industries that complement and support the move towards automation is theoretically possible – in robotic repair and maintenance, for instance – in reality this is challenging, slow and costly, and comes with no guarantee of a high rate of successful redeployment.

In light of these worries about structural unemployment, there has been increasing popular awareness of, and political support for, the idea of an unconditional basic income (UBI).

Under such a scheme, every adult will be given a sum of money each month – supporting not just their consumption but also the broader economy, which requires a sufficient level of demand to power growth and innovation.

Increased Inequality

The pandemic is likely to worsen inequality, not just within societies but between societies, and not just in general, but between races and genders.

Economic Inequality

In the first instance, economic inequality can be expected to rise as a result of the coronavirus. The pandemic hurts lowly-paid workers harder than highly-paid ones, with disproportionate levels of unemployment recorded for blue-collar service workers while white-collar professionals retain jobs.

Even in Europe, where countries have strong welfare states, the heavy reliance on pre-distribution measures – with equal access to education, health and strong labour protections resulting in relatively equal distribution of pre-tax income – means that the coronavirus-induced surge in post-tax inequality will not automatically be contained.

Moreover, with poorer students disproportionately lacking access to computers, educational disparities will worsen – in turn hurting long-term prospects for economic equality and mobility.

Racial and Gender Inequality

In the second instance, racial and gender inequality can be expected to rise. Racial minorities, such as those in the US, hold a disproportionate number of low-income and blue-collar service jobs, and with the pandemic hitting such workers harder, so too will racial minorities experience greater rates of job loss and poverty.

Women are affected to a greater extent than men – not just because the former are more likely to hold service jobs, but because unequal childcare burdens on mothers working at home will cause their performance to suffer, and, eventually, cost them pay and promotions.

Between-country Inequality

In the third instance, between-country inequalities will sharpen. Poorer countries, which have a greater proportion of people in poverty and living hand-to-mouth, and which have a lower state capacity to provide economic assistance to the unemployed, will see spikes in poverty and economic hardship.

Emerging market and developing economies (EMDEs) will also be especially hard hit given that they rely heavily on trade, tourism and remittances from abroad. In Asia, tourism-dependent economies have been severely hit, with a drop in tourist numbers leading to massive losses in tourism-related industries in countries like Thailand, Vietnam and Indonesia.

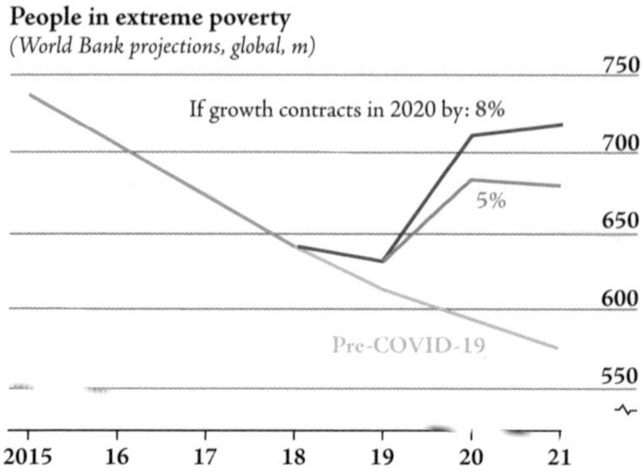

Figure 25: Impact of COVID-19 on Poverty (Source: World Bank)

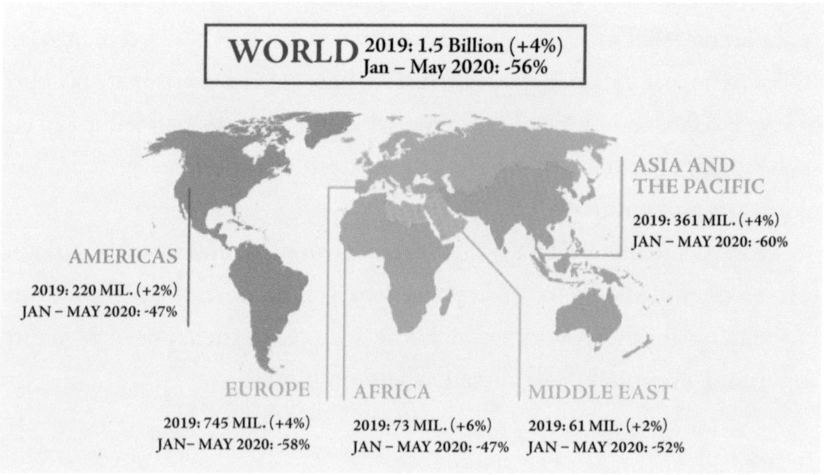

Figure 26: International Tourist Arrivals, 2019 vs 2020 (Source: World Trade Organization)

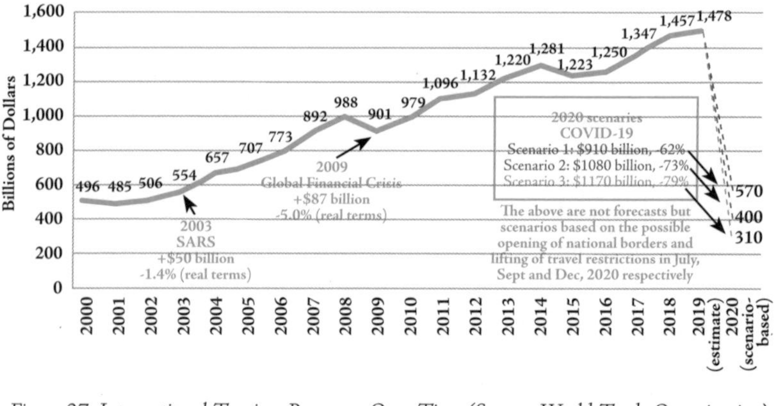

Figure 27: International Tourism Revenues Over Time (Source: World Trade Organization)

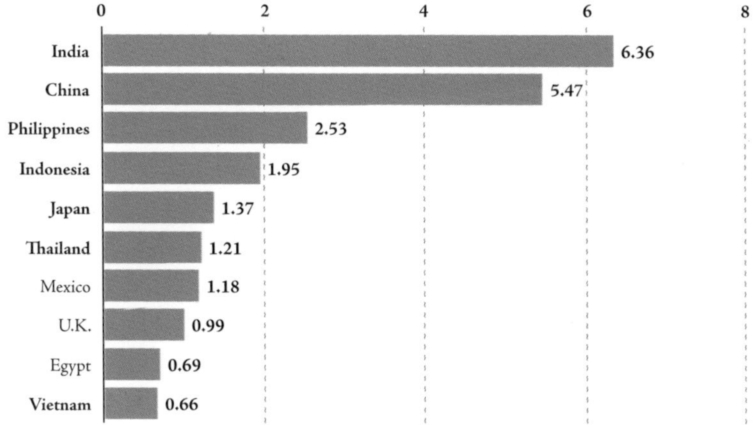

Figure 28: Top 10 Countries by Travel and Tourism Jobs Created from 2014-19 (Source: World Travel and Tourism Council)

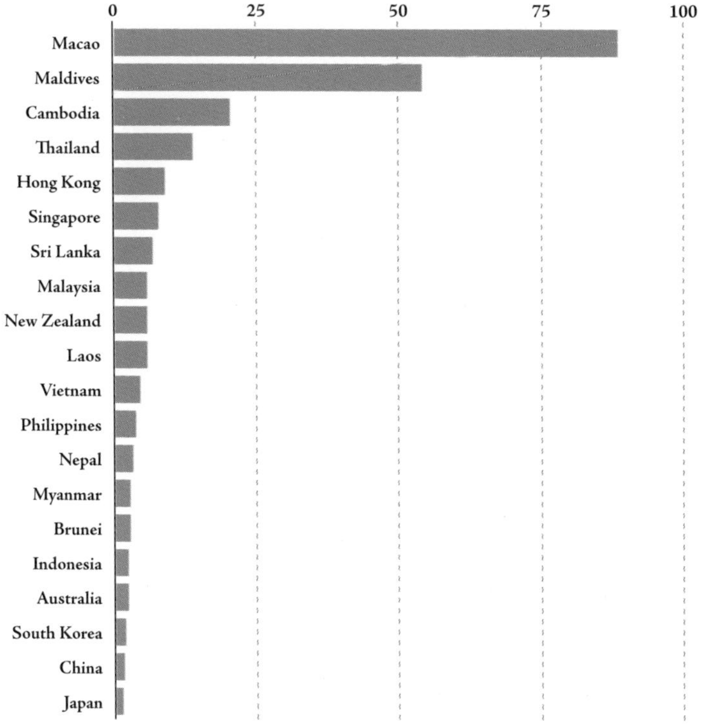

Figure 29: Countries by Percentage of Economy Dependent on Inbound Tourism (Source: World Travel and Tourism Council)

The airline industry has been badly hit, and with very few people travelling for either leisure or business, airlines are doing all they can to avoid collapse. International Air Transport Association (IATA) does not expect passenger traffic to recover until at least 2024, and foresees airlines losing more than $84 billion in 2020 alone.[43]

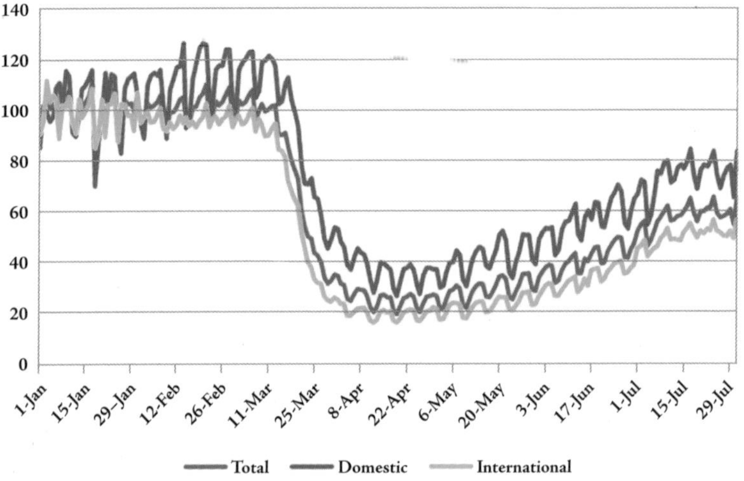

Figure 30: Number of Commercial Flights, 2020 (OpenSky and World Trade Organization)

Meanwhile, EMDEs also tend to have higher debt after the Global Financial Crisis, making them more vulnerable to financial stress.

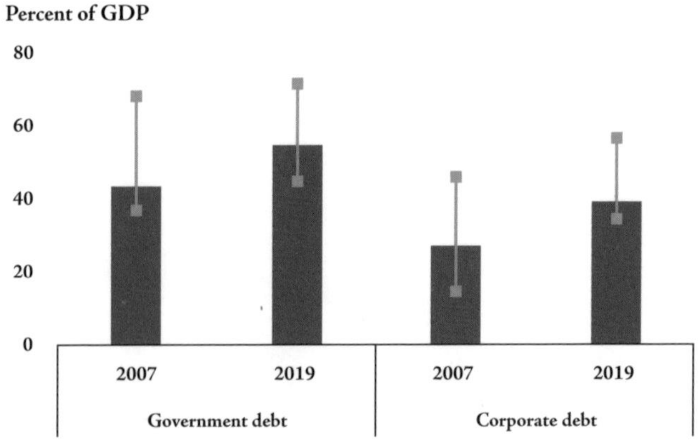

Figure 31: Government and Corporate Debt (Source: IMF and World Bank)

EMDEs are also more likely to have less diversified economies with their export portfolios being more concentrated on a small basket of primary products, whose prices can slump strongly in line with fluctuations in global demand. As Dana Vorisek, a Senior Economist at the IMF warns, "The long-term damage of COVID-19 will be particularly severe in economies that suffer financial crises and, in energy exporters, because of the collapse in oil prices. In the average EMDE, over a five-year horizon, a recession combined with a financial crisis could lower potential output by almost 8 percent while, in the average EMDE energy exporter, a recession combined with an oil price plunge could lower potential output by 11 percent."

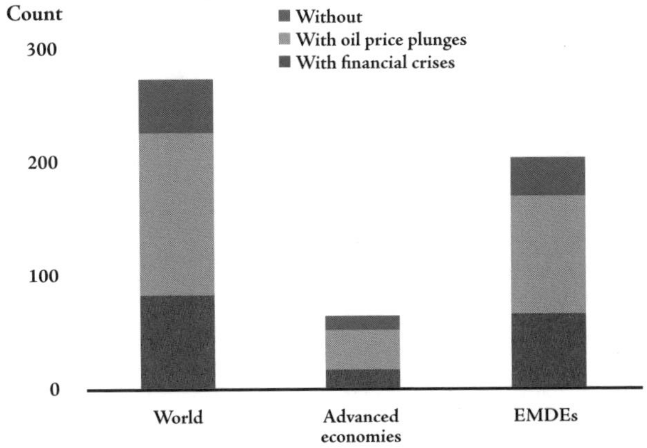

Figure 31: Frequency of Recessions (World Bank)

The impact is global. The decline of remittance flows this year is going to be historically a record.

Dilip Ratha
Lead Economist, Migration and Remittances, World Bank

Remittances have fallen during the pandemic, due to migrant workers being concentrated in hard-hit sectors, such as construction, and also because the pandemic lockdowns have made it difficult for workers to visit banks or to travel home with cash.

Countries such as the Philippines, Indonesia, Bangladesh, Pakistan and Myanmar, which rely heavily on remittances to manage their Balance of Payments (BoP), are finding these sources of hard currency inflows drying up which, at the same time, leaves them without the resources to provide adequate social safety nets for families dependent on such remittances for survival.

Moreover, recovery is uncertain, especially in the area of tourism. As Dana Vorisek notes, "Much is still unknown about the pace of tourism recovery in 2020. Peoples' desire and ability to travel abroad may continue to face headwinds going into 2021 due to the ongoing pandemic, leaving an uncertain outlook for tourism industries in economies both big and small."

Moreover, as Pulitzer Prize-winning journalist and tourism expert Elizabeth Becker cautions, any recovery in tourism will be uneven: "Smart travellers will trust places with good governance and health systems. They will take fewer trips and stay longer. They will see this pandemic as a forecast of what's to come from the climate crisis. They will act like responsible citizens as well as passionate travellers."

All these problems – trade, tourism and remittances being hit hard; pre-existing debt troubles; lack of diversified economies – are further compounded by the danger of "scarring". This is the permanent loss of productive capacity, with mortality, morbidity and worsened education outcomes depressing the population's future ability to produce goods and services.

The collapse of small enterprises that lack access to credit – and the overhand of debt on those companies that nonetheless survive – will also add to irrecoverable production disruption.

In the aftermath of the 2013 Ebola pandemic, Sierra Leone never returned to its pre-crisis growth path, and there is a danger that less-developed countries will face similar prospects, and a "lost decade" – with poverty increasing and the past decade's gains undone.

The IMF estimates that 100 million people could fall into extreme poverty as a result of the pandemic-induced recession.[44]

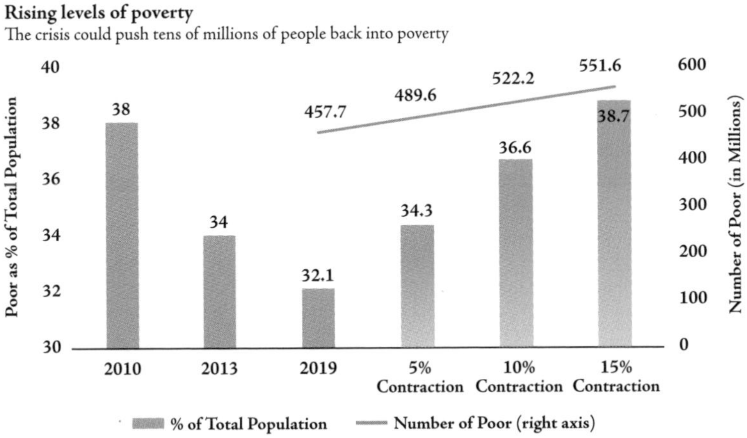

Figure 32: Global Rise in Poverty as a Result of the COVID-19 Pandemic (World Bank)

> *The crisis comes at a time when some countries were already in a crisis. It has taken away the means and the financial tools that these countries had to solve their problems in the first place. This is a very big problem for developing countries.*

John Baffes
Senior Economist, World Bank

MONETARY POLICY

Central banks are typically tasked with ensuring price stability and facilitating sustainable growth, along with maintaining foreign exchange stability. With COVID-19, a range of monetary policy options are available to economic policymakers and central bankers.

Interest Rates

To avoid deflation and a contraction in economic output, interest rates might be lowered, thereby stimulating investment and aggregate demand, and expanding economic output.

Historically, there has been a strong negative relationship between interest rates and aggregate real GDP, albeit one that has decreased over the decades. And with nominal interest rates near zero in many advanced economies, it is clear that reduction in interest rates alone cannot overcome the COVID-19 recession.

Quantitative Easing

This being so, central bankers might turn to unconventional monetary policy, particularly quantitative easing (QE). QE has several theoretical transmission channels for affecting output and inflation:

(i) It increases the amount of cash held by banks, and hence the amount of lending they do.
(ii) It reduces the liquidity premium in the financial markets and hence the effective interest rate faced by firms.
(iii) Bending the yield curve, with the purchase of short-term financial instruments like bonds, lowers short-term interest rates and pushes investors to riskier, long-term instruments like securities, thereby lowering interest rates there.
(iv) It raises inflation expectations, thereby lowering the real interest rate.
(v) It boosts confidence, and consequently consumer and firm spending.

Evidence from the Global Financial Crisis suggests that the Federal Reserve's QE was equivalent to a 200 basis point reduction in the federal funds rate[46] and that the Bank of England's QE measure measures were equivalent to a 150-300 basis point cut in the policy rate[47]; other estimates suggest that QE in the UK had a peak effect of +1.5 percent on real GDP.[48]

As can be seen from Figure 34, central bank balance sheets have significantly expanded since the Global Financial Crisis, and even more during the COVID-19 recession, as central banks engaged in aggressive quantitative easing, buying up significant amounts of financial assets to boost the real economy through the above-mentioned transmission channels.

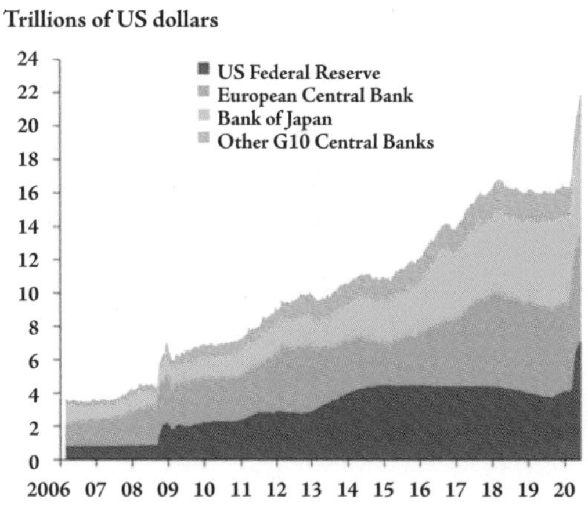

Figure 33: G10 Central Bank Assets (Source: IMF)

Of course, such radical expansion of central banks' balance sheets has raised worries. The Governor of the Bank of England, Andrew Bailey, has eloquently expressed this concern: "In the event that a crisis occurs, the pace of asset purchases as well as the stock of purchases matters for the overall macroeconomic effect. A reduction in the stock of assets held on the balance sheet provides more space for large and rapid purchase programmes in the future. We need to work through what lessons this may have for the appropriate future path of central bank balance sheets, including the pace and timing of any future unwind of asset purchases."

Nonetheless, despite such fears, there is no inherent risk to the expansion of central banks' balance sheets, as central banks are uniquely positioned to meet their liabilities with further money production.

The risk, as ever, is the inflation this would cause, but the experience of the past decade – low or no inflation in many advanced economies – and muted demand in the current crisis suggest that quantitative easing poses no real inflationary threat.

Helicopter Money

More radical sorts of monetary policy like 'helicopter money' might even be considered. Helicopter money is the transfer of money directly to individuals, as funded by the creation of new money. In effect, helicopter money constitutes fiscal policy supported by the monetisation of government debt.

Such a policy increases individual income directly, and is therefore highly effective at boosting consumption and demand. Inflation, while a theoretical concern, is unlikely to be a problem in practice for the foreseeable future, so long as output remains below potential.

There are two advantages of helicopter money over QE. Firstly, the stimulus impact per dollar is higher, and secondly, it avoids artificially inflating the value of stock markets as QE does, which can distort price signals and increase wealth inequality.

Securing Hard Currency

For countries with heavy import dependencies, ensuring the availability of US dollars would be a priority. In this regard, currency swap arrangements between the US federal reserve and various central banks globally for the US dollar – but also between the ECB and various European central banks for the euro are crucial.

These swap arrangements allow borrowing central banks to obtain reserve currencies like the USD using their own currency, on the promise to reverse the swap at interest at a pre-specified later date.

Credit lines through repurchase agreements (repo) are also important, in allow central banks to borrow reserve currencies like the USD with assets (denominated in the same currency) serving as collateral.

In the absence of such currency swap or repo arrangements, other options such as drawing down on official foreign reserves or asset sales might be considered. Alternatively, special drawing rights (SDRs) – supplementary foreign exchange reserve assets that are vested with the IMF that can be changed for tradeable currencies – might be utilised.

Macroprudential Policy

The banking system is facing a challenging task in the current crisis. On the one hand, they need to be able to distinguish viable borrowers from those who are unlikely to survive the pandemic.

On the other hand, an overly restrictive approach to lending will increase the likelihood of corporate defaults - and lead to a greater economic crisis and worsened balance sheets regardless.

To address this problem and encourage lending, central banks can consider relaxing capital buffets, easing regulations on nonperforming loans, relaxing liquidity buffers and bringing in miscellaneous measures like easing compliance costs.

Despite the risks inherent in such relaxation of financial regulations, this is appropriate given three considerations.

First, there is the vastness of the economic damage done by the pandemic, and the need to address it in any way possible.

Second, the current contraction in global growth differs fundamentally from the Global Financial Crisis, during which a badly regulated financial system was itself the seed of the crisis. However, the potential is real for drivers behind the Great Depression to reoccur and be amplified.

For instance, if there is a premature pull back of Central Bank support, or a failure to coordinate between Central Banks of major economies – especially when manifested by 'Beggar thy Neighbour' strategies adopted by countries like the United States – these represent non-trivial threats to confidence in a recovery. At the same time, they become frictional factors which inhibit the full potential for an organic recovery.

Third, such regulations can be put back in place when the worst of the crisis has passed, with banks made to build up their capital and liquidity buffers during and following the crisis.

Avoiding Procyclical Monetary Policy

Developing economies have long suffered from procyclical monetary policy – that is, monetary policy that reinforces the business cycle, rather than moderate it.

Expansionary policies during boom times that lead to an immense expansion in credit and debt, followed with contractionary policies during downturns, further intensify falls in output and employment.

The reason for such counterproductive policy is that downturns in developing economies typically involve large capital outflows, which causes significant currency depreciation and pushes inflation and the elevated risks of a sovereign debt crisis.

Liabilities denominated in foreign currencies become increasingly burdensome to service as the assets denominated in the local currency fall sharply in value. Central banks are hence incentivised to raise interest rates and defend the currency, even if this deepens the economic contraction. However, few countries have adequate official foreign reserves to arm their central banks to sterilise their currencies to maintain price stability for extended durations.

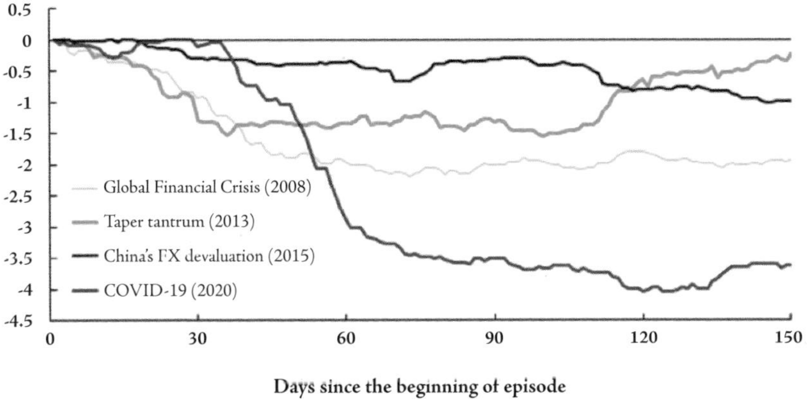

Figure 34: Capital Outflows from Emerging Market Economies During the COVID-19 Recession Relative to Past Crises (Source: VoxEU)

The solution to this is to have credible monetary frameworks and keep inflation low during booms, to allow greater space during recessions for interest rate reductions and expansionary monetary policy.

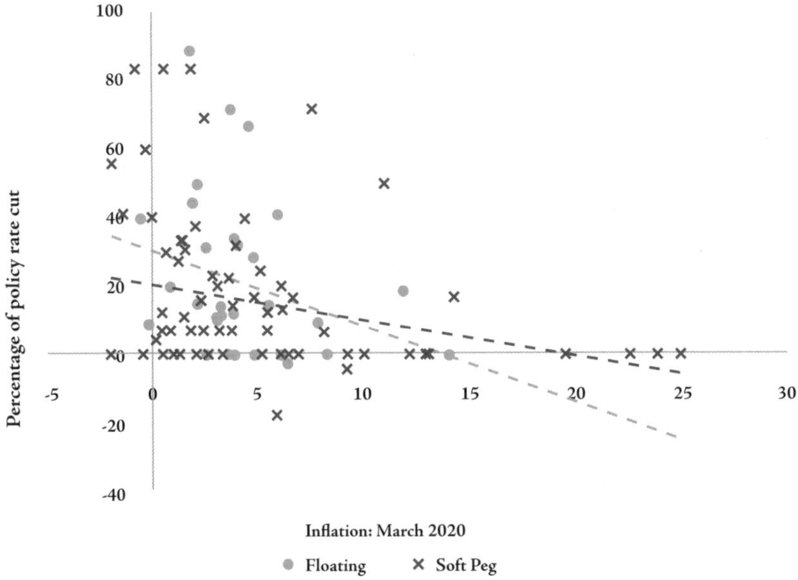

Figure 35: Relationship between Initial Inflation and Eventual Interest Rate Cut (Source: VoxEU)

FISCAL POLICY

The challenge for governments is to ensure growth and avoid unemployment in the short-term, even while balancing long-term concerns over debt.

Expansionary Fiscal Policy

Expansionary fiscal policy can expand aggregate demand, inducing the production of goods and services by firms, and in turn, expand employment. This increases consumption and further raises aggregate demand in a self-reinforcing cycle.

Estimates from the Global Financial Crisis suggest that the fiscal multiplier – how much output increases per unit of fiscal expansion – is positive, and ranges from anything between 0.9 to 1.7.[49]

Type of Stimulus

A fiscal stimulus can take the form of consumption-geared injections, which include direct transfers to households, wage subsidies and tax rebates; or it can take the form of long-term productive investments, in areas like public health, education and transport.

The former involves greater consumption multipliers and are more effective at bringing economies out of recessions, but have fewer long-term benefits.

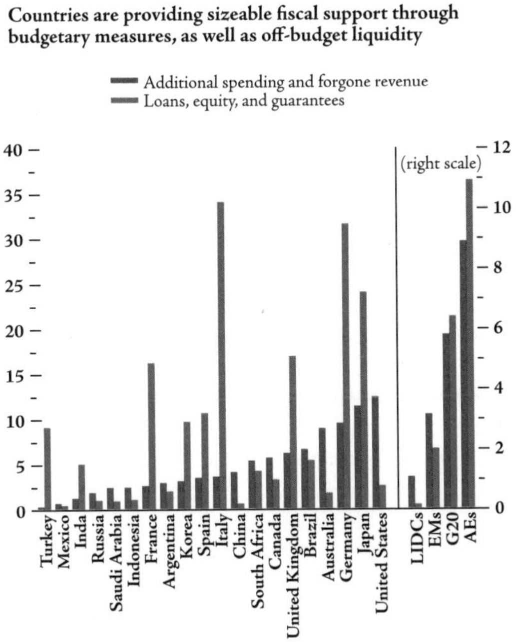

Figure 36: Countries' Fiscal Responses, in terms of Percentage of GDP (Source: IMF)

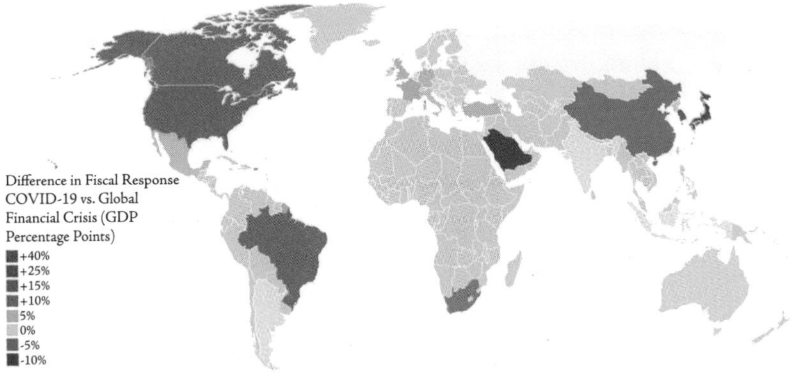

Figure 37: Difference in Fiscal Responses to COVID-19 Recession Relative to Baseline Action in the Global Financial Crisis (Source: Atlantic Council)

The latter boosts long-term growth but is more limited in its short-term stimulus effects. Policymakers must make a careful assessment when deciding on the appropriate composition of their stimulus measures, depending on specific national circumstances.

Funding Sources

Such stimulus can be funded through numerous sources, such as (i) the drawing down of government surpluses or past reserves; (ii) borrowing (for example, the sale of domestic government bonds in local currency, or the issuance of sovereign debt in foreign currency, or borrowing through state-owned enterprises); (iii) taxes; (iv) cancellation of prior budgetary commitments (infrastructure projections or defence acquisitions, for example); (v) sale of national assets; or (vi) international aid.

Crowding Out

If borrowing is used to fund the stimulus, crowding out of private investment will be unlikely, at least in the case of advanced economies.

As Douglas Elmendorf, a former director of the Congressional Budget Office and the current dean of Harvard's John F. Kennedy School of Government observes, "We're in an era where more government debt is not doing so much crowding out. I think the idea that we should not let the debt constrain our response to the pandemic is exactly right. But I think the idea that it never matters how much debt you have, because there's always some way around that, is wrong."

The lack of crowding out under present economic conditions is because of low prevailing interest rates, and also the reality of concurrent monetary expansion.

This factor shows the importance of coordinating fiscal and monetary policy in practice and remaining flexible and responsive to real world changes.

Debt and Growth

Borrowing also raises the issue of increasing government debt burdens. In theory, a government's increasing difficulty in meeting debt repayments can drive up default risk, and hence the risk premium and real interest rates, thereby depressing investment and growth.

That said, it is important not to overstate the case – especially for advanced economies capable of substantial borrowing in their own currency – and in any case, the empirical evidence in support of such theory is scarce.

For instance, prominent research from the economists Carmen Reinhart and Kenneth Rogoff purport to show that countries with a debt-to-GDP ratio higher than 90 percent grow slower than their peers below the threshold (1.7 percent vs 3.4 percent per annum growth),[50] but significant methodological errors in their research undermine their results.[51]

Moreover, correlation does not imply causation, and it is plausible that it is slow growth causing higher debt, as recessions trigger automatic and discretionary fiscal policy and consequent budget deficits.[52]

With all that said, even if debt does not in itself cause downside risks for growth, the increased burden on future generations is a concern, and governments might need to have a plan for meeting current debt commitments and paying off long-term debt.

Figure 38 indicates worldwide government debt in comparison to corporate debt, and COVID-19 can potentially worsen already heightened government debt burdens.

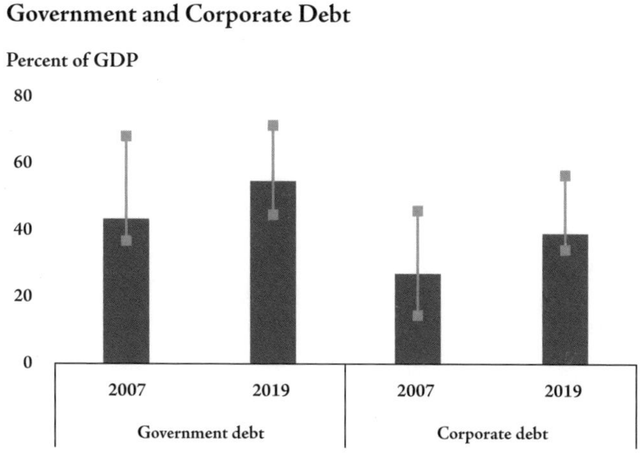

Note: Bars show unweighted averages. Whiskers show interquartile range. Based on data for up to 152 EMDEs.

Figure 38: Government and Corporate Debt (Source: World Bank)

Technological Innovations

Technological innovations can be used to facilitate economic policymaking and more timely fiscal action.

For instance, real-time mobility and location data from mobile phones while walking, driving or in transit, combined with data on different categories of places – be it retail and recreation, groceries and pharmacies, parks, transit stations, or workplaces and residences – can be used to infer the extent to which economic activity has fallen or risen.

The upshot is that with such real-time data, governments can conduct full macroeconomic assessments as well as engage in – and adjust the size of – fiscal interventions at a much earlier stage of the economic downturn without needing to wait for official macroeconomic and labour market figures collected in more traditional fashion.

This, in turn, allows the lever of fiscal policy to be used more speedily, to offset economic hardship and close the output gap. At the same time, it is important to acknowledge that there are limitations to such an approach, given the lower accuracy of such experimental indicators, and given the fact that such indicators only account for consumption, and not on the more volatile components like investment and capital spending that tend to drive the business cycle.

Containing this virus first is very important. Without containing the COVID-19 virus, the economic recovery will be very difficult. Protecting people's lives and their livelihood in the short-term period will provide the basis for economic recovery.

Changyong Rhee
Director of the Asia and Pacific Department at the IMF
29th July 2020

Financial Sector

Banks might need to be backstopped, to prevent financial panic and a breakdown in the supply of liquidity, as well as to head off a solvency crisis, which can impede lending in depressed times.

Risks

Beyond the direct issue of debt, monetary and fiscal planners must also be mindful of several varied risks.

Firstly, moral hazard can occur when support is extended to financial institutions, reducing the incentive to reform and to engage in responsible lending.

Secondly, a broad-based and poorly targeted stimulus can lead to deadweight, where generous government support allows inefficient and so-called "zombie" firms to continue operations. This frustrates the efficient reallocation of capital and labour to firms that could use such resources more efficiently.

Thirdly, speculative currency attacks can occur, as speculators sense an erosion in confidence in a currency's strength and take advantage accordingly.

Opportunities

For countries with appropriate reserves, a recession can offer the opportunity to acquire foreign assets, especially since deflation and correction in equity markets drive prices low, and since governments might be engaged in the sale of "crown jewels" to fund expenditures with the need to borrow or raise taxes.

The question is: how do we achieve resilience in a new global environment, including a pandemic-prone global environment, as well as growth – how do we avoid a sharp trade-off between resilience and growth?

Tharman Shanmugaratnam
Senior Minister, Prime Minister's Office, Singapore

INNOVATION

COVID-19 has significantly affected populations and economies. Consequently, it has spurred innovation in public policy, social behaviours, economic activity, organisational structures and processes. Research and development has been the benefactor of much innovation, with the development of rapid testing kits, vaccines and also technologies to make contact tracing, e-commerce and services, as well as remote working, more efficient and effective.

Innovations in Health

Testing

One common challenge faced by all countries is insufficiency in testing capacity – with shortages of chemicals or pipette tips – and the reliability of testing kits.

To overcome this, samples from several individuals can be pooled together for simultaneous testing. If the overall sample tests negative, this confirms the whole batch of individuals to be virus-free; but if the overall sample tests positive, further testing must be done on additional samples from each individual.

An ingenious method developed by Israeli scientists, however, allows just one round of testing; this method takes samples from hundreds of individuals and divides them into a small number of pools. For example, samples from 384 people may be divided into 48 pools, with each person's sample winding up in a unique set of six pools.

The pools are then tested, and because each person's samples are located in a unique combination of pools, positive results for that specific combination would indicate that the relevant individual is infected.

Meanwhile, an algorithm is also used to optimise the design of the tools according to the expected prevalence of the virus.

There are also limitations to this method; its usefulness drops as the community's rate of infection climbs, for a higher number of tests coming back positive makes it harder to distinguish which individual samples are virus-free.

Contact Tracing

While there are some 150 vaccine developments and trials in progress globally as of September 2020, there will likely not be a proven vaccine available till late 2021.

It has therefore become imperative for governments to rely on contact tracing, and the tracking of the movement and interactions of those who have tested positive for the virus. This is the best way to identify further groups of people who might have been infected, and to test and quarantine them, if necessary.

Technology can help immensely in this respect. China is using facial recognition and mobility data from both public and private sources to track movements.

Singapore's government technology agency, GovTech, has developed a national digital check-in system called 'SafeEntry' that allows individuals to "check-in" to venues including workplaces, schools, shopping centres, restaurants, whether by having their national identity card scanned or by scanning a QR code using their phone (see figure 43).

Commencing from September 2020, Singapore will introduce 'Trace Tokens', distributed free to every member of the public, which

Non-Random Binary Pool Testing

The method used by the Israeli scientists relies on the conception of non-random binary codes. Samples from individuals, such as from nose swabs, are split across a unique combination of testing pools, such that the eventual results (i.e. which pools come back positive) will indicate which specific individual is infected, and is causing his or her unique combination of testing pools to come back positive. Meanwhile, other individuals are cleared when the unique combination of testing pools their sample are in are found to be negative.

To illustrate this method in action, one can consider a case where eight individuals need to be tested. Under individual testing – one test per individual – 8 separate tests need to be administered. Under the non-random binary pool testing method, as little as four tests can be administered. Refer to Figure 39, where a "1" indicates that an individual's sample is included in the testing pool.

	Pool 1	Pool 2	Pool 3	Pool 4
Alice				1
Bob			1	
Cheryl			1	1
Daryl		1		
Eileen		1		1
Farah		1	1	
George		1	1	1
Hisham	1			

Figure 39: Distribution of Individuals' Samples into COVID-19 Laboratory Testing Pools under Non-random Binary Pool Testing

As can be seen, the distribution of eight samples into the four pools is not random, but deliberate. Each individual's sample has been put into a unique combination of pools, and in essence, each individual has been assigned a unique binary number – Alice is "0001", Bob is "0010", Cheryl is "0011" and so on).

Let us say then that, after testing, Pool 2 comes backs positive, as indicated by the blue column in Figure 40.

	Pool 1	Pool 2	Pool 3	Pool 4
Alice				1
Bob			1	
Cheryl			1	1
Daryl		1		
Eileen		1		1

Farah		1	1	
George		1	1	1
Hisham	1			

Figure 40: Hypothetical Results of Laboratory Tests under Non-random Binary Pool Testing

This result would show that Daryl is infected, and that no one else is, without the need for further tests. Him being the only one infected would explain why Pool 2 – and Pool 2 alone – comes up positive.

As his sample is included in Pool 2, his being infected would cause Pool 2 to test positive. Meanwhile, it could not be the samples from others such as Eileen, Farah and George who are causing Pool 2 to test positive, because the other pools that their samples are in have not tested positive – if George were infected, for example, Pools 3 and 4 would similarly test positive, but they have not.

And of course, all the others who do not have samples in Pool 2 at all – Alice, Bob, Cheryl and Hisham – would be in the clear, as the pools they are in – one or more of Pools 1, 3 & 4 – have tested negative.

As innovative as this method is for testing the same number of individuals with a smaller number of tests, there are limits. As the number of infected people in the community grows, the more those being tested are also likely to be infected.

This high proportion of infected individuals will – despite the non-random distribution of their samples – collectively cause all pools to test positive, leaving scientists unable to tell which specific individuals are infected or not. Refer to Figure 41, where the pools that test positive are again indicated by blue.

	Pool 1	Pool 2	Pool 3	Pool 4
Alice				1
Bob			1	
Cheryl			1	1
Daryl		1		
Eileen		1		1
Farah		1	1	
George		1	1	1
Hisham	1			

Figure 41: Non-random Binary Pool Testing Method Illustration

Alice, Bob and Daryl being infected would cause Pools 2, 3 and 4 to all test positive; hence, even though Cheryl, Eileen, Farah and George are – in reality – uninfected, the test cannot identify them as such. The "noise" from the infected samples end up swamping the test, degrading its usefulness and creating a situation where further rounds of testing are required.

will automatically synchronise with the SafeEntry app. This will make the process far more efficient and also much more effective in that it will allow for the automated detection of proximate persons if an individual is discovered to be infected.

Dr Vivian Balakrishnan who is both Minister of Foreign Affairs and Minister in charge of the Smart Nation and Digital Government Office, explained, "It is not enough to know who has been in this building in the last hour. You want to know, of this group of people that has been in the building, who actually has been in close proximity with one another."

Figure 42: Smartphone Screen Showing the use of SafeEntry (Source: GovTech)

In New Zealand, the 'NZ COVID Tracer' is an app that similarly allows people to create a digital register of places they have visited, through scanning official QR codes or via manual data entry. This then allows a contact tracer to identify and notify individuals who have been at the same location at around the same time as someone known to have COVID-19.

Quarantine Enforcement

Individuals identified as having a high risk of being infected, such as travellers returning from abroad, typically need to be quarantined to limit their interaction with the general public.

Technology can facilitate this process. An example is Singapore's Leave of Absence and Stay-Home Notice Tracking Solution, structured as an SMS and mobile web-based system that allows people serving their quarantines to report their locations to the government accurately and expediently (see figure 44).

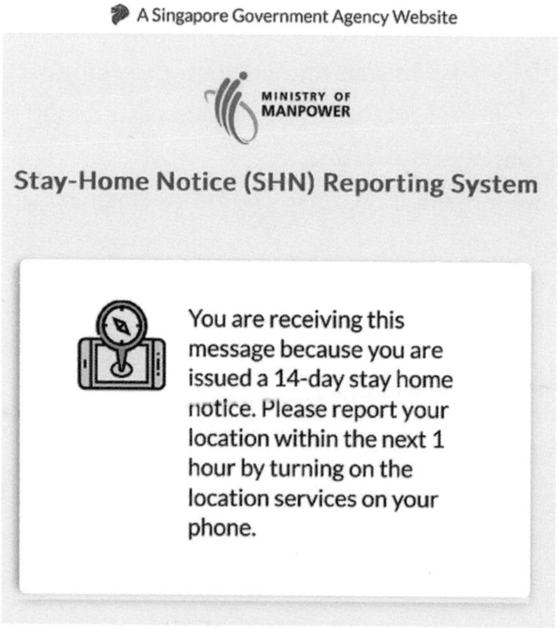

Figure 43: Leave of Absence and Stay-Home Notice Tracking Solution (Source: GovTech)

In South Korea, electronic wristbands have been deployed to allow the government to track individuals in quarantine, and to facilitate enforcement. This is a step up from the use of phone-based tracking apps, which uncooperative would-be curfew breakers could fool by leaving their phones at home.

Human Habits

Humans are creatures of habit, developing settled tendencies and practices from repetition.

A 2009 research study from Phillippa Lally and her team found that it takes an average of a little more than 60 days for habits to form out of constant behavioural repetition.[54]

This being so, the pandemic could well accustom people to habits such as mask-wearing, frequent hand sanitising and washing, and to some extent, even social distancing, especially during seasonal flu periods long after the COVID-19 pandemic itself has been contained.

This would represent an innovation in personal and societal conduct. At a systemic level, social distancing and remote working in the workplace may become a standard practice by organisations as a routine precaution rather than a contingency measure.

Furthermore, organisations may choose to fragment and distribute their operations and units rather than concentrate them in a single building, or even in the same city, state or even country.

Innovations in Scientific Research

The pandemic has had a silver lining in catalysing scientific innovations and driving efficiencies in the scientific research process.

Given the understandable desire to speedily develop a COVID-19 vaccine and to produce research on the effectiveness of various health measures such as mask-wearing, the scientific community has accelerated the way its traditionally sluggish research and adoption process works.

Grant-Making

In the first instance, the grant-making process has been expedited. Traditionally, it could have taken a scientist half a year to prepare a grant application, and many months more after that before approval is granted or rejection issued.

In response to the coronavirus, non-profit organisations such as Fast Grants have been set-up. Under the Fast Grants system, applications take not more than half an hour, while assessments and responses are provided within two days. Quality is maintained, and waste of money avoided, through the screening of a panel of 20 academic experts.

More generally, there is little reason to think that more time spent to make further, fine-grained distinctions in quality between submissions would be useful – research has shown that, above a certain threshold of grant quality, there is generally no correlation between a project's ex-ante score by reviewers and its subsequent success in terms of citations.

Pre-Print Servers

Meanwhile, scientists are increasingly using preprint servers, on which their research papers can be shared before being submitted for formal peer review with journals.

This allows new findings to be quickly shared with other scientists and researchers, and for them to then be built on; this can also allow policymakers to adjust their strategies according to whatever new evidence has emerged.

Such speed has inadvertently been purchased at the cost of deterioration in quality, with some articles not meeting the requisite scientific rigour being nonetheless widely reported by the media. Nonetheless, such issues in quality control are avoidable, and preprint servers are already engaged in efforts to screen out low-quality work.

Review of the Peer-Review Process

Further, scientific journals themselves have put in place expedited review processes, with editors, peer reviewers and production staff all working faster.

No loss in quality or scientific rigour is suffered, as intellectual standards are unchanged, and all gains in speed are obtained through cutting down preventable delays.

> *We feel very much that we are publishing research that is literally day by day guiding the national and global response to this virus. And that is both daunting and full of considerable responsibility, because if we make a mistake in judgment about what we publish, that could have a dangerous impact on the course of the pandemic.*

Richard Horton
Editor in Chief of The Lancet
21st April 2020

Innovations in the Economy

Technological Adaptations

COVID-19 is forcing both governments and companies to adapt, with digitalisation and automation both increasingly used to adjust to a new reality of providing services wherever human contact is a risk.

Telecommuting

Given the imposition of social distancing, companies have been forced to allow their employees to work from home.

In the United States, up to half of the workforce were telecommuting in June 2020 – more than double the percentage who occasionally worked from home in 2017-18.[55]

This change might prove permanent, as the clear feasibility of telecommuting during the crisis increases employees' willingness to demand the right to telecommute, and reduces the opposition of managers to permitting such working from home.

This, in turn, will lead to a rethinking of the need for expensive commercial office space. Simultaneously, travel budgets might shrink, as the rise of video conferencing makes travelling harder for companies to justify.

Social Distancing

Some organisations have become creative about ways to ensure social distancing, as when a bar in Tokyo introduced screens resembling fish bowls to lure customers back, by assuring them that they can drink and enjoy a night out without compromising their health and safety.

Automation

Companies are also deploying robots to discharge functions that would previously have been fulfilled by human staff. In the hospitality industry, serviced suites are using robots to greet and guide guests, while spas use automated systems to check guests' temperatures and to sterilise both visitors and their luggage.

The use of robots to perform cleaning and sanitation tasks is not just limited to the hospitality industry, however, as the travel sector – including airports – have also been investing in technological solutions.

The adoption of advanced autonomous robots such as those deployed for cleaning, service delivery, surveillance and policing is being accelerated and increasingly accepted by organisations and societies. These systems are equipped with 3D sensors, live feed cameras, artificial intelligence and machine learning capabilities.

COVID-19 has also accelerated the adoption of artificial intelligence to automate even white-collar jobs. In finance, the next half-decade will see perhaps an 80 percent rise in tasks carried out by machines, with time-consuming, repetitive tasks done by junior account executives being most susceptible to automation.[56]

A study conducted by the Institute of Singapore Chartered Accountants found that, "The rise in digitalisation has resulted in machines quickly taking over the tasks traditionally performed by humans, making room for humans to focus on higher-order tasks or new ones which require new skill sets. Accountancy and finance professionals will increasingly require knowledge beyond their main domain of accountancy and finance as well as their industries."

Contactless Delivery

With the health risks associated with in-person interaction, many companies have shifted from in-person provision of goods and services, such as restaurants shifting to supply takeout. Delivery platforms have in turn shifted towards allowing contactless delivery to further facilitate social distancing.

In Singapore, the food delivery app FoodPanda has implemented a system whereby delivery riders are required to check whether contactless delivery is requested, and if so, to deliver the takeout to a pre-designed drop-off point. Once this is done, the customer can be informed, allowing them to retrieve their order safely.

In California, as well as in Colombia and Taiwan, drones from the drone-delivery firm Kiwibot ferries both food and shopping. The pandemic – and the increase in popularity of contactless delivery – has allowed the company to grow its fleet by 150 percent in just a few months; and going forward, Kiwibot expects up to 1000 percent fleet growth to keep pace with demand.[57]

Digitalisation

The pandemic has also forced companies to increasingly provide their services digitally. The financial services sector, in particular, is rapidly evolving. Customers have shifted almost overnight to the digital opening of new banking relations, to the usage of mobile payment applications, and to the use of contactless payment.

Government services, meanwhile, are also increasingly digitalised. The LifeSG app in Singapore allows individuals to access more than 40 government services, including checking one's Central Providence Fund (CPF) savings and pension balances, or making housing payments on one's government-owned Housing and Development Board (HDB) apartment, to paying the annual road tax.

Though a predecessor to the LifeSG app was available even before the pandemic, the necessity of social distancing might see citizens increasingly shift to accessing government services digitally.

In Sweden, the Verksamt portal provides a one-stop portal for businesses and entrepreneurs to start, run, develop or close down their businesses, with easy access to permit applications and advisors provided.

Citizens, in general, can also access various digital government services – from applying for passports to registering for unemployment benefits, to paying taxes, to applying for driving licences, to changing addresses, to enrolling in universities, to obtaining healthcare information, and to reporting businesses for consumer rights abuses.

Open Data

Simultaneously, data has been used in increasingly innovative ways. Real-time data on personal mobility fed from mobile phones or wearable technology including watches and clothing made of smart-fabric can track walking, transit, driving and location with a high degree of precision and low latency.

Companies such as Google, Apple, Amap and Baidu are working aggressively to combine mobility data with data on different categories of places, such as retail and recreation, groceries and pharmacies, parks, transit stations, workplaces and residences, to generate inferences on the extent to which economic activity has fallen or risen.

This can in turn help governments react swiftly, with fiscal and monetary policy levers brought to bear to address economic problems – such as a contraction in growth – early, before they have had the chance to further deepen.

It will also allow mapping of changes in behavioural patterns, not only of individuals, but categories of people, which when matched with personalised biodata allow for triangulation of mobility, consumption and social-economic status information.

This will provide these companies with the ability to personalise technology-'pushed' marketing or to even anticipate demand and curate the lives of individuals around their preferences.

However, this also raises ethical and legal questions, regarding the benefits of data analytics versus issues of personal privacy and the unconscious curation of choices in consumption, knowledge and social interaction.

Green Technology

The coronavirus crisis is creating a growing impetus to focus on other large-scale challenges to humanity, most notably climate change. As a result, green technology can be expected to be more widely deployed.

In ports, where the crisis has caused a lull in shipping activity, there is scope to accelerate decarbonisation efforts. Already, ports in Singapore managed by the Port of Singapore Authority (PSA) are installing rooftop solar panels, AI-driven Smart Multi-Energy Systems to optimise energy usage, and battery-powered automated guided vehicles.

In Europe, the European Union is also leading a continent-wide effort at green transformation and ensuring a green recovery, with proposals being developed to support initiatives across a wide spectrum.

Proposals include subsidies and tax breaks for electric vehicles, funding for renewable energy projects and infrastructure, as well as R&D funding for the development of green hydrogen that can curb emissions in industries like steelmaking and cement production, where decarbonisation as a challenge is the most intractable.[58]

Organisational Optimisation

The sort of innovation that COVID-19 has demanded from companies has not just been technological in nature; organisations have also had to alter and optimise their organisational structures and processes.

Location Optimisation

Companies looking to expand into a regional market often choose to set up a regional headquarters (RHQs).

For example, in ASEAN, Singapore and Hong Kong have long been favoured destinations, due to excellent public safety, a highly educated workforce, strong aviation and marine connectivity, and a business-friendly tax and regulatory system.

Additional tax breaks provided by the Economic Development Board – Singapore's investment promotion corporation – for companies looking to expand internationally and set up RHQs also help increase the attractiveness of the country.

However, the pandemic is forcing many MNCs to reconsider their risk management strategies and to change their organisational structures and processes.

MNCs may elect to mitigate risk against future pandemics or shocks by distributing, rather than concentrating, their operations despite the undisputed 'trust and reliability' advantages offered by Singapore. Similarly, companies may elect to downsize their RHQs to become 'RHQ-lite' through a hybrid of smaller RHQs complemented by country offices.

Again, this may be a permanent shift as an organisational strategy, resulting from the extreme COVID-19 impacts in eroding Singapore's historical advantage of aviation connectivity. Other than the finance sector, most RHQs relied on that connectivity to monitor their regional exposures and operations.

The dramatic reduction in aviation links to and from Singapore stems not just from the generalised global precautions on travel, but is also linked specifically to the Singapore government's missteps in managing COVID-19 with respect to its foreign workers, resulting in larger gross numbers of infections making other countries reluctant to "Green Lane" arrangements.

Agility Matters

Certain companies have shown agility and daring in shifting out of their initial core businesses, and pivoting instead to new opportunities. Singapore-based Certact Engineering, whose core business is in the production of metal parts for semiconductor manufacturers, also had a niche business in plastic engineering.

The pandemic and trade tensions have caused demand for its metal products to plummet, but with increased demand for plastic parts in the manufacturing of DNA sequencing machines, the company rapidly adjusted to changing circumstances. It swiftly bought new machines, redeployed its workforce, and ran trials on new processes – all of which has borne fruit, with million-dollar contracts obtained in the relevant field.

Innovation: Macro Implications

Innovation across the spectrum, from changes in individual habits, to social acculturation, to the catalysation and accelerated adoption of technologies, will make societies, governments and organisations more resilient, and better prepared to 'shock absorb' future pandemics or challenges of a similar scale.

Naturally, there will be an unevenness across countries and regions depending on their level of development, quality of governance and market size and maturity. Those regions and countries which can adopt and absorb innovation – and optimised combinations of innovations – will become more competitive and attractive as locations for investments.

Fundamentally, however, successfully responding to COVID-19 requires accelerating digitalisation and permanently changing organisation structure, decision-making mechanisms and work patterns.

> *I want to emphasize that when we seek to recover from this unprecedented shock, it is not an option to return to business as usual.*

Masatsugu Asakawa
Asian Development Bank President

Part D: The Prevalence of COVID-19

This section contains analysis on patterns of prevalence and fatalities attributed to COVID-19. Country-level comparison on healthcare, government system capability and stringency of COVID-19 measures is made. Furthermore, cost projections for a potential vaccine are mapped out.

- Based on country-level analysis on 143 countries, GDP per capita showed a positive correlation with prevalence ratios whereas countries with a higher GDP per capita showed a lower Case Fatality Rate (CFR).
- In general, countries with a lower GDP per capita are expected to have lower prevalence ratios and higher CFRs, likely attributed to the lack of testing and medical infrastructure which understate prevalence ratios and negatively impact CFR.
- While it is challenging to tease out the relationship between the Stringency Index and either prevalence ratios or CFRs, there are some signals which indicate that stringent policy does help reduce infections and fatalities from COVID-19. And as will be seen later on in a discussion on public health policy recommendations, micro-level scientific evidence does support the efficacy of stringent policies such as lockdowns and mask wearing.

GEOGRAPHICAL EFFECTS

This segment explores the relationship between geographical regions and two important metrics:

- Prevalence of COVID-19 in the population, or the proportion of the population who are infected by the disease.
- Case Fatality Rate (CFR), or the proportion of the infected cases that have died from the disease.

The analysis combines similar regions to generalise findings based on important factors. The five groups are collapsed to take into account the following, in order of importance:

- Prevalence and CFR of COVID-19
- GDP per capita
- Geographical proximity

Characteristics of the five groups are as follows:

Group	Region (no. of countries)	Population Density	Stage of Economic Development
1	Central Asia (3) Western Asia (14) Australia and New Zealand (2)	Low to Moderate	Mostly developing, with few exceptions
2	Eastern Asia (4) Southeast Asia (10) Southern Asia (8)	High	Mostly emerging economies experiencing high economic growth before COVID-19
3	Northern Africa (5) Sub-Saharan Africa (42)	Moderate to High	Mostly developing with few exceptions
4	Eastern Europe (9)	Low to Moderate	Mostly emerging economies
5	Latin America and the Caribbean (32)	Moderate to High	Mostly emerging economies
6	Northern America (2) Northern Europe (10) Southern Europe (10)	Moderate	Mostly developed economies with few exceptions
7	Western Europe (8)		

Figure 44: Regions of Countries with Similar Geographical and Economic Demographics

The average values of prevalence and CFR of each region group as of July 2020 are provided, and the five groups are sorted in figure 46 below, in increasing order of CFR.

Group	Region (no. of countries)	Prevalence	CFR
1 (lowest CFR)	Central Asia (3) Western Asia (14) Australia and New Zealand (2)	0.4%	1.4%
2	Eastern Asia (4) Southern Asia (8) Southeast Asia (10)	0.07%	2.1%
3	Northern Africa (5) Sub-Saharan Africa (42)	0.06%	3.3%
4	Latin America and the Caribbean (32)	0.38%	3.8%
5	Eastern Europe (9)	0.20%	4.1%
6	Northern America (2) Northern Europe (10) Southern Europe (10)	0.45%	6.0%
7 (highest CFR)	Western Europe (8)	0.40%	8.5%

Figure 45: CFR and Prevalence Rates of COVID-19 across Major Geographical Regions (Source: Future-Moves Group; data from European Centre for Disease Prevention and Control)

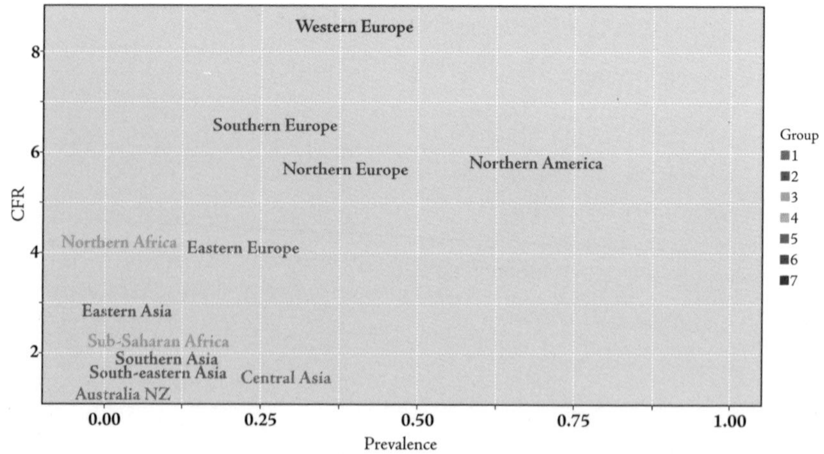

Figure 46: Scatter Plot of CFR and Prevalence (Source: Future-Moves Group; data from European Centre for Disease Prevention and Control)

Western Europe is expected to be most severely affected by the pandemic due to its ageing population. This geographical region has the highest CFR in the world.

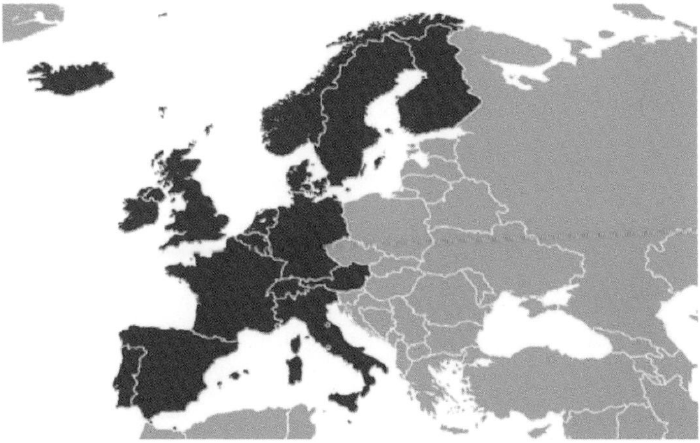

Northern Africa is an example of a geographical region that has a disproportionately high CFR relative to its prevalence ratio.

The disproportionately high CFR relative to Prevalence of COVID-19 in the populations of regions with lower GDPs, in general, can mostly be explained by two reasons:

(i) the under-reporting of infected cases due to lack of testing, awareness or otherwise, and/or;

(ii) the lack of medical infrastructure.

HEALTHCARE RESOURCE CAPACITY

This section will use the number of beds and number of nurses (per 1000 people) as a proxy for healthcare resource capacity, with all data sourced from 'Our World in Data'. This is then benchmarked against the proportion of elderly – defined as 65-years-old and above – in the population. For all indicators, the most recent information, or 2020 forecasts, are used for each country, where available. A summary of the group-level averages is shown in figure 47.

Group	Region (no. of countries)	No. of Beds	No. of Nurses	Proportion of Elderly	Remarks
1	Central Asia (3) Southern Asia (8) Western Asia (14) Australia and New Zealand (2)	3.0	5.7	7.4	
2	Eastern Asia (4) Southeast Asia (10)	3.0	2.9	8.6	Elderly Population <10%
3	Northern Africa (5) Sub-Saharan Africa (42)	1.3	1.2	3.9	
4	Latin America and the Caribbean (32)	1.9	2.2	8.6	
5	Eastern Europe (9)	7.5	7.1	17.6	
6	Northern America (2) Northern Europe (10) Southern Europe (10)	3.7	9.4	19.6	Elderly Population >10%
7	Western Europe (8)	5.6	12.1	19.4	

Figure 47: Healthcare Resource Capacity by Group
(Source: Future-Moves Group; data from UN)

There is a clear relationship between the proportion of elderly in the population and the CFR. The three groups that have the highest CFRs – 5, 6 and 7 – all have an elderly population above 10 percent. This is despite having generally better medical infrastructure.

STUDY OF GOVERNMENTAL EFFECTIVENESS

The study of governmental measures is important in achieving the key positive health outcomes of minimising prevalence and CFRs in the community.

Governmental effectiveness measures against the pandemic are referenced using the Stringency Index from the University of Oxford Coronavirus Government Response Tracker.[13]

The Stringency Index compiles 17 indicators of government responses, including eight policy indicators, four economic indicators and five health indicators.

The eight policy indicators used in the calculation of Policy Index include:

- C1: School closures
- C2: Workplace closures
- C3: Cancellation of public events
- C4: Restriction of gatherings
- C5: Closure of public transport
- C6: Stay at home requirements
- C7: Restrictions on internal movement
- C8: International travel controls

The four economic indicators used in the calculation of the Economic Index include:

- E1: Income support

- E2: Debt/contract Relief
- E3: Fiscal measures
- E4: International support

The five health indicators used in the calculation of the Health Index include:

- H1: Public information campaigns
- H2: Testing policy
- H3: Contact tracing
- H4: Emergency investment in healthcare
- H5: Investment in vaccines

The Stringency Index is calculated based on C1-C8 and H1 only. In calculating and comparing each region group's Stringency Level in figure 48, the average of each country's Stringency Index (at its maximum value) in each group is taken.

Group	Region (no. of countries)	Stringency Index C1-C8 + H1
1 (lowest CFR)	Central Asia (3) Southern Asia (8) Western Asia (14) Australia and New Zealand (2)	88.9 (highest Stringency)
2	Eastern Asia (4) Southeast Asia (10)	81.0
3	Northern Africa (5) Sub-Saharan Africa (42)	81.7
4	Latin America and the Caribbean (32)	84.1
5	Eastern Europe (9)	82.0
6	Northern America (2) Northern Europe (10) Southern Europe (10)	82.4
7 (highest CFR)	Western Europe (8)	82.7

Figure 48: Stringency Index by Region Group
(Source: Future-Moves Group; data: University of Oxford)

Based on the Stringency Index, the group with the lowest CFR – Central, Southern, Western Asia and Australia and New Zealand – also has the highest Stringency Index.

GDP, Prevalence and Stringency

A bubble chart displaying the pattern between GDP Per Capita, Prevalence and Stringency Index (denoted by the size of the bubble) across several key countries is provided below.

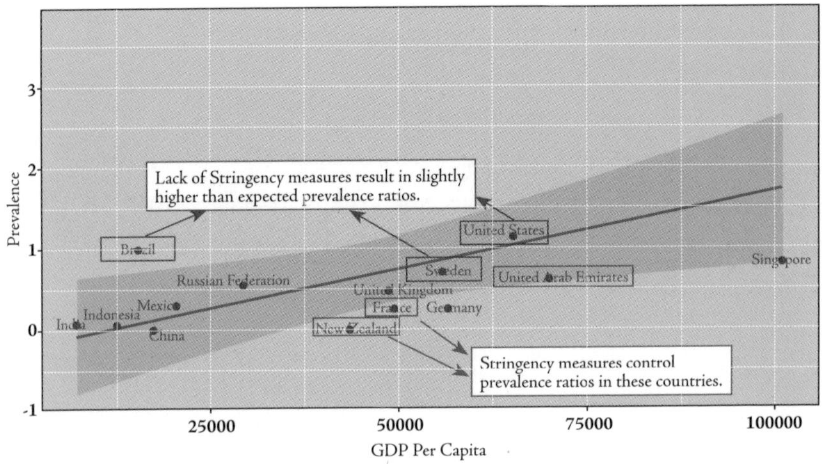

Figure 49: Bubble Chart of GDP per capita, Prevalence and Stringency (denoted by bubble size) (Source: Future-Moves Group; data from World Bank, University of Oxford, and European Centre for Disease Prevention and Control)

While countries with higher GDP per capita report higher prevalence ratios of COVID-19, this is likely due to greater public health system capacity and hence more extensive testing. In contrast, less testing has been taking place in poorer countries.

In Africa, 10 countries account for 80 percent of the new COVID-19 testing, with the rest of the African nations doing little testing themselves.

Countries in the latter group, which will be disproportionately poor, will have misleadingly low prevalence rate, thus skewing any resulting analysis.

Amongst the studied group of countries, those with a higher Stringency Index, such as France, New Zealand and UAE, fall below the best-fit line in the relationship between GDP per capita and Prevalence.

This suggests Stringency measures do reduce Prevalence ratios compared with countries with lower Stringency Indexes, such as the United States, Sweden and Brazil.

Notwithstanding some effectiveness of Stringency measures, they appear to have a greater effect on countries with a higher GDP per capita. The examples of France, New Zealand and UAE illustrate this point.

Some notable exceptions include Qatar, which has an extremely high GDP per capita and relatively high Prevalence ratio; and Singapore, which has an extremely high GDP per capita and relatively low Prevalence ratio.

These findings are not surprising given the small size of the population of these countries, which results in a much larger fluctuation compared with those of larger populations.

GDP, CFR and Stringency

A bubble chart displaying the pattern between GDP per capita, CFR and Stringency Index (denoted by the size of the bubble) across several key countries is provided below. This is the reverse trend of the previous relationship that studied Prevalence ratios.

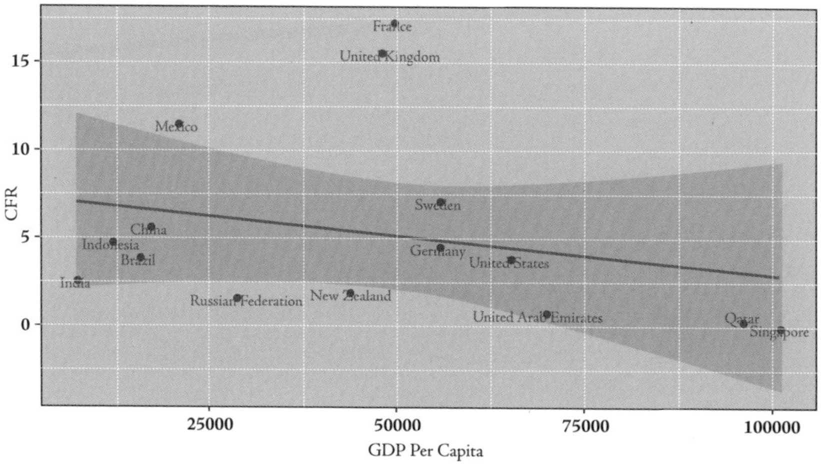

Figure 50: Bubble Chart of GDP per capita, CFR and Stringency (denoted by bubble size) (Source: Future-Moves Group; data from World Bank, University of Oxford, and European Centre for Disease Prevention and Control)

The findings include a negative relationship between GDP per capita and CFR, suggesting that countries with better GDP per capita – and therefore generally better medical infrastructure – have lower CFRs.

Notable exceptions include France and the United Kingdom, which have a disproportionately high CFR despite their wealth, which is likely attributable to their relatively aged population.

Compared to figure 50, it is not unexpected to see a less definitive figure as figure 50 does not take into consideration the proportion of the aged population or testing rates.

Examples of Archetypal Countries

Based on the variables studied, two countries from each group are contrasted with each other to show variation within each of the groups.

A summary of the highest and lowest Stringency Indexes is provided for each of the seven groups in figure 52:

I think this study [showing people underestimating exponential growth] shows how media and government should report on a pandemic in such a situation. Not only report the numbers of today and growth over the past week, but also explain what will happen in the next days, week, month, if the same accelerating growth persists. If we could have overcome the exponential growth bias and had convinced all Americans of this risk back in March, I am sure 99 percent would have embraced all possible distancing measures.

Joris Lammers
Professor of Social Psychology at the University of Bremen

Group	Region (no. of countries)	Min Group Stringency	Mean Group Stringency	Max Group Stringency
1	Central Asia (3) Southern Asia (8) Western Asia (14) Australia and New Zealand (2)	73.2 (Tajikistan)	90.3	100 (Jordan)
2	Eastern Asia (4) Southeast Asia (10)	47.2 (Japan)	85.0	100 (India)
3	Northern Africa (5) Sub-Saharan Africa (42)	33.3 (Burundi)	82.0	100 (Djibouti)
4	Latin America and the Caribbean (32)	16.7 (Nicaragua)	87.8	100 (Argentina)
5	Eastern Europe (9)	19.4 (Belarus)	76.5	92.6 (Ukraine)
6	Northern America (2) Northern Europe (10) Southern Europe (10)	46.3 (Sweden)	78.2	96.3 (Croatia)
7	Western Europe (8)	73.2 (Germany)	80.4	90.7 (France)

Figure 51: Variation of Stringency Indexes in each Group

GLOBAL COST OF MANUFACTURING AND DEPLOYING A COVID-19 VACCINE

This segment provides an analysis of the cost of implementing a global vaccine immunisation plan.

Vaccine Development Process

Currently, multiple possible vaccines are under development. Already, almost about 5.76 billion doses have been reserved by countries and organisations.

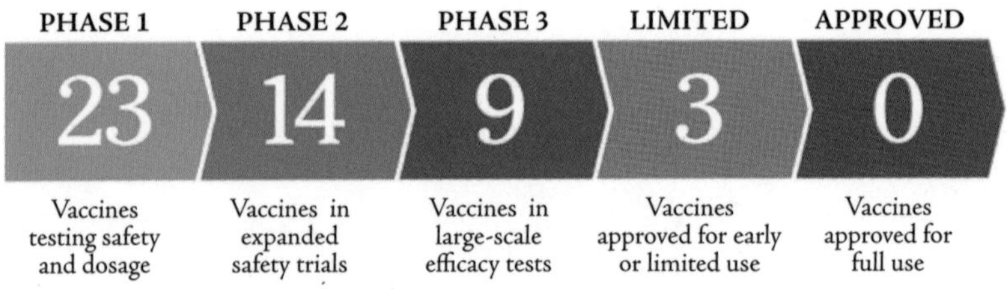

Figure 52: Vaccines under Development, by phases (Data from the New York Times; accurate as of 2 September 2020)

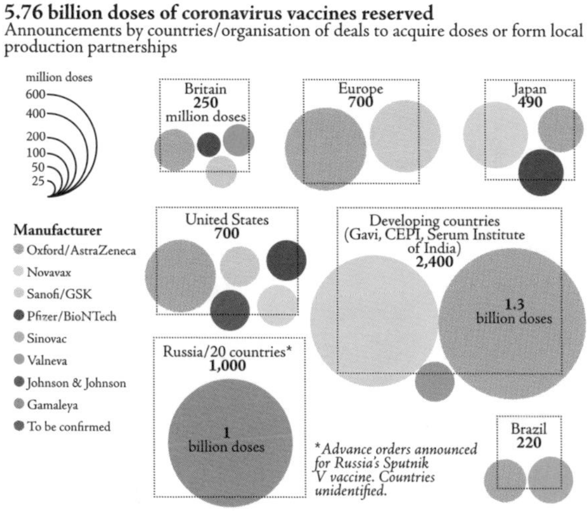

Figure 53: Reservation of Vaccines (Source: AFP)

Despite certain premature announcements – such as Russian President Vladimir Putin's, that his country has already developed a safe and effective vaccine – in reality, no vaccine candidate has yet passed the large-scale Phase 3 trials, or proven itself safe and effective for mass deployment.

Similarly, the Trump administration's political pressure on the FDA to approve a vaccine before the election is clearly politically-motivated.

Experts such as Dr Scott Gottlieb, a former FDA commissioner, as well as Dr Moncef Slaoui, who leads the Trump Administration's own 'Operation Warp Speed' initiative to develop a vaccine, agree that a vaccine will only become available in 2021, not before.

Going ahead with vaccine deployment without the appropriate trials conducted and evidence gathered would be immensely dangerous – not just because it would risk the lives of all those receiving the untested vaccine, but because this could fatally undermine the acceptance of vaccines by the population should anything go wrong. Indeed, it would be tragic if eventually, a proven vaccine were rejected by populations, because irresponsible political actors earlier pushed unsafe, unproven vaccines onto their own populace in a bid to appear effective and to shore up their political standing.

A reckless and foolish decision ... Mass vaccination with an improperly tested vaccine is unethical.

Francois Balloux
Director of the University College London's Genetics Institute
[On Russian President Vladimir Putin's premature announcement of a vaccine]

We have half a dozen or more vaccines. So if we wanted to take the chance of hurting a lot of people or giving them something that doesn't work, we could start doing this, you know, next week if we wanted to. But that's not the way it works.

Dr Anthony Fauci
Director of the US National Institute of Allergy and Infectious Diseases

The crisis is far from over. Many countries brought COVID-19 under the control and eased restrictions, only to see their cases rise sharply again. This can happen to us too, despite all our precautions. It will most likely take a year or two before a vaccine is widely available, and the threat of the virus is blunted.

Lee Hsien Loong
Prime Minister of Singapore

Cost Estimates

Estimates from the GAVI vaccine alliance,[61] as well as heuristic-based assessments by Future-Moves Group, suggest that an eventual SARS-CoV-2 coronavirus vaccine will cost between US$21 and US$41 per shot.

The model used in this book assumes a base price of US$20-$40 plus US$1 per shot for deployment costs (for logistics like storage and distribution), and takes into account economies of scale in production and deployment.

Given a world population of 7.8 billion people, comprehensive global immunisation will cost anything between US$160 billion and US$320 billion.

The situation is further complicated by the possibility of tariffs. These might be generalised import tariffs on medicine, as imposed by countries looking to protect the domestic pharmaceutical industry and to correct balance of trade problems.

There might also be export tariffs, as countries look to hoard the vaccine for their citizens. Already, the Asian Development Bank estimates that vaccine-related trade restrictions are only semi-open – or about a 3 on a scale of 1 to 5, where a higher number indicates greater restrictions. Tariffs could increase the cost of any future vaccine to perhaps US$61 (with a base price of US$60 and deployment costs of US$1), resulting in overall global costs of up to US$480 billion.

Such a situation disproportionately hurts developing countries who lack the capacity to manufacture the vaccine themselves and who need to source it from overseas suppliers

A further complication lies in the possibility that booster or multiple shots might be necessary during a future COVID-19 vaccination campaign, as is the case for polio, Hepatitis B, MMR and seasonal influenza. In such a scenario, the price of the vaccine would at least double.

There are three important caveats to note about such estimates.

First, these are highly speculative and subject to extremely uncertain conditions. Most vaccines are still far too early in the development process for final prices to be determined.

Seth Berkley, Chief Executive of the GAVI, cautions, "The truth is nobody has an idea what the price is going to be, because we have no idea which vaccine is going to work... The challenge is trying to come up with a cost. Anybody who tells you they know isn't being honest."

Even deployment costs are uncertain, for those can depend on the

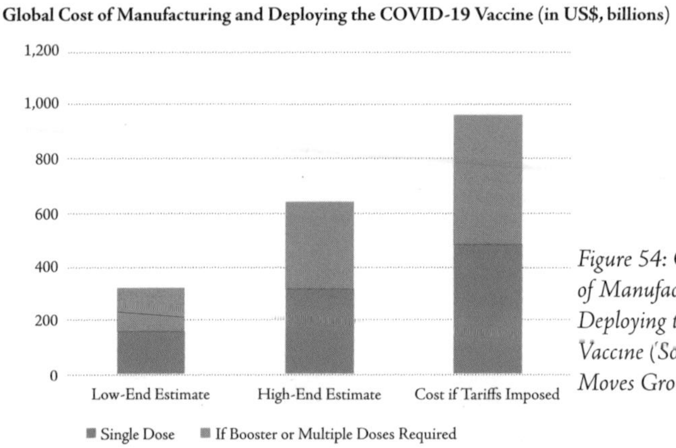

Figure 54: Global Cost of Manufacturing and Deploying the COVID-19 Vaccine (Source: Future-Moves Group)

nature of the vaccine itself. A vaccine like the DIOS-CoVax2 shot currently under development would not need to be stored at cold temperatures and could be delivered without the need for needles, making it easier – and cheaper – to distribute.

As Saul Faust, Director of the NIHR Southampton Clinical Research Facility says, such a vaccine "could be a major breakthrough in being able to give a future vaccine to huge numbers of people across the world."

Meanwhile, a second caveat to note about such estimates as provided is that not all countries will be equally able to vaccinate their populations. Two variables determine whether countries will be able to manufacture and deploy the vaccine accordingly.

First, vaccine access depends largely on pharmaceutical manufacturing capacity – the greater this capacity, the more capable the country will be in vaccinating its population.

Second, a country's fiscal position, as determined by their pre-existing debt levels and whether they are suffering persistent fiscal deficits, affects countries' abilities to source the funds necessary to support vaccine production and deployment.

Third, is the policy position of the Trump Administration, should he be successful in winning a second term of office.

In September 2020, the Trump Administration, having already withdrawn funding to the WHO, then withdrew its membership from the WHO and announced that it would pursue an 'America First' approach to acquisition and distribution of any eventual vaccine.

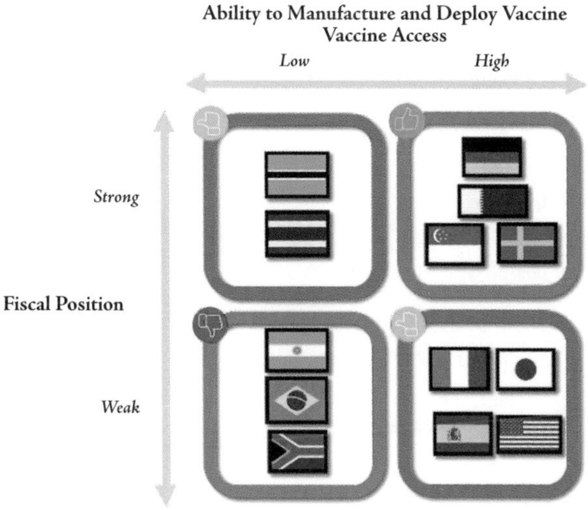

Figure 55: Matrix on Fiscal Position and Access to a COVID-19 Vaccine (Source: Future-Moves Group)

In the event that the singular or majority of successful vaccines are developed in America this would lead to a situation where the rest of the world be left behind in the race to safety. There would be the potential, given President Trump's past record, that he would impose usurious premiums on access to the vaccine formula, probably using national security as a premise.

The table below provides additional detail on the fiscal situations various countries can find themselves in, and how such situations will affect their ability to manufacture and deploy the vaccine:

Category	Notes
Advanced economies with reserves or fiscal surpluses • Able to purchase and deploy vaccine without taking on further debt. • Examples: – Singapore – Norway – Germany – Qatar	Singapore: With a population of about 5.85 million people, Singapore will need to spend about US\$123-US\$240 million dollars to vaccinate its population. • Only a small fraction of GDP (0.03-0.06%). • Also only a sliver of the US\$765 billion held by its sovereign wealth fund.

Category	Notes
<u>Advanced economies with debt overhang and fiscal deficits</u> There are two sub-categories of countries that are of interest, those with reliable access to credit and those without. ***Advanced economies with reliable access to credit*** • Able to purchase and deploy vaccine by taking on additional debt that does not materially increase long-term fiscal risks. • Examples: – United States – Japan – United Kingdom – France	<u>United States</u>: With a population of about 331 million people, the US will need to spend about US$6.95-US$13.6 billion dollars to vaccinate its population. • Only a small fraction of GDP (0.03-0.06%). • Given the US dollar's de facto status as the world's reserve currency, the United States can borrow freely regardless.
Unreliable access to credit • Able to purchase and deploy vaccine, but with increasingly unsustainable debt that materially increases long-term fiscal risks. • Examples: – Greece – Italy – Spain	<u>Greece</u>: With a population of about 10.42 million people, Greece will need to spend about US$219-US$427 million dollars to vaccinate its population. • A significantly higher fraction of GDP (0.1-0.2%) is required compared to other wealthy nations like the US and Singapore. • Debt problems from the aftermath of the Global Financial Crisis make borrowing less.
• Developing countries with debt overhang or fiscal deficits and with unreliable access to credit • Examples: – Brazil – Argentina – South Africa	<u>Brazil</u>: With a population of about 212.56 million people, Brazil will need to spend about US$4.46-US$8.71 billion dollars to vaccinate its population. • A significantly higher fraction of GDP (0.24-0.47%) compared to the advanced economies. • At pre-COVID trends, debt is projected to grow to the size of the entire economy by 2023; this makes issuing sovereign debt or borrowing on international money markets more challenging.

And as the figure below shows, debt levels amongst both advanced and emerging market economies have been rising going into the current crisis.

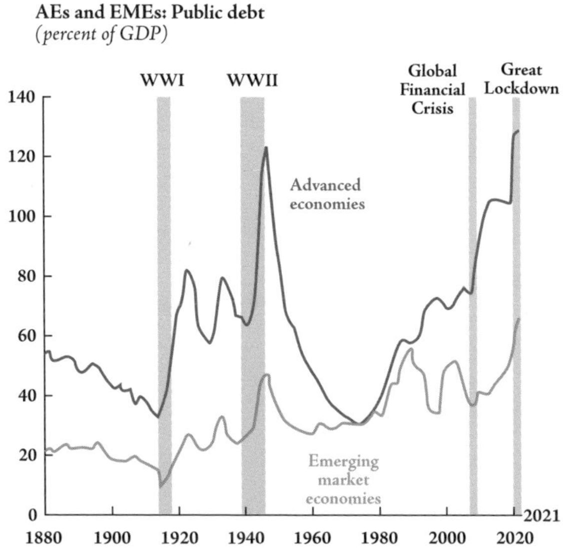

Figure 56: Public Debt in Advanced Economies and Emerging Market Economies (Source: IMF)

The upshot of all this is that certain countries – those with high quality of governance, strong public health systems, centralised government structures, high vaccine access and strong fiscal positions – will be better placed to recover from the pandemic. Poorer countries with debt problems and who might require help are in a difficult position.

> *Coming into this crisis, we had about 40 percent of low-income countries that were either already in debt distress or at high risk of being in debt distress... [they are] not able to borrow at reasonable terms on international markets... debt restructuring and debt relief will have to continue.*

Gita Gopinath
Chief Economist, IMF

SECTION III:
ANALYSIS AND RECOMMENDATIONS

This book began with framing the COVID-19 pandemic and proceeded to examine the evidence, supported by a comprehensive analysis of key aspects. This section deep dives into how countries have coped with the coronavirus pandemic.

By assessing the country cases, I find it useful to sieve out both unique aspects in the responses of selected countries and identify common patterns and distinctive trends across the cases. This exercise culminates in a summary of possible scenarios at the international level.

I have crafted these scenarios based on the building blocks of quality of governance, taken together with identified pre-determinants and critical uncertainties, and findings from country case studies. Given the scenarios, we provide key actionable recommendations at the global, regional and local levels. These constitute important steps forward and are recommended to leaders and decision-makers within the public sector, private sector, international organisations and NGOs.

Part E: Country Case Studies

The COVID-19 pandemic has led to divergent public health and economic outcomes. Country-specific cases are assessed according to measures of: (i) a combined view on public health and governance capacity, and (ii) with consideration of the state of a particular economy upon entering the pandemic, and subsequent economic repercussions contingent on the success of a response to the outbreak.

This section will study seven cases – a representative sample of large and small economies, having both centralised and distributed governance systems, and having very different cultural contexts.

The cases selected include New Zealand and Canada and their measured successes; the United States and Sweden and their muddled responses; as well as China, Hong Kong SAR and Singapore's mixed achievements.

These countries and polities have been chosen to provide contrasting perspectives to action taken in handling COVID-19 and the subsequent outcomes.

- Governance in a global health crisis builds on, in the first place, the fundamental strength of existing public health and government systems.
- Equally crucial is a country's ability to adapt governance to tackle domestic outbreaks via scientifically-guided approaches, with consistent monitoring of the evolving virus situation.
- It will benefit countries to learn from the experiences of others on how to handle the pandemic. Comparative study of varied approaches shows that while certain country-to-country variations are explained by unique pre-determinants, patterns still exist indicative of common flaws in public health and economic systems across countries.

**Data for Country Case Studies: World Bank,[63] Our World in Data,[64] and WHO.[65]*

NEW ZEALAND

New Zealand represents a best performing example of good governance. It acted swiftly, trusting in scientifically advised policies and cautiously eased lockdowns in May 2020, and managed to sustain 102 days with zero active coronavirus cases till early August 2020. At that point, a single failure to allow two infected travellers to leave a quarantine facility resulted in a personal assumption of responsibility by Prime Minister Jacinda Ardern and decisive action to place the quarantine operation under the supervision of the New Zealand Army to ensure discipline in the conduct of procedures. A senior General Officer was also held responsible to ensure that no such failures would reoccur.

The result of a proactive and strict disease control framework, clear communication strategy and sound economic recovery stimulus – together with the personal charisma and authenticity of the Prime Minister – combined to build a large joint 'trust account' between the Government and the populace, which ensured not just compliance with precautions, but also understanding on the part of the people when there were setbacks.

GDP Per Capita (2019) (US$)	42,084
Cumulative Number of Cases (As at 1st September 2020)	1,401
Total Number of Confirmed Deaths (As at 1st September 2020)	22
Case Fatality Rate (%) (As at 1st September 2020)	1.8

Advantageous Geographical Endowment

It is first important not to overlook that New Zealand possesses the specific advantages of geographical location and a low population density, as these traits constitute natural barriers to the transmission of the coronavirus across borders and between domestic regions.

The remote island nation of 5 million is also centrally governed, and, together, these factors made the country well-equipped to combat COVID-19 from the outset. Efficient governance is crucial, yet factors relating to a country's geography and demography have to be factored into the assessment.

Measured Public Health Plan

In January 2020, the healthcare regime worked to revise the country's existing national influenza pandemic plan as a starting point for the approach to COVID-19. This was done given the dissimilarity in the incubation period of COVID-19 infection in comparison to influenza.

Health authorities pursued an elimination approach, which is atypical to the mitigation model, which is more common to pandemic planning frameworks and requires a more forceful plan towards the aim of virus eradication.

The Ministry of Health established a COVID-19 Technical Advisory Group at an early stage, comprising experts on infectious diseases and public health to execute crucial decision-making in its ambitious goal of eliminating the virus. It was carried out via contact tracing and subsequent quarantine of infected individuals to break the chain of transmission.

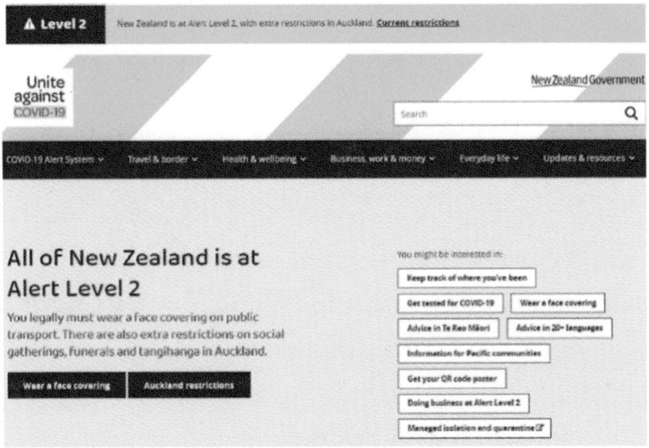

Figure 57: New Zealand Government's COVID-19 website (Source: New Zealand Government)

In a further demonstration of New Zealand's structured response to the outbreak, the nation's existing system of communicable disease control – comprising Public Health Units of medical nurses and officers – was tasked with immediacy to a National Close Contact Service (NCCS) hub in the Ministry of Health. The NCCS aided centralisation of contact tracing and was instrumental to the response when New Zealand transitioned to a level four alert in March 2020 as the number of cases rose.

Strict Lockdown and Contact Tracing

In March 2020, when about 100 people in the country had tested positive for the coronavirus, New Zealand imposed the closure of the nation's borders and transitioned into a level four lockdown.

The country implemented aggressive stay-at-home measures for citizens, except for healthcare personnel, and permitted movement outdoors was restricted to essential activity such as exercise and grocery shopping in the local vicinity.

By instituting one of the world's toughest lockdowns, border restrictions, setting clear alert levels and tightly defining the bounds of lockdown behaviour, New Zealand registered 1,504 cases and 22 deaths as of June 2020, which were comparatively low numbers. Efforts to ramp up testing led to capacity in processing approximately 8,000 tests per day, allowing for one of the highest testing rates per capita in the world. Notwithstanding that infections subsequently re-emerged in August 2020 after three months of no recorded cases, and that renewed tightening of quarantine measures had to be considered, it shows the importance of committing to strict lockdowns and rigorous contact tracing, and not letting up before the virus is truly eradicated.

Clear Public Information Campaign

Prime Minister Jacinda Ardern has charted a path of clarity in the face of an emergency, in clear and consistent messaging to citizens supported by public health professionals and a team of scientists. The slogan of "be strong, and be kind" repeated by Ardern served to foster a sentiment of national unity for citizens enduring strict shelter-in-place restrictions.

Ardern's government-directed New Zealanders to "stay home to save lives", demonstrating transparency on the state's decision-making processes and offering purpose to compliance with containment measures via near-daily televised briefings and regular Facebook Live sessions.

Public trust in government at the later stages of the pandemic continued to be bolstered by the administration's reassuring stance in communication and preparedness, such as encouraging persistent vigilance even as cases dropped to zero.

The New Zealand government's consistent, clear direction and swift response in coping with the developing pandemic situation, has proven successful in rallying its people to comply with the country's strict measures.

Balanced Economic Response

Nonetheless, New Zealand has not been able to avoid the economic repercussions to its heavily tourism-dependent economy. Service and construction industries contributed most to the fall in economic activity, which was down 1.6 percent in March 2020, the first quarterly fall since December 2010.[68]

The New Zealand government has in response introduced a COVID-19 Response and Recovery Fund worth NZ$50 billion (US$32 billion), allocated to wage subsidy extension, funding to the New Zealand Trade and Enterprise (NZTE) and establishment of a Tourism Sector Recovery Plan, amongst other plans for the Fund.[69]

And that is why we as a country took the challenge of staring down COVID-19 – because we believed that decisive action, going hard and going early, gave us the very best chance of stamping out the virus. And it has.

Jacinda Ardern
Prime Minister of New Zealand
20th April 2020

SINGAPORE

Strong and prompt government response to the COVID-19 situation in Singapore is juxtaposed by the major oversight that led to a relatively severe outbreak driven by mass cases in migrant worker dormitories in late March 2020.

The Singapore case exemplifies how despite robust governance, gaps in detecting and taking decisive action with regard to vulnerable groups – in its case the large foreign worker population densely housed in dedicated dormitories – can lead to an 'explosive' outbreak of the coronavirus.

Singapore went from being globally regarded as the 'gold standard' for COVID-19 management in February 2020 to becoming a case study on 'dropping the ball'.

However, in the time since, its government has shown itself willing to rapidly respond to negative developments and to also maintain sustained communication to the public through media conferences, as well a daily update via Whatsapp and other digital channels.

GDP Per Capita (2019) (US$)	65,233
Cumulative Number of Cases (As at 1st September 2020)	56,812
Total Number of Confirmed Deaths (As at 1st September 2020)	27
Case Fatality Rate (%) (As at 1st September 2020)	1.8

There were also several keynote speeches delivered by the Prime Minister Mr Lee Hsien Loong. It is notable that the Prime Minister not only addressed the nation, but also consciously spoke directly to the foreign worker population and their families overseas to provide assurance that the Singapore government would provide them the same level of care as it would to Singaporeans.

Robust Governance and Handling of the Pandemic

A combination of a politically centralised state, a 'whole-of-government' approach and a high-quality healthcare system in Singapore meant there was adequate state capacity to enforce an effective quarantine and testing regime.

Efficient contact tracing measures through the use of the SafeEntry and TraceTogether applications, the speedy imposition of border controls upon eruption of the virus in China, and a 'circuit breaker' lockdown to lower community transmission numbers were all put in place.

In July 2020 Singapore also held general elections, with the ruling People's Action Party calling for a renewed mandate to lead the country out of the coronavirus pandemic, at a point when fatalities remained low and the country had kickstarted a phased reopening process.

With physical rallies forbidden, opposition parties in the city-state sounded out difficulties in reaching out to the electorate while campaigning in adherence to COVID-19 containment measures, and communication moved primarily to digital channels.

Prime Minister Lee Hsien Loong has indicated that the decision on when he will step down from leadership will depend on getting Singapore back on track post-COVID-19. This shows leadership and ownership in managing a national crisis..

The coronavirus pandemic has intervened in leadership succession plans in the country and made imperative the renewed goal of reorganising the state in the wake of COVID-19 to a level ready for a handover.

I had expressed the hope that I would be able to hand over by the time I celebrate my 70th birthday. But I do not determine the path of the COVID-19 pandemic, and it will also depend on how events unfold. And all I can say is, I will see this through. And I'll hand over in good shape as soon as possible to the next team, and into good hands.

Lee Hsien Loong
Prime Minister of Singapore
25th July 2020

Government Oversight

In April 2020, Singapore jumped to the unwanted top spot in Southeast Asia for the number of reported coronavirus cases, a fivefold jump recorded in two weeks.[70]

The surge was attributed to the steep rise in infections within the migrant worker population, residing in overcrowded dormitories and living conditions that do not allow for any form of physical distancing.

At the end of April 2020, 85 percent of 14,951 cases comprised workers living in dormitories,[71] with one of the largest clusters located in a Punggol dormitory complex that houses 14,000 workers in cheap four-storey buildings spanning about 5.8 hectares.[72]

The problem has not been quick or easy to solve and even after measures were put in place to quarantine and test workers, cases have slipped through the cracks and new cases have again emerged in the largest dormitories. In one example, on 12 August 2020, 800 migrant workers were recommitted to quarantine due to the discovery of an infected individual amongst them, despite their dormitory having previously been cleared and identified as virus-free.

The outbreak has focused attention on the systemic neglect of the foreign worker population in a city-state that operates with lax controls and loose thresholds on the number of persons allowed in a single room, with 12 to 20 men sharing a single room at present.

The largest of these facilities houses around 200,000 workers, which are operated by independent companies charging employers between US$200 to US$300 a month per worker.[73]

The lauded response of Singapore to its handling of the pandemic before the sudden outbreak in migrant worker dormitories signifies a blind spot in governance and highlights the grossly unequal treatment of the foreign worker population, which perpetuated long before the onset of COVID-19.

Income and Sectorial Inequality

Singapore has one of the highest GDP per capita but also the lowest wage share (43 percent) amongst advanced economies. This means that a sizeable amount of GDP is captured in corporate profits or government taxation. This is further evinced by a Gini coefficient of 0.452 (0.398 after government transfers), and one of the largest income inequalities in the world.

With COVID-19 causing significant unemployment, particularly amongst the lower-paid working in the blue-collar service sector, such income inequality can only be expected to deepen.

Meanwhile, Singapore also evinces inequality between the various sectors that make up its economy. Small and medium enterprises (SMEs) consist of 99 percent of all firms in Singapore, and employing 71 percent of Singaporeans and Permanent Residents, but only contribute to half of Singapore's GDP.

With firm failures more prevalent in the SME sector, and MNCs being better able to weather the crisis given their greater cash reserves, the Singapore economy which emerges from the pandemic will be certain to see further deepening in sectorial inequalities.

Dimming Economic Forecasts

Singapore has, since the final quarter of 2018, tended to consistently project a higher GDP growth rate compared with the actual growth rates. The initial full-year GDP contraction for 2020 provided by the Ministry of Trade and Industry (MTI) in March 2020 was -4 to -1 percent, before being subsequently corrected to -7 and -4 percent, having taken into account: (i) the prolonged effects of the "circuit breaker" measures, (ii) the lack of clarity of the length and severity of the economic effects of the pandemic both locally and abroad, and (iii) the expectation that the brunt of the contraction will come in the second quarter of 2020, as indeed it did, with a -12.6 percent plunge.

My projections have been consistently less sanguine. In March through July 2020, prior to the General Election, I publicly noted the prospect of elevated levels of unemployment once the wage support wanes.

Since then, in August 2020, the government has committed a further SG$8 billion to extend wage support into 2021. However, this measure cannot countervail falls in final demand, erosion of investor sentiment and cashflow crunches for many SMEs.

Several factors motivate this assessment: global demand will be worse than anticipated – not least the improbability of a vaccine being developed and distributed before mid-2021 – and the lack of further coordinated economic response both in key economies like the US and globally.

The initial overestimate of GDP performance could be attributed to the time lag of events as the crisis began to shift from a public health focus to an economic one, as well as a reluctance to prematurely weigh-in negatively on market sentiment.

With that said, in response to these darkening economic conditions, the Singapore government has taken strong action, by announcing a series of five stimulus packages as of 1st September 2020, which together amount to SG$101 billion.

Measures include support for households, in the form of cash payouts and wage subsidies, as well as additional targeted support for low-income individuals and the unemployed.

Help is also extended to businesses, through the waiving of the foreign worker levy, rental rebates, enhanced financing schemes, direct aid to self-employed individuals and badly affected industries, such as aviation and tourism, and the provision of working loan capital to businesses. There will also be direct government spending on R&D as well as on stockpiling food supplies and enhancing food security.

However, in my view the government's five budgets – counting the SG$8 billion as a *de facto* budget – represent 'overkill', which has caused many Singaporeans to have a false sensation that the situation is not as serious as it truly is, and has also induced a moral hazard among workers, households and businesses that the government will catch their fall each and every time.

This is 'pushing on a string' and is not fiscally sustainable, which will lead to a 'cliff fall' effect over the next 12 months. I forecast that resident unemployment will reach 6 to 8 percent. Underemployment will reach similar proportions while structural unemployment may reach 3 to 5 percent.

There needs to be a serious reckoning with the hard truths of the economic situation, not political platitudes. This is necessary to prepare workers and households whose consumption patterns seem unaffected by the crisis, notably with speculative expenditures.

Macro-Economic Performance

Singapore's traditional tripartite arrangement, whereby the government, employees and unions collectively manage labour issues, is also being updated to include the Fair Retrenchment Framework (FRT), which seeks to protect Singaporean citizens and permanent residents, as well as preserve jobs and provide job support.

The Monetary Authority of Singapore (MAS) has also taken measures to expand the range of collateral that banks in Singapore can use to access US dollars from MAS's own USD facility. This strengthens the banking sector and allows banks to continue extending funding and support to businesses and individuals.

Unlike the Asian Financial Crisis of 1997 and the Global Financial Crisis of 2008-2009, Singapore is entering the economic crisis resulting from the COVID-19 pandemic with recent weak economic growth.

Total merchandise exports dropped by 19.8 percent from October 2018 to June 2019, and non-oil domestic exports dropped 28.5 percent from May 2018 to June 2019.

Non-oil domestic export (NODEX) in Singapore is concentrated primarily in a few sectors, with Machinery & Transport Equipment (37.3 percent) and Chemical & Chemical Products (30.4 percent) comprising the bulk of NODEX volume in 2019.

This means that Singapore is reliant on the increased demand in these sectors from economies of final demand, which is unlikely in the short-term due to the impact of Covid-19.

The proportion of professionals, managers, executives and technicians (PMETs) has risen from 62 percent of the total workforce in 2006 to 71.6 percent in 2018.

This is a reflection of investments in the public education system that prepares its workforce for cognitive labour. However, this also means that they are most vulnerable to pay cuts and job losses as they are expensive to hire and retain.

One clear winner in the pandemic is the technology sector. Firms are looking to automate processes where possible, and PMETs who are retrenched from this economic crisis might add to a growing pool of structurally unemployed Singaporeans.

Citizens are likely to be increasingly displaced by technology advancements, which will, in turn, create social and political challenges that the government needs to address and navigate.

This involves pre-empting how these workers can be effectively and efficiently redeployed into sectors that best match their skills and needs with those of Singapore's.

Singapore's economy is heavily service-oriented. In 2018, services consisted of 64.4 percent of GDP. This exposes Singapore's economy to more vulnerabilities during a financial crisis due to the greater volatility in services.

Unlike the 2008-2009 Global Financial Crisis, it is questionable that we will see a quick rebound, particularly in the financial services sector, due to the muted global recovery as a result of the pandemic.

Therefore, the asymmetry between a fast contraction and a slow rebound will be greatly felt within the next two years.

Besides, the services sector, while more volatile to economic shocks, is also harder to downsize in times of economic crisis. This is because of the heavy concentration of labour costs.

The government recognises the need to retain workers, and the five budgets announced have a common overarching goal – to retain jobs for Singaporeans while keeping labour costs low for employers.

In September 2020, the MAS's survey of private-sector economists showed that they have on aggregate, revised their forecast for FY2020 GDP from -5.8 to a -6 percent contraction.

In March 2020, I issued a forecast of a -9 to -7 percent contraction, which I revised mid-year to -10 to -8 percent. I note the strong counter-cyclical measures implemented by the government. Without which actual GDP performance would already be much worse.

I expect the MAS to revise their Q2 figures to reflect an even worse performance than -13.2 percent, once lagging data is imputed. I continue to be more pessimistic than the conventional sources and as of the time of writing, maintain a forecast for a -10 to -7 percent contraction range, with loading to the midline.

This is due to structural damage to the economy from government policy, free falls in the US and Indian economies from poor governance of COVID-19, and the anaemic performance of EU nations and degrading performance of ASEAN nations.

I also price in the upside potential for further shocks from sovereign debt bubbles, a continuation of the rising costs of trade as well as the outside chance of a US-China conflict.

I acknowledge the government's efforts but I expect much of it to be dead weight and obstructive of necessary creative destruction, which may weaken long term prospects for growth.

The Singapore Commercial Credit Bureau (SCCB) released a report on 8th September 2020 stating that business sentiment for the fourth quarter of 2020 was -4.97 percent. This is a marginal improvement from the -5.16 percent expectation reported for the third quarter.

However, the deeper story is to be found in the year-on-year comparison. In the fourth quarter of 2019, business sentiment was at +4.98 percent. Hence, the deterioration of business sentiment year-on-year is not only a symmetrical inversion, but in statistical terms this represents a nearly 10 percent spread.

This is unprecedented in Singapore's economic history. As business sentiment tends to be sticky and forward-looking it implies the expectation of retrenchment of workers and a decline in investments heading into the first half of 2021.

Risk tolerances will shrink and risk premiums will rise. This 'scissors' effect will act as a dampener of organic growth, thus keeping Singapore in a recessionary mode beyond 2020.

There should be no illusions of a V-shaped recovery. Nor can there be exaggerated expectations of the fiscal impulse effects from the massive, collective counter-cyclical measures introduced by the government in 2020.

Business failures are likely to rise steeply in the fourth quarter of 2020 and into the first half of 2021. The creation of new businesses will also fall sharply. The implications of this second scissors effect go beyond job losses to structural damage to the economy.

Deflationary Threat

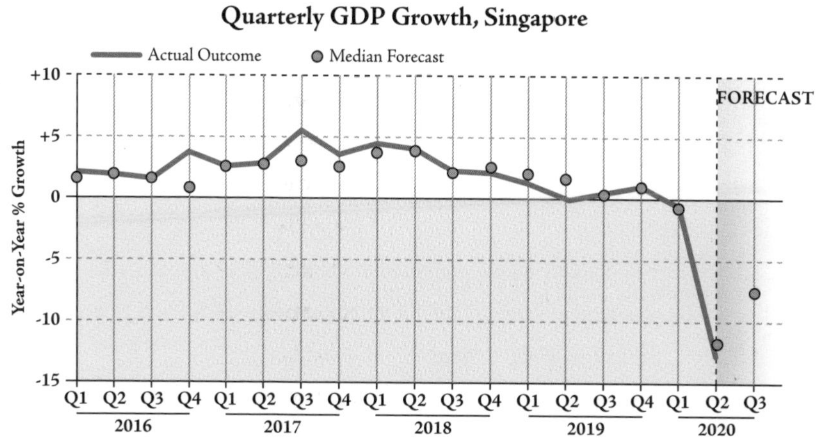

Figure 58: Quarterly GDP Growth in Singapore (Data: Monetary Authority of Singapore)

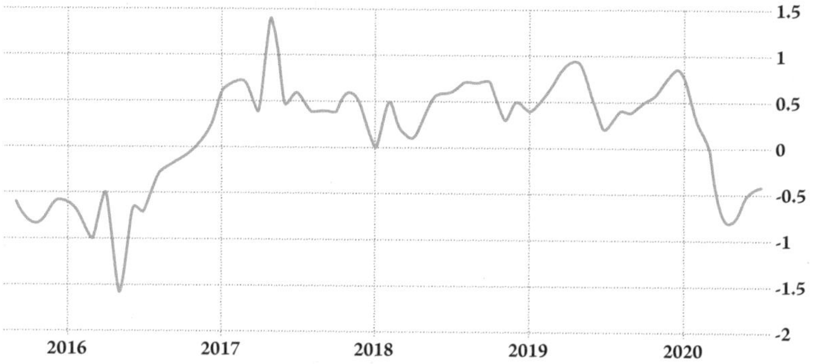

Figure 59: Singapore Consumer Price Index, 2016-2020 (Source: Trading Economics)

Singapore's economy is on a deflationary track despite the extraordinary five budgets. Low inflation combined with severe and sustained contraction of growth deep into negative terrain, are a recipe for deflation once it translates into rising unemployment, erosion of business and investor sentiment, and falls in consumption.

As counter-cyclical measures are tapered off through the remainder of 2020 and the first half of 2021, if global growth remains subdued to the point of neutral or negative growth, and if Singapore's connectivity remains constrained – it is notable that while Singapore has announced "Green Lanes", these are not reciprocal arrangements and none are with our major trading partners – then we will enter the lose-lose condition of deflation and contraction.

It is not possible to spend one's way back to growth, so fiscal measures are limited to supporting functions rather than truly catalytic ones, at least in the short term.

Deflationary conditions, if protracted, have the propensity to become sticky and have a longer-term inertial effect which then infects consumer psychology and investor sentiment.

Anti-Foreigner Sentiment

As the economic performance has worsened there is growing negative sentiment both on social media and amongst the general population against foreigners on the assumption that they are 'stealing jobs'.

My position on the matter of displacing expatriate talent through policy action to tip hiring in favour of locals is that it must be nuanced.

First, it is important to understand that if Singapore aims for long term economic success it must compete globally, something it cannot do with a small and ageing population and if it adopts protectionist labour policies.

Second, it is necessary to distinguish between skilled and unskilled expats. While there is some justification to substituting a percentage of skilled expats with equally skilled locals, none or negligibly few Singaporeans are willing to substitute for foreign unskilled workers.

So the premise for displacing each category cannot be the same. With regard to foreign unskilled workers it can be more clearly justified by economic contraction. But with respect to skilled expats, a blunt and knee-jerk protectionist policy undercuts competitiveness which makes local workers better off but smacks of populism.

The concern is the longer-term impact on the perception that Singapore is going from being long-sighted, confident and rational, to short-sighted, insecure and populist. The short-term political benefits of blunt protectionist policies may result in long-term erosion of economic competitiveness, leading to even more future job losses.

Adaptation

Singapore took an early, aggressive and Bayesian approach – inducting new knowledge to adjust policies – which to the public seemed inconsistent but in fact, represented the intelligence and will to rapidly change course based on new information.

Similarly, Singapore will prove naysayers wrong on its economic future. However, that will require a Whole-of-Nation effort, a rethink of fundamentals and strategic patience. In my view, Singapore is not at the end of the crisis but at the end of the beginning. The recovery will be slow and painful. I do not expect a return to growth anytime soon, but I do expect a return of confidence in our potential for future growth.

A prerequisite for this is long-term adaptation, to make Singapore more resilient.

Singapore is a 'test-tube' nation. Every decade it has endeavoured to reinvent itself to remain relevant to the global economy. The challenges confronting it today are as profound as those it faced upon its sudden assumption of independence in 1965.

But it has many more advantages today than it had 55 years ago. Its population is highly educated; its public transport, education and health infrastructure are sound, abundant and modern. Its financial position is very strong and its international reputation renowned. Unlike in 1965, there is no question or doubt over the viability of its continued sovereignty.

However, the major challenge lies in the coincidence of the timing of the pandemic and the generational change in political leadership from the '3G' to the so-called '4G' leaders. The latter are untested by crisis, predominately former civil servants and military officers with little private sector experience, and whose entire careers have been curated for success and largely insulated from economic realities.

Whether they can weather the crisis and win the confidence of the people will have long-term path dependency effects for the political future of Singapore.

COVID-19 will remain a problem for a long time yet. It will take at least a year, probably longer, before vaccines become widely available. We must all adjust the way we live, work and play, so that we can reduce the spread of the virus, and keep ourselves safe.

Lee Hsien Loong
Prime Minister of Singapore
7th June 2020

CHINA

China's case exemplifies the efficacy of a draconian approach to lockdown and containment, supported by a public health system readied to ramp up and respond to an evolving crisis.

Success in China's case is mixed, especially when taking into account its role in global diplomatic and economic systems, where repercussions of weakening trade and manufacturing activity, as well as international criticism over a lack of transparency with information, dent an otherwise largely successful containment strategy.

GDP Per Capita (2019) (US$)	*10,262*
Cumulative Number of Cases (As at 1st September 2020)	*89,914*
Total Number of Confirmed Deaths (As at 1st September 2020)	*4,723*
Case Fatality Rate (%) (As at 1st September 2020)	*5.3*

Equipped Disease Control and Healthcare Capability

Emerging from the 2002-2003 SARS outbreak, Chinese health authorities worked to enhance its disease control infrastructure, led by the Chinese Center for Disease Control and Prevention. Improvements to scientific research laboratory facilities and public health surveillance systems were made in the wake of SARS, are now helping to tackle the onset of COVID-19.

Domestic response to imposing shelter-in-place measures and organising critical care and testing systems was set in motion at a remarkable pace in January 2020, a testament to the meaningful progress in healthcare and disease control. In the span of four weeks in January, close to 50 million people in Wuhan and bordering cities had been placed under quarantine.

The Chinese government fast-tracked approval of testing kits, constructed new laboratories and authorised participation for a higher number of private actors in response to the rapidly rising testing imperative in the first months of the outbreak.

Further, China leveraged digitalisation to combat spread of the virus, with tele-response bots running on 5th generation wireless technology aiding communication between healthcare personnel and patients in several cities, tracking health indicators and delivering medical supplies.

Lack of Political Transparency

In January 2020, the WHO gave public recognition to China's quick response to the novel coronavirus, thanking the Chinese administration for speedy sharing of the COVID-19 genetic map.

An investigation carried out by the Associated Press thereafter exposed the hidden truth, where critical scientific information on the virus – including its initial discovery and the related first death – was withheld by China for six days.[74] In fact, the decoded genome sequence of the virus took over a week to be revealed to the public eye.

Secrecy in a global health crisis impedes international cooperation and squanders time that is crucial to halting the spread of a virus.

China's actions likely stalled diagnostic test developments and drug research, prompting comparison to the country's handling of SARS, where the international community at the time had to similarly wrestle information from China.

Vulnerable Position in Global Supply Chains

Primarily active in manufacturing, consumer goods, retail and food production, China's 50 million SMEs have been hit hardest by the pandemic despite the gradual reopening of the economy and government attempts in previous years to strengthen SME competitiveness.

China President Xi Jinping's intention to bolster support for large state-owned enterprises stands in stark contrast to a worrying SME landscape, where financial reserves, credit lines and government support are lacking. Containing the outbreak through China's drastic measures has driven its SMEs to the brink. A Tsinghua University survey in February 2020 reported that 85 percent of firms studied were unable to remain in business for three months or more with existing cash reserves.[75]

Struggling SMEs

The effect of SME downturn will be felt in China's banks, especially ones that have increased exposure to small and mid-tier firms. As SMEs remain liable to loan repayment, operating costs and employee salaries in a poor business climate, the situation of cash flow shortage is expected to further deteriorate.

Manufacturing activity looks set to remain at depressed levels as supply shocks continue to ripple through the global economy. Drop in production fell by 13.5 percent in January and February 2020, a stark drop exceeding those experienced during the 2002-2003 SARS epidemic and 2008-2009 Global Financial Crisis.[76]

As international businesses begin to evaluate post-COVID plans, a pattern of pivoting away from the Chinese production powerhouse is starting to surface. In adjusting supply chains in the aftermath of the pandemic, some countries are encouraging domestic firms to exit China and shift plants back home.

The world's second-largest economy now encounters a worsening situation of firms from the US, Japan and Europe leaving. This has already been set in motion thanks to the effects of the US-China trade war and rising costs of manufacturing.

Looking ahead, the capacity to recover production to normal levels will remain dependent on the speed at which factories return to work, as the effects of the pandemic on global consumption remain largely uncertain.

China supports a comprehensive evaluation of the global response to the epidemic after the global epidemic is under control, to sum up experiences and remedy deficiencies.

Xi Jinping
President of the People's Republic of China
18th May 2020

Hong Kong SAR

GDP Per Capita (2019) (US$)	48,756
Cumulative Number of Cases (As at 1st September 2020)	4,823
Total Number of Confirmed Deaths (As at 1st September 2020)	90
Case Fatality Rate (%) (As at 1st September 2020)	1.9

Hong Kong's strategy is to keep the pandemic at a low level rather than trying to achieve zero cases. Such measures consume fewer medical resources in the short-term, but might inflict higher social and economic costs in the long term.

Zhang Wenhong,
Director of Huashan Hospital's Department of Infectious Diseases in Shanghai
19th July 2020

Measured Approach to Phased Closure

Hong Kong, while a part of sovereign China, has been permitted to have a distinctiveness in its governance model through the 'One Country, Two Systems' arrangement. Hence, it is permissible to consider Hong Kong as a separate case study from Mainland China.

Hong Kong implemented drastic early response measures at the onset of the pandemic, closing schools, ordering civil servants to telework, imposing a strict quarantine on visitors from outside the country, and close contact tracing and hospitalisation of individuals tested positive for the coronavirus.

However, a renewed outbreak in July 2020 saw local hospitals reach 80 percent capacity for quarantine isolation rooms and stretched testing facilities. Before this, Hong Kong had received wide praise for its quick response to the pandemic, tightened border restrictions and quarantine rules soon after cases were first identified in Mainland China.

More recent outbreaks puzzle health experts. As the ongoing outbreak unfolds, Hong Kong's case is similar to Singapore, illustrating how COVID-19 remains a situation to be closely monitored because complacency can have dire consequences.

Given the second wave in cases – which is being blamed on quarantine exemptions for some business travellers and the crew members of aircraft and ships – the government has moved to a regime of mass voluntary testing, with the hope that at least 5 million people will participate.

Civil Society Action

Public and community-led action has seen voluntary and rapid adoption of mask-wearing and adherence to social distancing rules, partly attributed to the experience of the 2002-2003 SARS outbreak.

Robust testing, quarantine for more serious patients and a monitoring framework for those in lockdown at home were measures that benefitted from frictionless community buy-in, a result of having learnt from SARS, which killed 299 people in the city.[78]

The population of Hong Kong has come forward where its government has failed. More than 2,400 healthcare workers staged a strike in early February 2020 to pressure the government to shut borders with Mainland China as the city recorded 15 confirmed cases of the virus.

The pro-democracy movement has shifted to digital organising, where activists have highlighted deficiencies in the government's pandemic response and even organised mask distribution to underserved communities.

Poor Government Communication

Chief Executive Carrie Lam's mixed messages early on in February 2020 on mask-wearing and closure of the border with Mainland China raised mistrust in Hong Kong's population, with an episode of medical workers and residents organising to strike and opposing the choice of housing estates selected as quarantine sites.

Further complicating the situation on masks was the ban on their use that was introduced in October 2019 in response to widespread violent protests in the city. Since the onset of the coronavirus pandemic, the law has been criticised for contradicting public health measures.

In a separate episode of unclear communication on the subject of mask-wearing, Chief Executive Lam had to publicly apologise for remarks she made discouraging public officials not to wear masks unless in limited and specific situations, citing a shortage of supply.

This move has come under fire as the comments only served to raise panic in the population that there were no masks available in the market.

Severe Economic Effect and Countermeasures

The pandemic has hit Hong Kong's economy badly, with the economy shrinking 8.9 percent year-on-year in the first quarter of 2020.[79] This contraction is deeper than any other on record and is worse than the previous nadir during the Asian Financial Crisis.

This is partly driven by local factors affecting supply and demand. In the first instance, local lockdowns terminated the supply of certain goods and services.

This included the closure of schools, entertainment and sports facilities and limiting diner capacity in restaurants for the sake of social distancing. Then, as sectors shut down and unemployment – particularly in the blue-collar services industry – rose north of 4 percent,[80] there was a knock-on effect on demand.

Being a small, open economy for which trade to GDP ratio stands at more than 350 percent,[81] Hong Kong is especially vulnerable to global economic conditions.

With the pandemic also negatively affecting its biggest trade partners – Mainland China, the US, and other East Asian countries – Hong Kong experienced a slump in global demand for its goods and services, as well as supply chain disruptions.

Together with the pre-COVID-19 headwind of the US-China trade war, Hong Kong's exports slumped 9.7 percent in the first quarter of 2020.[82]

Hong Kong has announced HKD$287.5 billion – or 10 percent of GDP – in fiscal expansion, with measures including: (i) the establishment of a new Anti-Epidemic Fund to enhance facilities and services used to combat disease outbreaks; (ii) tax relief and fee waivers; (iii) direct cash payments to Hong Kong permanent residents; (iv) wage subsidies; (v) a temporary job creation program; and (vi) support for specific sectors.[83]

These specific sectors singled out for aid are the ones hardest-hit by the pandemic. For service providers and suppliers to schools and universities, which have been forced to close, one-off grants have been provided, helping the likes of catering outlets, lunchbox providers, school bus drivers and sports coaches.

In the passenger transport sector, taxi and minibus drivers have been provided with both monthly and one-off subsidies, while their vehicle repair and maintenance costs, as well as insurance premiums, have been reimbursed.

In the creative industry, while digitalised entertainment service providers like Netflix have benefitted from the lockdowns imposed globally, traditional entertainment sectors like theme parks, cinemas and tourist locales have suffered.

Recognising this, Hong Kong has provided subsidies to cinemas, as well as to the tenants of the historic Police Married Quarters site.

Tourism has been especially hard hit by global border closures, which has resulted in the government issuing direct cash subsidies to travel agents, tourist guides, licensed hotels, coach drivers and cruise lines. In the construction sector, subsidies have also been provided to workers, contractors and non-profit organisations running projects.

I think the situation is critical and there is no sign the situation is being brought under control. We can't just make a simple and extreme move to cut everything at once. We haven't adopted that in the last six months because we wanted to maintain a normal life for everyone.

Carrie Lam
Chief Executive of Hong Kong
19th July 2020

SWEDEN

The Nordic state's COVID-19 plan stands as a cautionary tale to tackling the pandemic. Its light-touch strategy led to more than 5800 deaths, as of early September 2020, in a country of 10 million people.[84]

Economic suffering is on the horizon too, with growth projections set for steep GDP contraction. More than 90 percent of deaths recorded as of end-April 2020 were of patients over the age of 70; half of whom were nursing home residents and the remaining receiving care at home – a sign of clear neglect of the country's elderly. Sweden's decision to take an alternative approach to the lockdown strategies as seen in most of the rest of the world has not produced successful outcomes.

GDP Per Capita (2019) (US$)	51,610
Cumulative Number of Cases (As at 1st September 2020)	84,406
Total Number of Confirmed Deaths (As at 1st September 2020)	5,820
Case Fatality Rate (%) (As at 1st September 2020)	6.9

Laissez-Faire Approach

Sweden has adopted a controversial strategy of aiming for herd immunity while keeping businesses and schools running – a stark contrast to the strict lockdowns imposed by other countries.

This strategy is facilitated by a high level of public trust in government, with the populace exhibiting low levels of fear of the pandemic – taking their cue, perhaps, from the government itself.

An effect of this lax approach, however, is a death toll per capita far exceeding those of its Nordic neighbours who imposed strict lockdowns – Sweden's death rate is roughly eight times higher than Denmark's and 19 times that of Norway's[85] – sparking domestic debate and doubt in the effectiveness of the Swedish government's distinct strategy.

In the region, the gradual reopening of borders in Nordic and European states has excluded Sweden. In Denmark, Norway and Finland, where the situation has stabilised, Sweden's worrying death rate means a preference to keeping borders closed to the Swedish people and products – a bad sign for business and regional integration.

As holders of one of the best passports for global travel, Swedes now find themselves with little option to move around in the European Union.

While most countries in the bloc have reopened borders to member nations, only France, Italy, Spain and Croatia are open to Swedes without restrictions.

Ill-preparedness in Healthcare Governance

Sweden's Public Health Agency was delegated to lead pandemic response by political leaders, and healthcare in the country is also highly decentralised to regional governments.

Regional variation in performance, however, marks a longstanding quality of the healthcare sector, one notable disparity being the quality of end-of-life medical intervention where the care of patients and familial support differ according to the location of treatment across the country.

Concerns with large differences in waiting times for specialist and out-patient treatment, especially between capital Stockholm and the northern region, also remain.

Command and control mechanisms to disseminate political agenda in tackling the pandemic made necessary the use of communication channels across agency lines and toward regional-level administration.

In a case of poorly coordinated action, key agencies of the Public Health Agency and National Board of Health and Welfare found that it lacked crucial information on the stockpiles of personal protective equipment in local medical facilities, leading to shortages.

Falling Consumer Confidence and Weakening Export-based Economy

Both business and consumer confidence indexes as presented in the National Institute of Economic Research's (NIER) 2019 Economic Tendency Survey fall short of normal levels, with consumer confidence only a slight margin away from a seven-year low and dwindling for its fifth straight month in September 2019.[86]

As customers tighten spending in the current global economic downturn, consumer confidence indicators in April 2020 plunged to the lowest level since records began in 1996,[87] despite a slight improvement in May.

Demand for Swedish exports have in recent years demonstrated weaker growth despite a well-performing manufacturing sector and depreciation of the Krona.

As global supply chains were disrupted and consumer bases diminished as the COVID-19 crisis took hold, reduced demand for Swedish products understandably extended into the current year.

The drop in manufacturing PMI (purchasing managers index) began in March 2020 – and while many of their European neighbours suffered the same fate – this confirms that Swedish manufacturers have been considerably hit by a fall in exports.

Given that the significant dip in demand is being further worsened by the pandemic, the Ministry of Finance forecasts a 9.3 percent unemployment rate in 2020, while a system of short-term retrenchment is expected as an alternative to sharper drops in employment, as companies will, in the long run, maintain the capacity to keep their workers.[88]

Consistent with this prediction is one from the Riksbank, the country's central bank, which expects a 9 to 10.4 percent peak of the unemployment rate.[89]

The Riksbank has further drawn out two possible scenarios for economic contraction – either a 6.9 percent contraction or in a more negative prediction, a worst-case forecast of 9.7 percent GDP contraction.[90]

[This crisis] is a reminder that the society affected by the pandemic was not a perfect society, therefore we will not go back to how everything was before.

Stefan Löfven
Prime Minister of Sweden

THE UNITED STATES

The US response to the coronavirus pandemic has exposed foundational weaknesses in its public health system and the Trump administration's command of governance. This has led to a public health crisis with deep economic and societal repercussions, and a vast under-performance for a high-income country that is traditionally a global leader in public health.

Figures in mid-June 2020 saw the seven-day average of new COVID-19 cases increase more than 24 percent compared to the previous week, with cases growing by 5 percent or more in 25 states across the US.[91]

Worryingly, the rise in cases is found to outpace the growth in testing rates. As of early September 2020, US coronavirus cases has passed 6.25 million, and 185,000 people have died of the coronavirus in the United States.[92]

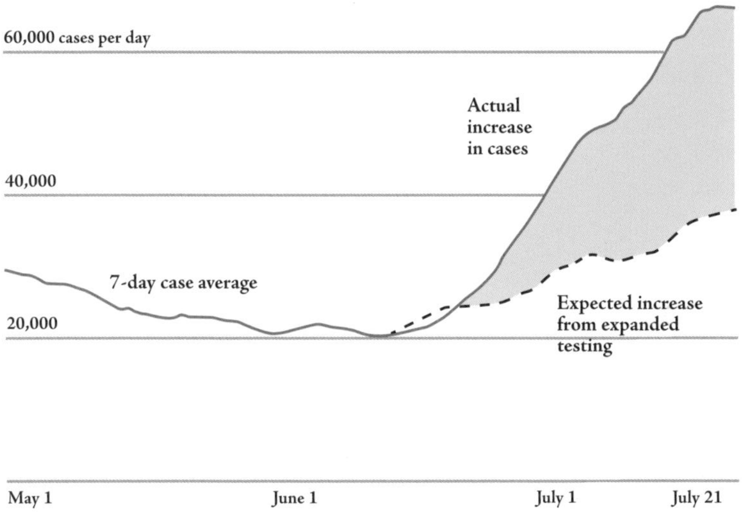

Figure 60: Growth in US Case Numbers, May–July. Expanded testing – increased by 80 percent since early June – is not the sole reason driving the steep growth in case numbers. This implies a worsening outbreak.[93]

Fragmented Healthcare System

In comparison to other countries with a similar status of wealth and size to the US, the US has fewer practising physicians per capita but comparable numbers of licensed nurses per capita.

Stark numbers concerning hospital density, with 17.1 hospitals per million people in 2016 – by comparison, South Korea has 73.9 hospitals per million people – are an important indication of a steep healthcare facility shortage in the US.

The fragmented health system is marked by the divide between richer and poorer institutions within the system, a rift set to widen with COVID-19.

The US healthcare system has high levels of medical debt and the likelihood of fatality from preventable causes is generally higher for Americans than in other parts of the world.

In an American Medical Association study last year, the US wasted at least US$760 billion in inessential healthcare spending.[94]

Although the US spends large amounts on public health, the country has become somewhat of an outlier that has failed to translate a highly-funded system into a provider of affordable healthcare.

Uncoordinated Communication

From the start, US leaders have displayed unclear communication in the country's pandemic approach, forwarding contradictory messages when relaying information on the outbreak and causing anxiety in the American public.

At the onset of the virus, President Trump's downplaying of the pandemic's severity stood in contrast to Dr Anthony Fauci, a leading expert on infectious diseases, who warned of the lethality of the viral strain.

In a recent instance of perpetuating untruths to the American public, Trump, in an interview in July 2020, claimed the US had low mortality rates, despite the US standing in 10th place globally in the number of COVID-19 deaths at the time.[95]

Conflicting advice between federal leaders on safety measures, such as the back-and-forth situation of the Center for Disease Control and Prevention's (CDC's) decision to impose distancing restrictions and wearing of masks, is one of many episodes that have contributed to public distrust in US leadership and impeded progress in the formulation of public health policy.

But when you talk about mortality rates, I think it's the opposite. I think we have one of the lowest mortality rates in the world.

Donald Trump
President of the United States
20th July 2020

Ill-prepared Response System

In 2018, the National Security Council's Global Health Security and Biodefense unit, established by the Obama administration in the wake of the Ebola experience, was largely disbanded with the departure of well-respected health security official Timothy Ziemer. This prompted domestic doubt on American readiness to respond to a prospective health emergency.

Creation of the President's Coronavirus Task Force in 2020, an exclusively male team of a dozen advisors, seems a move at improvisation in the absence of a formal framework to health crisis response.

With a constitutional system that places key responsibility for public health in the hands of individual states via diffused chains of commands that branch into cities and counties, the federal government in these extraordinary circumstances has done too little.

The dangerously slow federal reaction to the viral outbreak is in large part attributed to disunited national leadership, with leaders of localities at the helm of response exercising only limited health legal authority in the rapidly developing outbreak.

This failure of governance has meant that America has experienced a high number of deaths, even relative to other countries such as Russia, which are poorer and also burdened with ineffective, autocratic government.

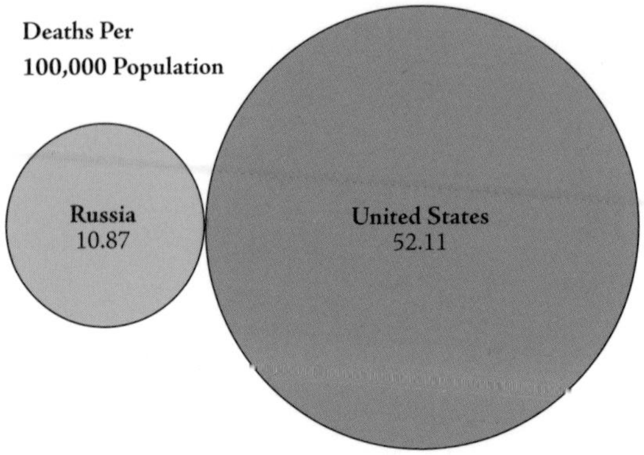

Figure 61: Comparison of COVID-19 deaths in the United States vs Russia (Source: John Hopkins Coronavirus Resource Center)

Struggling Economy

With a severe outbreak that killed at least 180,000 people by 1st September 2020,[96] the economy has been forced to stay closed for an extended period, and attempts at reopening bars and other recreational venues had to be reversed after a surge in cases.

Employment fell by an unprecedented 22 million in March and April 2020 – a rapidity unseen even during the Great Depression itself.

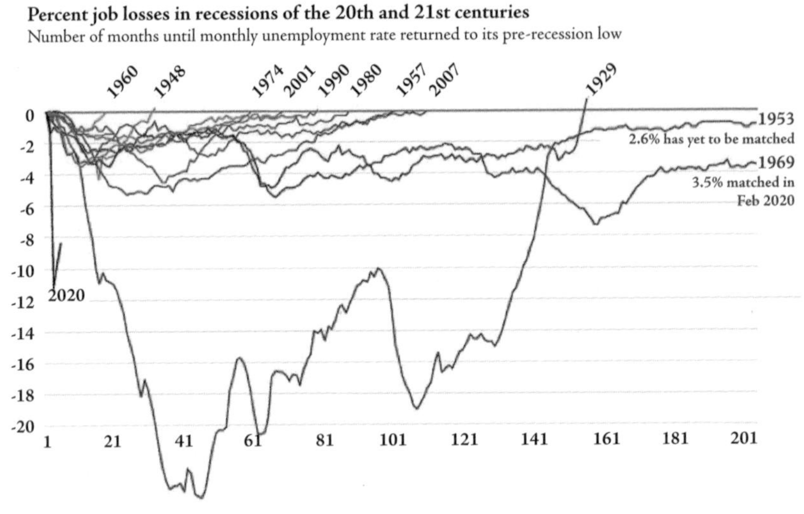

Figure 62: Fall in US Unemployment in 20th and 21st Century Recessions (Source: Time)

The World Bank projects that US GDP will shrink by 6.1 percent in 2020.[97] And while the US government initially implemented an ambitious US$2.2 trillion emergency relief bill that would have sent money directly to households, boost unemployment insurance and set up loan programmes for businesses,[98] there was no follow-up. The enhanced unemployment insurance benefits terminated at the end of July 2020.

Termination of these increased unemployment insurance benefits will not just increase the economic hardship and privation suffered by households, but it will also prove a negative demand shock.

This is because the individuals these benefits are targeted at are those most likely to spend the additional income. The result will see GDP at 3.7 percent lower and the number of unemployed persons 5.1 million higher, relative to a baseline where the increased unemployment insurance benefits are extended through to the middle of 2021.[99]

As of September 2020 Congress is actively working towards passing a bill extending these support measures into 2021. However, these expenditures represent unfunded liabilities that will incur a large budget deficit and have to be financed through borrowing, which will further burden the national debt which will add drag to the progress of future generations of Americans.

Long-Term Political Consequences

Beyond the death toll and the economic damage, the pandemic has also deepened polarisation in America – raising the stakes, and further embittering both those opposed to Donald Trump and those who support him.

The pandemic has also weakened America abroad, as its failure of governance makes the American political system less attractive, and weakens the confidence of both allies and enemies that the United States is willing and capable of asserting global leadership.

As writer and *TIME* senior editor Alex Fitzpatrick has suggested, "Regardless, the pandemic seems likely to leave the US weakened and adrift for at least the near term, with hundreds of thousands, possibly even millions, of its citizens dead. It has already exposed significant foundational flaws, from a disastrously frayed social safety net to life-threatening systemic racism. It has made clear that many of us do not think of ourselves as our brothers' keepers, perhaps forever damaging any sense of community among neighbors. And it has crippled our standing on the world stage – who would want to import American ideals when those ideals bring death on a mass scale? Many Americans will not survive this pandemic. Those who do will be left with considerable work to fix ourselves – and our country."

You have to have responsibility for yourself but also a societal responsibility that you're getting infected is not just you in a vacuum. You are propagating the pandemic.

Dr Anthony Fauci
Director of the National Institute of Allergy and Infectious Diseases
16th July 2020

CANADA

Canada represents a good comparison case with the US, where the federal government has largely mounted a concerted response to COVID-19. In contrast to the US, Canada has fared better, with approximately three-times fewer cases of infections and two-times fewer deaths per capita.[100] In terms of demographic characteristics, Canada has just over 10 percent of the US population, and cities in the country are not as densely populated as its neighbour's, which partially contributes to the relative ease in imposing widespread measures.

GDP Per Capita (2019) (US$)	46,195
Cumulative Number of Cases (As at 1st September 2020)	128,948
Total Number of Confirmed Deaths (As at 1st September 2020)	9,126
Case Fatality Rate (%) (As at 1st September 2020)	7.7

Funded Healthcare Provision

Canada's publicly-funded healthcare system covers the cost of coronavirus testing, medication and hospitalisation where necessary, vastly lowering the barrier to seeking medical attention and incentivising early detection.

In contrast, approximately 27.9 million Americans lack health insurance,[101] and 44 million are underinsured, meaning that the cost of care acts as a severe deterrence to seeking medical help in this public health emergency.

Canada practices a single-payer universal health system that ensures all citizens receive quality and accessible healthcare in the event of detection in COVID-19 symptoms, without the individual having to foot out-of-pocket costs.[102]

Yet, numbers in early-April 2020 were already indicative of a higher occurrence of deaths in residents of nursing homes – approximately 80 per cent of all cases[103] – and larger outbreaks in vulnerable communities in prisons and the foreign worker populations. This demonstrates a neglect of the needs of varying demographic communities within the country, leading to inadequate safeguards for vulnerable groups.

Integrated Governance

Handling of the coronavirus pandemic has largely not become a partisan or politicised issue in Canada, and authority to guide outbreak containment plans was generally deferred to public health officials, supported by federal government directives and action.

Prime Minister Justin Trudeau took swift action to work with opposition leaders and put bitter partisan issues largely aside, despite heading into the pandemic with a minority government.

Minister of Health Patty Hajdu and Chief Public Health Officer Theresa Tam have led the Canadian response, along with provincial counterparts.

Across federal-provincial boundaries, the federal government provides strong support to provinces and Prime Minister Trudeau has taken the consistent stance of the coronavirus as a serious threat requiring a united federal response.

While provincial premiers have overall mounted varying responses to the pandemic, there was no disagreement from local leaders over the need to impose strict measures. Provinces under the leadership of different political parties have forwarded similar social distancing and public health guidelines, demonstrating country-wide coordination.

The Federal government has further taken the responsibility to acquire personal protective equipment centrally, and distribute supplies to provinces where demand is high, providing support to provincial efforts to secure supplies. In a massive effort following the outbreak of cases in March 2020, federal authorities fast-tracked the import of medical devices and test kits to be distributed to provinces and provide supply in excess given rising case numbers.

Contraction of the Economy

Nonetheless, Canada's economy has suffered a drastic contraction as a result of the pandemic, with GDP falling 8.2 percent in the first quarter of 2020 relative to the previous year.[104]

The policy measures Canada has used to manage the pandemic, including travel restrictions, social distancing, and the closure of non-essential businesses, has had the unavoidable side-effect of drastically curtailing certain sectors of its economy, notably the restaurant business, aviation and tourism.

This has been a negative supply shock, as unemployment spiked – to a record 13.7 percent in June 2020[105] – alongside plummeting consumer spending and aggregate demand, which drove down GDP performance.

Fiscal Measures and Recovery Effort

In response to the pandemic-induced recession, the Canadian government has moved decisively, introducing fiscal measures worth CAD317 billion, or 15 percent of GDP.[106]

Such measures include: (i) additional money to the health system to support an expansion of testing, the development of a vaccine, and the acquisition of additional medical supplies; (ii) aid to households and firms in the form of wage subsidies, help for workers lacking sick leave and employment-based insurance, increased tax credits, expanded child care benefits; (iii) tax deferrals to boost liquidity and avoid cash flow problems; and (iv) specific support for the indigenous community, including the creation of a new Indigenous Community Support Fund.

Complicating any possible recovery efforts, however, is the fact that Canada's neighbour and largest trading partner, the United States, is struggling to get the pandemic under control.

Given US Senate Republicans' hostility to further generous spending to households – which would prop up demand and GDP despite the disruption brought by the pandemic – additional robust fiscal stimulus by the US government seems unlikely unless and until a Biden administration takes action in 2021.

The upshot of this is that muted demand from the US will prove a drag on growth in Canada over the next year and for the foreseeable future, making Canada's economic recovery difficult.

We have to recognize that things will change in this world, even after the end of this pandemic, even after a vaccine," he told reporters. "COVID-19 will be one of the things that create changes in our society. There will be adjustments.

Justin Trudeau
Prime Minister of Canada
15th May 2020

Part F: Long-Term Forecast Model for Global Growth

This section examines the longer-term economic prospects for the global economy and forecasts some possible growth trajectories depending on how events develop.

- Conventional forecasts like the IMF's predict a rapid recovery from the COVID-19 recession.
- I take a considerably more pessimistic outlook, for two reasons:
  - A vaccine may take longer than the expected 12 to 18 months to develop, and;
  - COVID-19 has the potential to set off further crises on political, geopolitical, economic, financial and societal fronts.

LONG-TERM FORECAST MODEL FOR GLOBAL GROWTH

The IMF's global economic forecast, published in April 2020, was relatively optimistic in projecting a strong recovery after the initial sharp contraction. Refer to figure 64 for an illustration of such a "V-shaped" recovery.

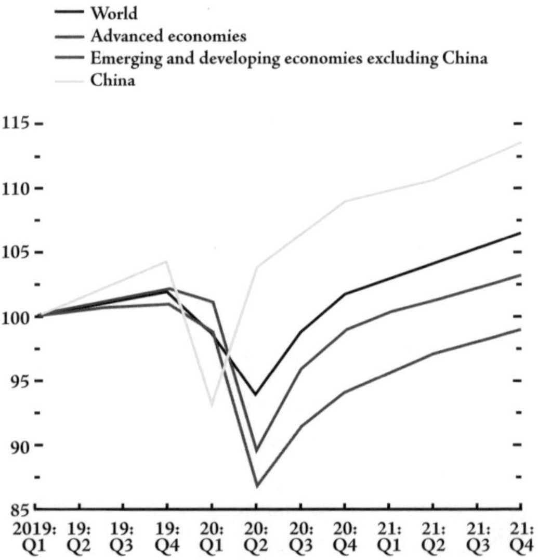

Figure 63: COVID-19's Impact on Global GDP Growth (Source: IMF)

In contrast, my forecast models are more pessimistic. These forecasts are predicated upon the following rationale:

Multiple Crises

First and foremost, I take the view that COVID-19 is not an isolated phenomenon but a trigger that can potentially detonate several latent 'time bombs' in the political, geopolitical, economic, financial and social dimensions.

Protracted Vaccine Development

It can be assumed that a COVID-19 vaccine will not be available until at least mid-2021. Although scientific progress is being made in gaining a better understanding of the nature of the virus, there is still no consensus of its exact pathology, its modes of transmission or the latency of its potency.

I am also circumspect of the several optimistic announcements by private companies competing to produce the vaccine.

I believe these are largely self-promotional to entice private investors or, if in the case of publicly listed companies, are attempts to 'goose' their share prices. There has also been no definitive valid peer-review of any prototype vaccine which is close to maturity.

Similarly, and as noted before, despite President Putin's announcement that Russia has already developed a safe and reliable vaccine, no such thing has occurred. This is merely a political stunt, with Russia's vaccine candidate not yet having undergone large-scale Phase 3 trials.

Indeed, the fact that this is political theatre can be evinced from Russia eventually announcing large scale trials on 40,000 people; the need for further testing and development is far from over.

Moreover, even workable vaccines may vary in effectiveness, and studies have shown that if a vaccine is only 80 percent effective, then 75 percent of the population would need to be vaccinated for the pandemic to be fully ended.[107]

With any lower vaccine effectiveness or coverage rate, then some degree of current pandemic control policies would need to remain. As Dr. Bruce Y. Lee of CUNY Graduate School of Public Health and Health Policy has written, "[a vaccine with lower efficacy] would mean social distancing and mask-wearing likely would have to continue until the pandemic runs its course or a vaccine that is actually 'good enough' arrives." This will mean continued drag on economic activity even after the arrival of an initial vaccine.

Meanwhile, even once an effective vaccine is developed, manufacturing and deploying it will take time. UNICEF estimates that global vaccine manufacturers will be able to produce unprecedented vaccine quantities over the next one to two years, but this is also highly dependent on factors like advance purchase agreements, confirmation of funding, and the streamlining of regulation and registration pathways.

Exceptions are not the Rule

The pandemic is truly global in nature and yet it has not completed its full penetration of populations around the world. New Zealand is the singular exception where the virus has almost been eradicated, with no other country coming close to reaching such a goal.

The special circumstance of New Zealand is created not only by the good governance of its government and its civic community but its isolation, which makes it a case study onto itself. Its success is impossible to replicate elsewhere even if similar policies are pursued and with the same degree of commitment.

The other exception is China, where the virus originated. However, here again, the special circumstance of a strong central government with exceptional powers and a compliant population make it impossible for democratic nations to replicate. Even authoritarian regimes such as Venezuela lack the resources to implement similar counteractive measures as China.

Poor Governance, Politicisation and Conspiracy Theories

The rate at which new infections are occurring is still high and rising, with total cumulative cases climbing ever higher. Moreover, the rate of new infections is increasing in several large economies in Western Europe.

Globally, the death toll from the coronavirus approached 800,000 in late August 2020 and then blew past it, with countries like the United States, Brazil and India leading the rise in fatalities.

India, in particular, has seen a record number of cases, with the country hitting 3.7 million infected cases as of 1st September 2020. In Brazil, meanwhile, as in the rest of Latin America, death counts have been especially high.

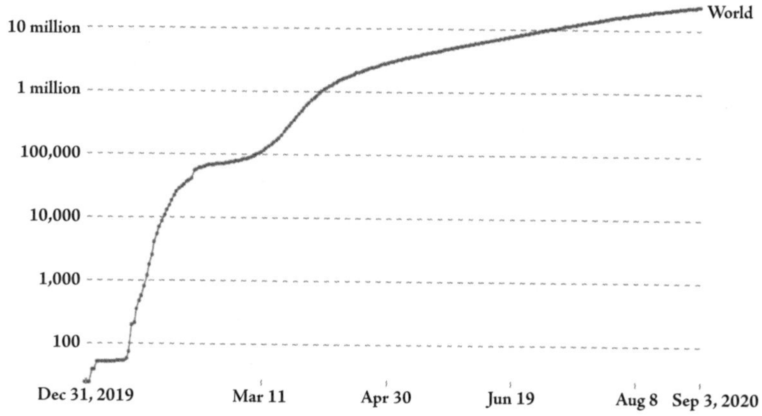

Figure 64: Cumulative Number of Confirmed COVID-19 Cases as of 4th September 2020 (Source: Our World in Data)

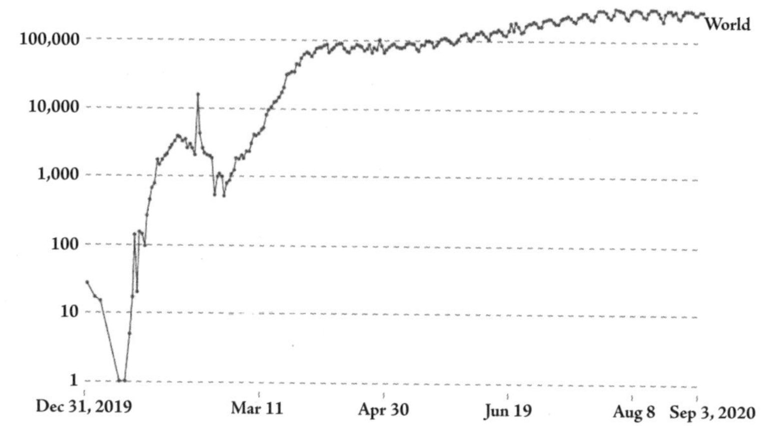

Figure 65: Daily Number of New Confirmed COVID-19 Cases as of 4th September 2020 (Source: Our World in Data)

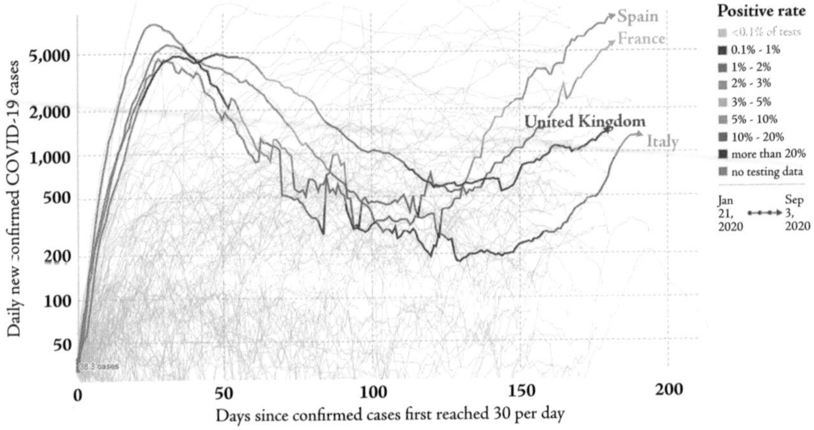

Figure 66: Daily Number of New Confirmed COVID-19 Cases by Country as of 4th September 2020 (Source: Our World in Data)

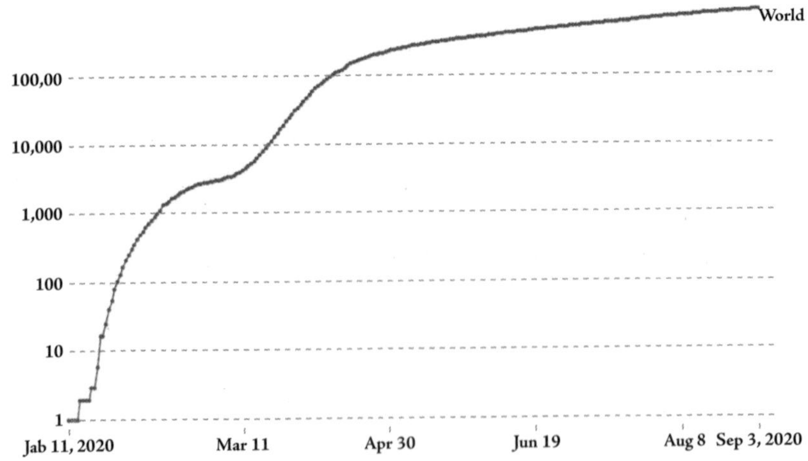

Figure 67: Cumulative Number of Confirmed COVID-19 Deaths as of 4th September 2020 (Source: Our World in Data)

All this is due to poor governance, polarised politics, complex governance structures and large segments of populations having a poor appreciation of-, or respect for, the science of epidemiology. Many are even susceptible to conspiracy theories.

In the United States, in particular, there is a small but not insignificant population of 'anti-vaxxers' who absolutely refuse to subject themselves or their families to any form of vaccination. This presents a danger of the virus continuing to spread in the population even after a vaccine becomes widely available.

The numbers of Americans who already say they are hesitant to receive a COVID-19 vaccination if and when one becomes available, are a small proportion of the population but not so small that their resistance to vaccination will not have a negative effect on communities being fully protected from COVID-19.

Given recent research suggesting that "natural" herd immunity to this virus is all but impossible to achieve, a vaccine is our only way back to anything resembling normal life – but mass vaccination will only work with enough buy-in from a trusting public.

The damage that the President and others are doing to Americans' trust in science and professional expertise could have significant consequences on the country's ability to get past this pandemic, even if Trump does not win a second term this November.

In several countries, such as Spain, Germany and Italy, there is growing 'COVID Fatigue', in which segments of the population are becoming increasingly uncooperative and non-compliant with government mandates and prescribed precautions.

In Germany, thousands of people – including far-right and neo-Nazi extremists – have engaged in protests across the country, against mask-wearing and vaccines; some even attempted to storm the Reichstag.

In Singapore, too, surveys have shown that 44 percent of people are tired of following the requisite health measures. Mask-wearing is cited as the most vexing requirement, but checking in for contact tracing and the limitation of physical gatherings were also sources of frustration.[108]

Such fatigue has put politicians under severe pressure to lift precaution measures, only for a resurgence in the number of infections to occur, as happened in the state of Victoria in Australia in August 2020. Despite the empirical evidence to guide policymakers and political leaders, there is a growing propensity to open up economies and lift internal precautions.

Wave Effects

This point further develops to my 'Wave Theory' of the COVID-19 phenomenon, as previously articulated when framing the COVID-19 pandemic.

Economies open and shut on an iterated basis due to sequential waves of infections, and the longer this continues, and the longer it takes for the vaccine to develop, the greater likelihood there is of two dangerous negative developments.

The first is that the virus mutates to become more dangerous. This may possibly have already occurred, with the emergence of COVID-G, which is more infectious and produces greater viral loads.[109]

While there is no evidence that the increased viral loads increase disease severity or raises the Case Fatality Ratio,[110] the strain's greater infectiousness risks raising population-level transmission and hence total deaths.

If it emerges that what makes a person a super-spreader (i.e. someone who is unusually contagious) is elevated viral loading, COVID-G could see far more super-spreaders and exponentially higher infections.[111]

A second and even more lethal possibility is the potential for further mutations to render certain virus strains immune to the vaccines currently in development, as these vaccines would have been developed off earlier strains.

Presently, there is no evidence of such an occurrence, with COVID-G responding similarly to antibodies from patients who had the original D-variant. This suggests that vaccines developed based on COVID-D would also retain effectiveness against COVID-G.[112]

"Nuts and Bolts" of Global Vaccine Programme Implementation

The funding, coordination, prioritisation and distribution of a vaccine will be very uneven globally and even within countries. The rich in most countries are likely to access the vaccine first, and richer nations with domestic pharmaceutical production capacity will be able to produce and immunise their populations faster.

However, weak governance in countries such as Spain, Italy and the United States, with volatile politics, inadequate and uncoordinated public health systems, will – despite their advanced economy status – have great difficulty and take much longer to complete a population-wide immunisation programme.

Less Developed Countries (LDCs) – who lack funds, have weak institutions and poor infrastructure – will be completely dependent on international aid to implement national programmes.

Migrants drifting across the African continent, particularly in the North African region, and undocumented immigrants such as those already present in several Western European nations, the Rohingya in Bangladesh, and Syrian refugees in Turkey, Saudi Arabia and the United States, are all likely to be placed at the end of the queue or be unable to access the vaccine.

The shared nature of this shock – the novel coronavirus does not respect national borders – has put a larger proportion of the global community in recession than any other time since the Great Depression.

Carmen Reinhart
Chief Economist, World Bank Group

Sovereign Debt Risks

All advanced economies have considerable public debt and are confronting recessions. The combination of these two forces will make it an imperative to assume even more public debt to undertake COVID-19 precautions, attempt fiscal stimulus to prop up their ailing economies and, ultimately, finance the procurement and distribution of a population-wide vaccine programme.

For several Western European countries with social welfare state models such as the United Kingdom and France, there is the additional burden of providing unemployment benefits, supporting patient cost-free national health systems and national pension schemes.

Exceptional countries include Japan, where the borrowing is internal, and the United States, which can exercise its 'exorbitant privilege' of the US dollar being the world's reserve currency. Even in its case, the budget deficit, already large, will increase significantly.

The net result of these large assumed public debt piles is the elevated risk of sovereign debt defaults, which can become a contagion as international capital markets bring pressure on governments to service debts even whilst public revenues are falling.

The debt servicing ratio will take up ever-larger proportions of the fiscal balance, creating 'fiscal drag' but also severely limiting the fiscal space available to finance longer-term investments in productive public investments, such as skills training, technology adoption, improved education, health and transportation systems; all of which will be essential for economic recovery.

There is a significant risk of a debt crisis in developing and emerging market economies, as higher debt-to-GDP ratios cause both domestic and international lenders to lose confidence in governments' ability to repay the debt.

If governments become unable to borrow, government spending can fall precipitously, causing a significant demand-deficient recession; this recession will be exacerbated by the fact that heightened uncertainty will reduce private sector investment.

Many countries are already likely to have a weak debt-carrying capacity, as defined by the IMF-World Bank Debt Sustainability Framework (see figure 69). Those currently under high risk at the moment might move into outright debt distress, with the country unable to service its debt.

Even if governments were able to negotiate debt relief or an international bailout, there will still likely be remaining credit access issues; and any debt relief or bailouts might end up merely kicking the can down the road if the interest rates payable – especially with a high-risk premium imposed – are unsustainable.

Debt Burden Thresholds and Benchmarks under the DSF

	PV of external debt in percent of		External Debt service in percent of		PV of total public debt in percent of
	GDP	Export	Export	Revenue	GDP
Weak	30	140	10	14	35
Medium	40	180	15	18	55
Strong	50	240	21	23	70

Figure 68: IMF-World Bank Debt Sustainability Framework (Source: IMF)

In such a scenario, another debt crisis and the possibility of default will emerge with a vengeance at the end of the refinancing or bailout period, as has happened numerous times, as seen in the cases of Greece, Spain and Italy in the aftermath of the Global Financial Crisis.

Even prior to the COVID-19 pandemic, the IMF had been warning about developing countries' public debt burdens, with half of such countries either already in debt distress or at high risk of it. The problem will only worsen as the economic crisis deepens – the need for massive expenditure to combat the pandemic and its economic consequences, plus the economic contraction itself, will combine to sharply raise debt-to-GDP ratios.

It is possible that about two-fifths of developing economies' sovereign external debt could be at risk of default – and to further complicate matters, attempts to engage in fiscal consolidation in response to this debt crisis might then undermine future global efforts to combat crises like climate change, for which significant public investment and spending will be necessary.

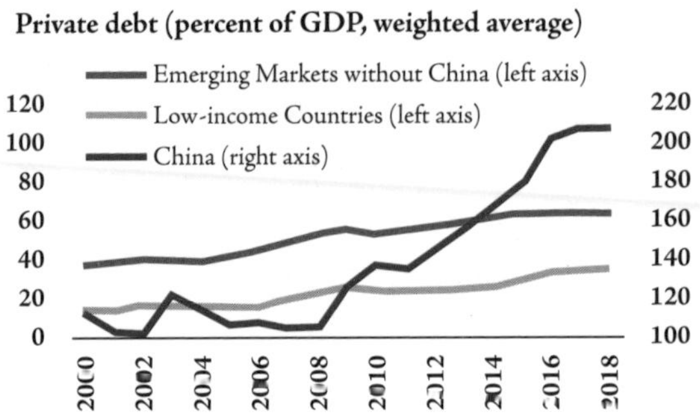

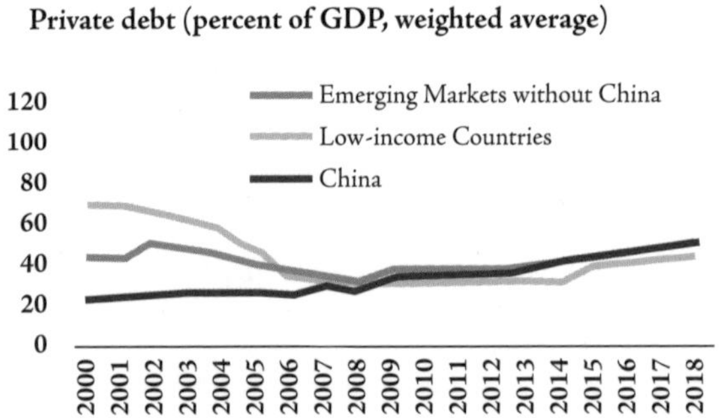

Figure 69: Debt Trends (Source: IMF)

Deflationary Risks

The combination of increased borrowing from international capital markets, shrinking fiscal balances, rising budget deficits and recessionary economies can create elevated risks of deflationary conditions in several advanced economies. Deflation is a severe inhibitor of investment and consumption.

While this can increase national savings, this gain would be offset by a drain on savings by the large scale unemployed and underemployed and growing size of the population of the structurally unemployed and discouraged workers.

The growing propensity to save may not be matched by rising commercial loans due to negative investor sentiment despite attractive interest rates, and due to a negative or zero bound interest rate environment depleting banks of their deposit base. Deflationary scenarios tend to be protracted and difficult to reverse.

GIC's Assessment of the Global Economic Environment

There is a risk of both higher debt and higher inflation going forward, given looser fiscal policy as well as more accommodative monetary policy.

GIC, formerly known as Government of Singapore Investment Corporation, is a sovereign wealth fund that manages Singapore's foreign reserves, and they made the following assessment.

"Two fundamental changes are happening to policymaking. The first relates to monetary policy. The major central banks are now unlikely to respond pre-emptively to signs of higher inflation and are instead willing to accommodate periods of above-target inflation. This is a marked change from the past when interest rates were usually raised in response to leading indicators of inflation, which subsequently dampened economic activity.

The second is the bigger role played by fiscal policy in stimulating the economy, given limited policy room for central banks to cut rates. The size of fiscal stimulus packages is expected to be US$11 trillion, almost 20 percent of GDP for advanced economies and about 5 percent of GDP for emerging economies.

Alongside the impact of lower tax revenues and higher government transfers due to the deep recession, these stimulus packages are expected to contribute to an increase in public debt of around 19 percent of global GDP in 2020 alone.

Not all countries can afford such large-scale stimulus, and concerns over how these programmes are financed will likely weigh on debt markets, particularly in lower-income economies and those that are reliant on foreign capital flows.

These shifts in policymaking have the potential to change the investment environment in two ways.

Increased risk of higher inflation over the medium term: If central banks deliberately keep rates low even as economic activity increases, economies could overheat, resulting in upward pressure on prices.

This risk scenario is only likely to play out over the medium term given the strong disinflationary forces in the present environment. Should it materialise, however, it would imply a very different investment landscape relative to what investors have been used to. In particular, the correlation between equities and bonds could become positive, making it difficult for asset allocators to achieve diversification.

Currency moves could play a larger role in asset returns for a global investor: As the effectiveness of the interest rate channel for monetary policy decreases, more emphasis will be placed on increasing purchases of government debt and potentially capping interest rates, which could lead to capital flight and currency depreciation."

Recessions and Depressions

Emerging markets such as economies in Sub-Saharan Africa and India are struggling and will continue to struggle to contain COVID-19 due to internal political complications, weak fiscal balances and inadequate and inefficient public administration.

Meanwhile, advanced economies – i.e. the markets of final demand – are facing protracted economic recessions, sovereign debt risks and vulnerability to deflationary scenarios. Together, these factors combine to impede global growth.

While all economies will confront recessions in 2020 and most also in 2021, some economies may have to deal with depression-level recessions, as defined by a greater than 25 percent contraction of their 2019 GDP levels for a multi-year period.

Some economies will stabilise due to good governance and the ability to form beneficial trade and travel partnerships with other economies that have similarly stabilised, such as between New Zealand and Australia, and potentially between select countries in ASEAN and the East African Community (EAC).

However, their economic performance will not be 'growth', but 'recovery'. These economies, at best, will stabilise at a neutral growth or marginal recessionary levels because their economic outreach will be limited due to the fall in final demands and weak inflows of capital and tourism.

Taken as a whole, at the global level there is a greater-than-marginal risk that recession can transform into depression due to a combination of the aforementioned risks occurring in combination, either concurrently or sequentially.

I am not alone in my pessimism here. 80 percent of panelists surveyed by the US's National Association for Business Economics believed that there was a 25 percent chance of a second economic downturn as a result of the coronavirus, and that the median panelist expectation was that 40 percent of all business closures would be permanent rather than merely temporary.[113]

And while the economists surveyed were confident in the Federal

Reserve's monetary policy being appropriately accommodating – with most agreeing that near-zero rates would be kept until the end of 2021, and with about a quarter believing that rates would stay as such until at least 2023 – this is also an implicit admission that the economy will weaken over the next 3 years, and will be in need of constant fiscal and monetary support.

Indeed, only about a fifth of these economists expected to see non-farm payrolls recover to pre-pandemic levels in 2021, and a third assessed that a pre-2023 recovery was unlikely.

Any recovery, when it comes, will be slow and uneven, rather than fast and consistent – not a "V-shape" so much as a "jagged swoosh".

Jagged Swoosh Recovery

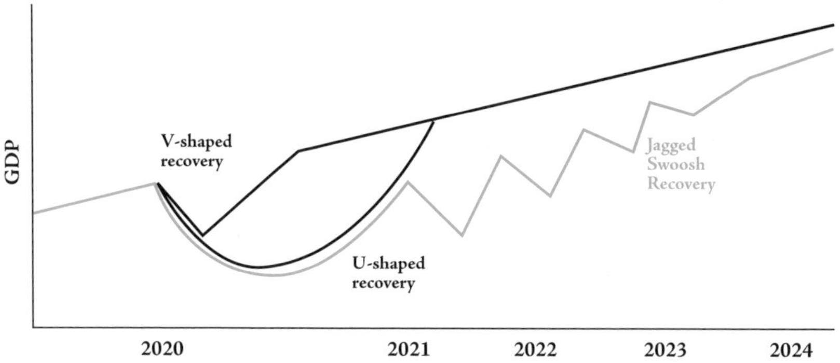

Figure 70: "Jagged Swoosh" Recovery

Destruction of Economic Capacity

The economic recession, with the potential for depression, will cause mutually reinforcing large-scale firm failures and stress on supply chains. This will manifest itself most severely in the SME sectors where the majority of the workforce is concentrated.

Ultimately, under prolonged economic and financially-stressed conditions, large firms, including transnational corporations and banks, may also fail or require public-financed recapitalisation to avoid a liquidity and solvency squeeze.

Many public and private projects may be abandoned or rendered financially unsupportable. It will take considerable time to rebuild the SME sector and to restart productive investment projects, even though large enterprises may recover faster and – in the case of the technology sector – even thrive under COVID-19 conditions.

Technological Substitution and Organisational Change

A protracted COVID-19 crisis, with repeated 'lockdowns', will accelerate the adoption of technology and prompt organisational changes in process and management.

The adaptation will go beyond the use of remote working platforms to general digitalisation, machine learning and artificial intelligence to save costs. This technological substitution will come at the price of cognitive labour.

Hence, during the eventual recovery, we may see productivity-driven growth but lagging labour force expansion. Countries which invest in appropriate skills upgrading and technology infrastructure will do better in resolving the challenge of 'matching' the unemployed with the new technology-focused jobs.

Countries that do not make such investments and focus solely on stimulus or populist measures will be burdened by a long tail of structural unemployment, with associated stress on social support systems, political backlash and social frustrations and divisions driven primarily by widening inequality.

Political Extremism

Protracted recessionary or depression scenarios have the propensity to create political destabilisation. This will be both national and geo-political. Such destabilisation can be within the political systems, or in extreme cases, transform political systems through revolution, either peacefully or violently.

The United Kingdom, for instance, may see the secession of Scotland from the Union, as well as potentially the unification of Northern Ireland with the Republic of Ireland. In Spain, Catalonia may succeed in achieving independence.

Current populist leaders may lose credibility but retain power through a hardening of their base, or even resort to extra-judicial actions to maintain their grip on office.

Under protracted negative economic and financial conditions, it is possible that even more extremist and fringe leaders may take their place by playing upon the anxieties, fears and frustrations of populations.

Wars: Cold to Warm to Hot

There is also the potential for 'Cold Wars' between America and China; between America and Iran; and between the Gulf Cooperation Council and Qatar. The 'Warm Wars' between Russia and Ukraine; between Russia and Georgia; between India and Pakistan; and between China and Taiwan, could potentially turn into actual 'Hot Wars'.

This could be due to a political need to create an external political distraction; states might engage in 'blame-ification' to distract from domestic political problems, and political miscalculations could be made as governments under prolonged stress of crisis management misjudge confrontational situations.

Countries may also act opportunistically as the international community is too distracted or hamstrung to intervene, and as the United States has ceased to play the role of 'global policeman' but adopted "America First", and increasingly "America Only", foreign and trade policies.

Forecast Models

Based on the above factors, I forecast three outcomes for the global economy: Central, Favourable and Unfavourable.

My central forecast involves approximately an 'L-shaped' economic pattern for the next 10 years, wherein the world economy experiences a sharp fall and a slow, unsteady recovery (see figure 72). I assign a 50 percent probability to this outcome.

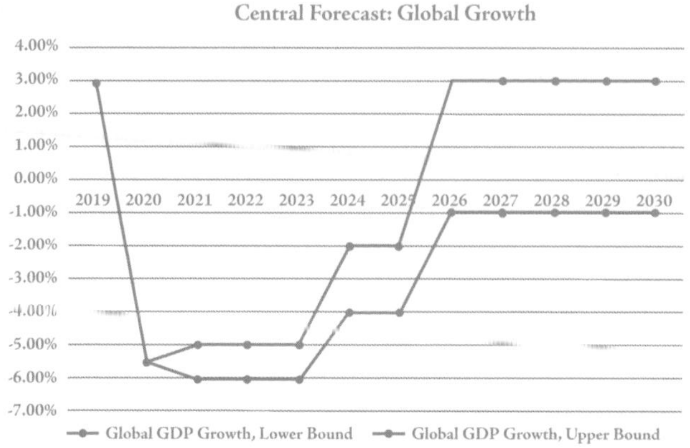

Figure 71: Central Forecast of Global Growth (Source: Future-Moves Group)

Beyond the central forecast, I also make two marginal forecasts.

One is for a more favourable global growth performance due to an earlier-than-expected development of a vaccine, as well as private and multilateral cooperation to ensure funding, distribution and implementation of vaccine programmes in most of the globe at an accelerated pace.

Meanwhile, matters will be helped by certain outcomes of elections in advanced economies over the next three years, if more sober and centrist leaders come to power.

These leaders would be willing to cooperate and also provide greater support to multilateral institutions such as the World Bank, the IMF, the WHO and the United Nations Development Programme (UNDP). See figure 73. I assign a 30 percent probability to this scenario.

My third forecast is for a global depression combined with the potential for multiple geopolitical security conflicts. This unfavourable forecast factors in a delayed arrival of a vaccine and lack of funding, coordination, cooperation and 'beggar thy neighbour' nationalist approaches to control vaccine capacity.

Additionally, in this forecast, political destabilisation in both developing and advanced economies will create confusion, erratic policy trajectories and mismanagement of public finances, leading to a triggering of sovereign debt risks and systemic failures in national financial sectors (see figure 74). I assign a 20 percent probability to this scenario.

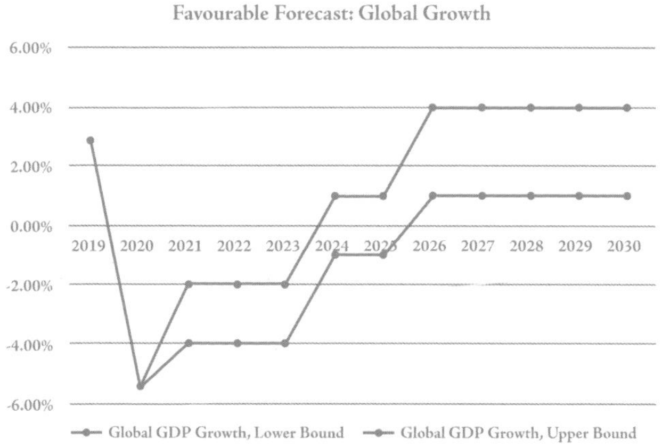

Figure 72: Favourable Forecast of Global Growth (Source: Future-Moves Group)

Figure 73: Unfavourable Forecast of Global Growth (Source: Future-Moves Group)

In the event of a major conflict, however, the already unfavourable circumstances could further worsen, and growth could further contract. In contrast to the mainline unfavourable forecast, which can be termed *Variant A*, this worst-case forecast can be termed *Variant B*. For the severity of the global economic contraction in the eventuality that *Variant B* occurs, see figure 75.

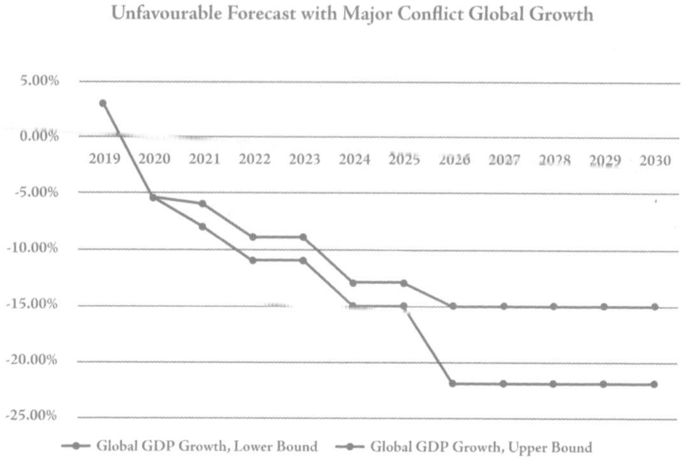

Figure 74: Unfavourable Forecast of Global Growth in the Event of Major Conflict (Source: Future-Moves Group)

Fundamentally, such pessimistic projections are also borne out of a recognition that fiscal and monetary policy are of limited value in this recession, relative to previous ones.

At its core, this recession is caused by the need to prohibit economic activity so as to prevent the spread of the virus; so long as that remains true, businesses cannot open nor can consumers go out. In this context, injections of money into the economy, whether through expansionary fiscal policy or accommodative monetary policy, will not do as much as hoped.

As Michael Spence, a winner of the Nobel Prize in Economics explains, "In previous economic crises, the origin was a set of dynamics that resulted in balance sheet damage that, in turn, caused a drop in consumption followed by investment and employment. In the Great Depression, banks failed and because of a lack of credit, businesses failed. In the pandemic economy, [in contrast], the origin is a direct hit on demand, supply, and employment via containment policies and risk aversion.

"In normal times, fiscal stimulus that replaced lost income and/or assets would produce a fairly immediate uptick in consumption, and to some extent investment and employment. In the pandemic economy, this effect is muted because of regulations and self-imposed restrictions on mobility and activity."

Admittedly, there is room for optimism, as WHO Director-General Tedros is when he says that "... we have also the technology ... and the knowledge to stop [the virus]. So we have a disadvantage of globalisation, closeness, connectedness but an advantage of better technology. So we hope to finish this pandemic (in) less than two years."

However, many things will have to come together for the pandemic to be stopped. These include the development of a viable and affordable vaccine, excellent quality of governance, international cooperation and the avoidance of counterproductive nationalism – and to the extent that one or more of these are unlikely to be forthcoming, there is, unfortunately, reason to be pessimistic

Summary of Forecasts

	Favourable Forecast	**Central Forecast**	**Unfavourable Forecast** *Variant A: No Major Conflict*	**Unfavourable Forecast** *Variant B: Major Conflict*
Average Annual Global GDP Growth (2020 – 2030)	0.08%	-1.68%	-8.76%	-12.51%

Figure 75: Summary of Forecasts (Source: Future-Moves Group)

Part G: Possible Scenarios

This section indicates three scenarios on a best, middle and worst-case basis, highlighting prominent characteristics unique to each scenario that describe the effects of COVID-19 on an international level.

Core factors of critical uncertainties and pre-determinants, when taken together with the quality of domestic governance, will produce a distinct predicted scenario of either (i) cooperation, (ii) fragmentation, or (iii) an undermined situation.

Pre-Determinants	Critical Uncertainties
Demography, Size and Geographical Location	Vaccine Development and Distribution
Existing State of Political and Healthcare Systems	Elections and Political Leadership
Foundations of Private Sector Mobilisation	International Cooperation and Leadership

Figure 76: Pre-Determinants and Critical Uncertainties

Given these scenarios, the global trajectory to collective action should be steered toward a "cooperative" scenario.

Figure 77: Possible Scenarios (Source: Future-Moves Group)

- Based on the current state of response to COVID-19, countries must steer toward a cooperative scenario, as elements of cooperation and fragmentation are observable at present.
- While pre-determinant factors are in motion, which affect the efficacy of country and international action in COVID-19, it will serve governments well to re-evaluate the foundations on which its systems of governance, public health and economy are built upon.
- The critical uncertainties that the pandemic has brought to the fore constitute lessons for governments moving forward and should compel leaders to work on political leadership and coordination, both nationally and internationally. In anticipation of another potential crisis, these critical uncertainties serve as key focal points that should command enhanced attention from governments and policymakers.

COOPERATIVE WORLD

In a "best hope" scenario, countries around the globe, including the great powers, will come together to combat the coronavirus and its effects. American leadership is crucial, given its status as the world's sole superpower – and it is also likely to be forthcoming, in the event of Democratic nominee Joe Biden's victory in the 2020 US Presidential Elections.

Biden is supportive of a coordinated international response to the pandemic, in line with past US administrations' approaches to global crises like the 2008-2009 Global Financial Crisis, and in stark contrast to predecessor Donald Trump's mistrust of multilateralism and failure to lead a coordinated global response.

The Chinese leadership will play an important role as well, given its rising power and influence. While the Chinese government has engaged in "mask" diplomacy, this approach has yielded limited dividends, given concerns over the quality of the masks, and in view of the confrontational "wolf warrior" diplomacy being employed at the same time.

In a best-case scenario, China steps back from a bellicose approach, and instead works to bring together its neighbours and the wider world in combating the coronavirus.

Evidence-based Approach

Under the best hope scenario, national governments and intergovernmental organisations will come together to implement an effective test-and-trace approach, with wider society-level lockdowns implemented as necessary.

In this approach, used to great success in South Korea, individuals suspected of being infected due to past contact with people with COVID-19 are quickly isolated and tested for the virus. If they prove infected, everyone they have had physical contact with is traced, after which they are isolated and the whole test-and-trace process is repeated.

Beyond South Korea, all successful responses to the pandemic have involved early action and extensive testing of individuals, tracing their contacts and physically isolating patients, even while adapting to changing conditions.

Simultaneously, lockdowns can be used to prevent the virus from spreading out of control – buying time as the test-and-trace regime works to identify and isolate all cases of COVID-19 in the community.

Lockdowns can vary in severity, from China's full-scale lockdown of entire provinces, and South Korea's relatively moderate approach of extensive and transparent testing paired with occasional re-impositions of restrictions. It will be important for countries to pick the best strategy appropriate to their situation, which will differ based on the strength of their health system and the extent of their administrative capacities.

A poorer country with a weaker ability to engage in test-and-trace might need to impose relatively more stringent lockdowns; and in contrast, a wealthier country with strong state capabilities might be able to avoid the need to put in place an economically damaging, full-scale lockdown.

Unconditional cash transfers can also be used to support the people economically for the duration of the necessary lockdowns. These can be extremely effective, as demonstrated in the case of the United States, where vast federal aid has prevented the poverty rate from rising despite record unemployment levels due to the nationwide lockdown.

Mutual Aid and Cooperation

Poorer countries are disadvantaged in having poorer access to test kits, and from lacking the administrative capacity to engage in contact tracing. International cooperation and mutual aid are therefore necessary, with wealthier countries exporting test kits, rather than just restricting them for domestic use. Money can also be provided to hire contact tracers, as happened during the Ebola epidemic.

International cooperation concerning the development and distribution of a vaccine will also be of the utmost importance so that any scientific breakthroughs by researchers in one country can be built on by those in another, and so that any eventual successful vaccine can be mass-produced. Given the globalised supply chain, the ingredients and spare parts needed to manufacture vaccines will not come from any single country alone.

Autonomous Private Sector Mobilisation

The pandemic demands governments and firms to be more creative than ever, especially through the use of technology.

In Israel, the government's use of mobile data, intended originally for counterterrorism operations, is now being capitalised upon as a virus containment measure. This is one of many indications of how global privacy regulations are struggling to stay relevant when lives are at stake.

Besides, firms completely unrelated to healthcare can do their part, such as when alcohol distilleries switch to producing disinfectant, or when computer gaming firms set up an automated face mask manufacturing line.

FRAGMENTED WORLD

The second scenario is a central scenario that is fragmented politically, socially and financially. Countries might individually engage in some, but not all, of the necessary health and economic measures described in the first scenario.

At the same time, there will be no clear leadership or global cooperation, as countries focus exclusively on their domestic containment efforts.

Instead of the coronavirus becoming a social and political leveller, it becomes a source of division by exposing the blind spots in society. Singapore's foreign worker dormitories as a hotspot for coronavirus cases is a prime example of how traditional "social distancing" measures do not work in some settings.

Inequality

Wealthier countries might eventually succeed in getting the virus under control, while their poorer neighbours struggle to do so. The latter face an uphill task, given the disadvantages they suffer from – denser urban slums, low state capacity, the risk of population outflows from urban centres to rural areas, greater existing poverty, and a lack of ventilators and trained medical personnel. All of this makes containing the virus and limiting fatalities much harder.

Distribution of a ready vaccine will run into global supply roadblocks and inequitable access will characterise the situation, albeit less severely as in the third scenario.

And even within individual countries, inequality in mortality outcomes can grow. Early indicators from the United States are indicative of what a central scenario will look like, where black and Hispanic patients are dying at higher rates than other ethnicities in New York State.

Patchiness

The number of new cases reaches a peak in many major cities around the world but takes a longer time to reach suburban and rural areas, where health infrastructure is lacking. Early examples of this inability to handle the pandemic in the suburbs include Waverley, near Sydney, and Vertova, near Milan.

ANTAGONISTIC WORLD

In a worst-case scenario, the lack of leadership both nationally and internationally leads to the appropriate public health measures and economic policies as described in the first scenario not being taken.

Deaths will mount, economic hardship will deepen, and there will be systematic and permanent damage to entire sectors of the economy, especially service-oriented ones like hospitality, tourism and aviation.

Multiple Waves

Countries end the lockdown prematurely, resulting in the continual spread of asymptomatic cases and resulting in a second or even third wave of infections.

This will put governments around the world in a catch-22 situation, having to make a calculated risk by not prolonging lockdowns for too long, while understanding the collateral damage involved by extending lockdowns for a prolonged period.

Missing Leadership

In this scenario's undermined leadership, countries – despite holding Member State status to international organisations – will see the disintegration of international cooperation and a lack of credible leadership directing a global response.

The Trump administration represents an example of missing national and global-level leadership, as illustrated by the botched handling of the pandemic within the US's own borders and mirrored at the international sphere in the formal move to withdraw from the WHO.

The Trump's Administration's announcement of an America First policy with regard to vaccine acquisition and distribution increases uncertainty and anxiety across the globe in whether and how countries will cope if the vaccine(s) is solely or primarily American sourced.

The US was formerly the single largest contributor to the WHO, providing around 15 percent of the global health agency's total budget in 2019, so its withdrawal amid a global pandemic undercuts effort not only to curb COVID-19 but toward other global vaccine programmes and global health activity.

Specifically, and concerning the uncertainty of progress in vaccine development, the pathway to obtaining a readily-available vaccine in 12 to 18 months will be disrupted by a lack of success in human clinical trials.

Even in the event of successful vaccine development and licensing, distribution will be severely limited to wealthier countries. Lacking global cooperation and an effective international supply chain, access will essentially be cut off to poorer countries – where COVID-19 rages on but their capacity to obtain the vaccines are vastly inadequate.

Political Disruption and Inflamed Political Hotspots

This crisis will move beyond being a public health issue to being a political one. Failure to control the coronavirus effectively will lead to further destabilisation, as mounting deaths cause increasing political unrest.

US-China

The United States and China will further escalate tensions, bringing potential confrontations to a flashpoint, with perhaps even military skirmishes in the South China Sea.

India-Pakistan

Economic turmoil has traditionally been used as a pretext used by India and Pakistan to assert control over the disputed area of Kashmir.

North Korea-South Korea

As in the past, the Kim regime can engage in military and political provocations to extract economic aid from the South – aid that might be necessary given the devastation done to the already sanction-battered North Korean economy.

Russia-Ukraine

Russian President Vladimir Putin has seen his popularity suffer due to his poor handling of the coronavirus crisis, a crisis that has reduced the Russian state's ability to provide services and decent living standards to its people.

Meanwhile, in the Russian Far East, anti-Putin protests initiated by the arrest of a popular local governor continue to rage, despite a crackdown. Given such domestic difficulties, there might be the temptation for Putin to escalate the military conflict in eastern Ukraine, to create a rally-around-the-flag effect and to use patriotism to boost his own popularity.

China-Taiwan

China has ramped up its military activity around Taiwan, which Mainland China claims as part of its own sovereign territory. Additional aggression is possible, as a rising China looks to assert itself, and as it judges the US too distracted by the COVID-19 crisis at home to properly thwart it in the Western Pacific.

Given that Taiwan intends to push back against Chinese air and naval incursions into its territory, the possibility of military skirmishes, which then escalate into a large-scale war, is not negligible.

As the Taiwan defence ministry declared in a statement on 20th August 2020: "Absolutely do not treat lightly our resolve to defend Taiwan. The most arrogant country can easily provoke a war, and the most ignorant government can be caught in the flames of war. These provocations will only further unite Taiwanese and recognise the essence of the Chinese Communist's militarism. In the end, it will have the opposite effect, inciting the wrath and antipathy of Taiwan's people, seriously hurting peace and stability across the Taiwan Strait."

A Brexit-Busted Britain

COVID-19's impact on the economy and domestic politics of the United Kingdom has been profound. Prime Minister's Boris Johnson's grand plans for Britain to form a new network of bilateral and multilateral economic relationships has been fatally compromised by the steep decline in the British economy.

The timing of the pandemic, which followed soon after the culmination of the Brexit settlement, has meant that the United Kingdom is in a lose-lose economic world. Prime Minister Johnson's poor management of the COVID-19 situation has also eroded confidence in his leadership, while his erratic and abrasive relationship with the EU leadership has meant that there is little sympathy or empathy for Britain's plight.

The effects have been the erosion of his political standing domestically and a rapidly contracting economy, coupled with a growing public debt overhang from support measures committed by his Chancellor of the Exchequer, Mr Rishi Sunak. Mr Sunak pledged to do "whatever it takes" to support the economy, which has taken the form of a GBP350 billion rescue package for business, which is impossible to fund without recourse to massive borrowing.

Confidence in the economic future of the United Kingdom and especially in its ability to finance its debt is reflected in negative yields for two- and five-year Gilts, while its 10-year Gilt remains at a historically low level.

These factors have exposed Mr Johnson to challenges from the Scottish First Minister to call for another referendum on Scottish independence, and this time, there is a good possibility of such a referendum succeeding, given Scotland's opposition to Brexit.

Northern Ireland, once considered inseparable from the British mainland, may also see greater political and economic sense in an eventual *de jure* union with the Irish Republic through economic ties and a free border.

Thus, COVID-19, in combination with the questionable competence of Mr Johnson and his loose association with facts, has led to a historic situation where the United Kingdom may not remain united for much longer.

Its position as a First World power is also under threat, as its economy shrinks, defections from its financial sector – which generates 7 percent of national GDP and nearly 50 percent of the City of London's GDP – grow, and human capital flight accelerates as skilled young Britons look for opportunities abroad, thereby stripping Britain of the talent it needs to drive its future.

SUMMARY OF SCENARIOS

	Scenario 1: Cooperative	Scenario 2: Fragmented	Scenario 3: Antagonistic
Unemployment (%)	*5-10*	*10-15*	*20-25*
Structural Unemployment (% of unemployment)	*25*	*33*	*50*
Firm Closures (%)	*10*	*20*	*40*
Deaths (in Millions)	*1-2*	*2-4*	*4-8+*
Likelihood of Occurrence (%)	*20*	*50*	*30*

Figure 78: Summary of Scenarios (Source: Future-Moves Group)

According to my forecasts, the table above provides measures of (i) unemployment, (ii) structural unemployment, (iii) firm closures, the (iv) likelihood of occurrence of each scenario, and (v) estimated numbers of fatalities in each predicted scenario.

Part H: Recommendations

This section delineates key recommendation points derived from prior analysis on country case studies and scenario planning. What COVID-19 has laid bare is the persistent potential for governance to be bettered at the national, regional and global levels.

In a circumstance of urgency where situational developments and outcomes of action are fluid, response to the pandemic needs to be guided by tried-and-tested approaches that are effective and evidence-based.

Global	Regional	National
Coordinated action must leverage on strengths of multiple stakeholders to establish standards and guidelines, harmonise country-level strategies and provide support via international public health frameworks to fight COVID-19.	Regional coordination should plug the gaps where international or national efforts cannot organically address. Coordination should build on the collective strength and shared history and interests of regional blocs.	Targeted action needs to be supported by robust governance. Countries need to adopt best-practices and contextualise international and regional strategies to their local context to ensure effective implementation.

Figure 79: Overview of Recommendations

- Cooperation in a public health emergency should be led both by international organisations and independent initiatives directed by sovereign governments, scientists and researchers, non-profit organisations and business leaders. Similarly, organisations of regional states will benefit from forging a collective response to the coronavirus pandemic.
- Global, regional and local action requires balancing of interests and incentives of diverse stakeholders, countries and actors, these which cross-cut areas of public health, economy and organisation of society.
- National governments and regional and international organisations need to respond to COVID-19 in readied, swift and outcome-focused approaches, taking into consistent account a longer-term view of recovery.

RECOMMENDATIONS AT THE GLOBAL LEVEL

Global cooperation in a public health emergency should be led both by international organisations and independent initiatives directed by sovereign governments, scientists and researchers, non-profit organisations and business leaders.

Coordinated international action on both the public health and economic side is necessary.

Medical capacity for treatment and testing must be scaled up, a vaccine developed and deployed, surveillance continued to detect virus re-emergence, provision of strong and sustained support extended to less developed countries, and pandemic preparedness improved over the longer-term

Strong fiscal policy to counteract the recession is needed, which must be paired with coordinated monetary policy to support liquidity. Governments must cooperate to ensure that trade and supply chains are protected, and as barrier-free as possible.

General

Public health-related intergovernmental organisations have – especially at early stages of the pandemic – displayed ineffectiveness. Most notably, the

WHO's early response to the pandemic was poor.

Generalised recommendations for international organisations in this section indicate the key flaws to be remedied to bolster the ability of institutions to direct collective action in a global crisis.

First, international organisations need to contend with the common situation of a lack of mandate powers, which situates organisations as easy punching bags by health authorities and civil society groups.

The WHO has been accused of responding to and identifying epidemics and pandemics late, both for COVID-19 and Ebola in particular. It similarly faced accusations of overreacting towards pandemics in the past, such as the H1N1 Swine Flu, resulting in an oversupply of H1N1 vaccines, especially in developed countries.

An international public health organisation needs to leverage its community of experts, scientists, researchers and policymakers to craft effective action in an emergency and avoid missteps that harm its credibility.

Second, the information and public health advisories communicated by international organisations, especially in an urgent epidemic or pandemic situation, need to be structured and credible.

The WHO's initial reporting of the virus was extremely fluid and perceived as inconsistent. The discouraging of using surgical masks for healthy persons by the WHO, for example, contradicts the earlier advice provided by the Center for Disease Prevention and Control in the US.

International organisations that possess a macro-perspective on global affairs in a public health crisis, which have pooled resource bases and diversified country support, need to act as key channels of information to countries and their populations.

Third, the WHO has seen its reputation as an impartial, apolitical organisation come under intense criticism by President Trump, who argues that the WHO has been excessively deferential to China by endorsing early Chinese declarations that human-to-human transmission had not been proven, and that they moved too slowly to declare a global pandemic.

America has since pulled out of the WHO, and with the WHO's top ten donors being Western countries, the organisation is vulnerable to further punishment in the form of funding cuts. It has also refused to participate in multilateral efforts to develop vaccines.

The lack of independence from its membership renders an international organisation vulnerable to the whims of individual powers, especially those with the most influence.

While never truly independent, organisations need to bolster autonomy in action and exercise authority over member states to not allow power rivalry or strategic competition between states to hinder response in a crisis.

Specific

Coordination in global data-sharing and vaccine development is crucial for knowledge-sharing and learning in a global pandemic. Where international organisations have traditionally taken the lead, governments and researchers gradually look to other avenues to forward collective responses and bolster open-source databases.

This section provides actionable recommendations for cooperation both at the level of international organisations, and via independent-from-government, non-profit or private actor-led initiatives.

International Organisations

Managing Stakeholders

In a global pandemic where diagnostics, vaccines and treatments are dependent on a complex stakeholder ecosystem, international organisations should mediate to determine actors responsible to pay the costs, offset risks and intensify medical research in an aligned global response.

The UN-led COVID-19 Supply Chain Task Force, coordinated by the WHO and World Food Programme, represents an initiative created due to a complex multi-stakeholder environment of market suppliers, sovereign governments and logistics companies.

The Task Force leveraged expertise of UN funds and programmes to identify procurement needs of countries that needed supplies to better negotiate with suppliers and consolidate fragmented procurement processes.

In the context of scientific research, the WHO's Strategic Preparedness and Response Plan has activated a network of specialised referral laboratories, commercial and non-commercial agencies and the WHO's own regional and country offices to strengthen global diagnostic capability for COVID-19 detection.

To improve surveillance and track the spread of the disease, WHO can better detect COVID-19 transmission patterns with the support of partners and key stakeholders.

Supporting Global Scientific Research

International organisations need to distil the lessons learned from past epidemic outbreaks on a global scale, compel swift action to detecting a new virus and provide a platform that facilitates scientific research across borders.

Building on experience from the Ebola epidemic, the WHO early on in January 2020 activated the R&D Blueprint, a global preparedness plan allowing rapid activation of scientific research and treatment development in epidemics.

Following activation, the global research and innovation forum convened 400 scientists soon after to draw a roadmap for tackling epidemiological questions the coronavirus pandemic has brought, with the WHO facilitating research that builds on the experiences of SARS and MERS outbreaks.

The R&D Blueprint was created to reduce the time between the declaration of a public health emergency and the availability of diagnostics, treatment and vaccines, thus allowing for rapid intensification of global coordination in the novel coronavirus outbreak.

Medical Equipment Supply

The pandemic has exposed public health system deficiencies even in high-income countries, and supply of personal protective equipment, nasopharyngeal swabs and other required medical resources have been compromised.

International organisations equipped to coordinate logistics for global shipments, procure supplies from a range of sources and appeal for critical funding can better distribute medical supplies to countries hardest-hit by the pandemic.

International organisations that do not primarily centre on a public health agenda have stepped up to bolster global supply chains of necessary equipment.

The UN's World Food Programme partnered with the WHO to provide 'Solidarity Flights' carrying medical equipment including face masks, goggles and ventilators to African nations in April 2020.

This flight ensured supplies for testing and treating more than 30,000 patients and was part of a larger effort to ship lifesaving medical supplies to 95 countries.[115]

Public Health Funding

Especially in low-income and emerging market countries, poor healthcare systems and lack of financial capacity impede a swift response to a health crisis.

International organisations with the ability to tap on varied sources of funding should make funds and debt service relief available and accessible at relatively short notice to help quicken the response.

Financing needs of countries in the recovery process should also be supported by international organisations. Existing lending programmes need to increase in scope and flexibility to allow a larger number of countries in need to acquire funding.

The UN's Response and Recovery Fund, projected at US$2 billion, helps to support low- and middle-income programme countries to tackle the health emergency, mitigate the socio-economic impact of the pandemic on people and generally recover better.

The IMF has made available about US$250 billion under its various lending facilities and debt service relief financed by the Catastrophe Containment and Relief Trust.[116]

Member states can access emergency financing through the Rapid

Financing Instrument and Rapid Credit Facility to respond to the crisis, especially where public health systems are weaker.

The Fund has also approved the establishment of a Short-term Liquidity Line to enhance liquidity and strengthen economic stability for member states in need of short-term payments support.

Similarly, the UN Global Humanitarian Response Plan (HRP), launched for the April to December 2020 period, acts as the international community's primary fundraising vehicle to respond to the humanitarian impacts of the coronavirus in low- and middle-income countries.

The Global HRP complements existing government responses and national coordination systems to stem pandemic outbreaks. It aggregates COVID-19 appeals and funding inputs from international organisations and other UN funds and programmes for NGOs to access funding and provide direct service delivery of COVID-19 testing and protection measures.

> *The world is only as strong as the weakest health system. This COVID-19 Global Humanitarian Response Plan aims to enable us to fight the virus in the world's poorest countries, and address the needs of the most vulnerable people.*

António Guterres
Secretary-General of the UN

Independent Sources of Cooperation

Vaccine Development

Governments around the world, in coordination with the global scientific community, should forward the vaccine development agenda collectively. The urgency at which a vaccine is required makes it necessary that there is information and expertise-sharing in early stages. Discussions on ensuring equitable access to a safe and effective vaccine should be advanced immediately.

Global coordination in vaccine development can be seen in the work of the Coalition for Epidemic Preparedness Innovations (CEPI), which reaches out to global health authorities and vaccine developers to maintain a vaccine development database and provide funding for ongoing programmes.

In February 2020, CEPI, together with the World Bank, hosted a consultation on the launch of a Vaccine Development Taskforce that now works to plan financing and manufacture of vaccines for global access.

CEPI was able to take rapid action on the outbreak of the coronavirus, directing the attention of four existing vaccine programmes towards the agenda of a COVID-19 vaccine in early February, with parallel effort in calling for other vaccine programme proposals.

As of early September 2020, 76 wealthy nations – including Japan, Germany and Norway – have committed to COVAX. This group will help finance the purchase of vaccines out of their own national budgets, and will also partner with 92 poorer nations so as to ensure that the global deployment of vaccines is equitable.

"As we accelerate the science, solidarity is needed to provide a joint solution to the pandemic. The COVAX Global Vaccines Facility is the critical mechanism for joint procurement and pooling risk across multiple vaccines, which is why today I sent a letter to every Member State encouraging them to join.

Like an orchestra, we need all instruments to be played in harmony to create music that everyone enjoys. One or two instruments playing by themselves just won't suffice when the world is waiting and listening intently. We will work to bring the band together, to promote science, solutions and solidarity because we believe to our core that we do it best, when we do it together.

Dr Tedros Adhanom Ghebreyesus
Director General of the WHO
18th August 2020

Gavi and COVAX

In 2000, the Bill & Melinda Gates Foundation with a group of founding partners created the Global Alliance for Vaccines and Immunisation. Today, Gavi, the Vaccine Alliance, continues to improve access to new and under-used vaccines for vulnerable children in the world's poorest countries.

Gavi draws from the strength of core partners the WHO, UNICEF, the World Bank and the Bill & Melinda Gates Foundation. It works with donors including sovereign governments, the private sector and NGOs to increase immunisation in children and strengthen primary healthcare.

COVAX was developed as the vaccines pillar of the Access to COVID-19 Tools (ACT) Accelerator by Gavi, CEPI and the WHO. The ACT accelerator represents a global collaboration to accelerate the development and manufacture of COVID-19 vaccines and to guarantee fair access to every country in the world.

The WHO has pushed for nations to join COVAX, as the European Union, The United Kingdom, Switzerland and the United States have arrived at agreements with vaccine producers, and as Russia and China are separately working on vaccines. The WHO's concern in this context is the global efforts are undermined by individual countries pursuing their own national interest; this is the problem of "vaccine nationalism", whereby finite supplies are not shared strategically where it will do the most good, but instead hoarded at the national level.

(Source: Gavi)

COVAX is the only truly global solution to the COVID-19 pandemic. For the vast majority of countries, whether they can afford to pay for their own doses or require assistance, it means receiving a guaranteed share of doses and avoiding being pushed to the back of the queue, as we saw during the H1N1 pandemic a decade ago.

Dr Seth Berkley
Chief Executive Officer of Gavi, the Vaccine Alliance
15th July 2020

COVAX offers an innovative solution to the gravest public health crisis in living memory. It will speed up the availability of safe and effective vaccines through early investment in manufacturing capacity, and maximise the chances of success by backing a broad and diverse portfolio of vaccine candidates.

"Through COVAX our aspiration is to be able to vaccinate the most vulnerable 20 percent of the population of every country that participates, regardless of income level, by the end of 2021. Ensuring fair access is not only a matter of equity; it is the fastest way to end this pandemic.

Dr Richard Hatchett
Chief Executive Officer of the CEPI
15th July 2020

COVID-19 has focused researchers and scientists all over the world on an urgent mission, calling for other research agendas to be put on hold.

To increase the capacity for evidence-based intervention to the coronavirus pandemic, restrictions on data and information-sharing need to be removed and scientific research should be globally integrated.

Signatures from 117 scientific and non-profit organisations on a commitment to share research data with the WTO has called for all peer-reviewed publications to be made immediately open-access, and interim or final data to be shared as rapidly and widely as possible.

This 'Open COVID Pledge' includes signatories of technology giants and research institutes that commit to make intellectual property freely available upon request of the WHO.

This aims to accelerate the rapid development and deployment of diagnostics, vaccines, therapeutics, medical equipment and software solutions.

Researchers have also identified and shared information on viral genome sequences and related clinical and epidemiological data through real-time data sharing platform GISAID.

In June 2020, a new coalition of more than 500 scientists coordinated by the University of Manchester, the COVID-19 MS Coalition, pledged to share data gathered from mass spectrometry research to work together in examining the structure and presence of the coronavirus in patients' blood.

"*Microsoft is always looking for ways to use our patents to contribute to positive outcomes, and the fight against COVID-19 is one of the most urgent issues of our time. Pledges and open licensing like this effort can help spur innovation, especially in a crisis like this one. Researchers, scientists, and others working against the virus should be able to develop and deploy effective solutions at scale without needing to worry about the threat of patent litigation.*"

Jennifer Yokoyama
Chief IP Counsel of Microsoft
20th April 2020

RECOMMENDATIONS AT THE REGIONAL LEVEL

A region's resilience in the face of COVID-19 will hinge upon the cooperation taken to ensure the safety of public health and safeguard economic growth.

With close regional ties meaning easier transmission of the coronavirus and tightly-linked ripple effects of adverse repercussions, so a shared regional response is crucial.

How ASEAN countries respond to this crisis will decide whether ASEAN will forge ahead of the competition or fall behind.

Lee Hsien Loong
Prime Minister of Singapore
26th June 2020

General

Consolidate Goals

Cooperation within regional blocs should be guided by articulated and shared goals that provide direction to all member states navigating the coronavirus pandemic. Concerted effort to communicate experiences in the course of the pandemic and a rallying of resources to mount a shared response should stem first from an alignment of goals.

In ASEAN, member states reaffirmed their collective commitment to combating the pandemic via joint video conferences, similarly extending coordination to the ASEAN Plus Three group of states as well.

Ministers of Health in the Gulf Cooperation Council established a joint operations room to hold regular meetings discussing updates on the situation in each member state, exchange information on the spread of cases and discuss contingency measures and possible procedures moving forward.

In the EU, a robust collective response at the outset has guided numerous plans and initiatives within the bloc, with a 'Team Europe' approach aimed at providing targeted financial support to partner countries in the immediate neighbourhood.

The European Commission coordinates a common EU response on all fronts – an economic recovery plan for Europe, supporting diagnostic and vaccine research, guidance to healthcare sectors and border management measures. This has mobilised member states to coordinate their responses to the pandemic.

Share Public Health Expertise

Containing the coronavirus pandemic within a regional area is important to the wider goal of halting transmission of the virus globally.

Regions with broadly similar experiences in public health management, social conditions and economic wealth should intensify efforts to ensure that the quality of case detection, treatment and eventual dissemination of a vaccine is widespread and equitable.

The European Commission committed in the early stages of the pandemic, via the joint ERAvsCorona Action Plan, to take utmost action in supporting coordinated scientific research both within the EU community and worldwide, setting out research and innovation action steps in the short to longer-term.

A data-sharing platform enables research findings to be disseminated to public health agencies and other scientific groups; meanwhile, resources are allocated to the development and deployment of vaccines by member nations, while regulatory frameworks are reviewed to better facilitate the whole process.

Similarly, the ASEAN Plus Three Senior Officials Meeting on Health Development saw sharing on information, technical updates and existing challenges in dealing with the pandemic.

The ASEAN Emergency Operations Center Network for public health emergencies coordinates on-the-ground situational assessments in each member state, providing information on its online-based platform and fostering real time information sharing.

Stimulate Joint Economic Recovery

Regions need to act with the foresight of stimulating economic and social recovery in the longer term, be that through the establishment of long-term economic recovery plans or bolstering existing trade and economic agreements.

On funding, a topping-up of current EU financial programmes, incentivising private investments in the bloc and reinforcing healthcare funds form part of a plethora of initiatives.

A €750 billion proposal by the European Commission to finance collective economic recovery has been approved – the first time that such a large amount of common debt in capital markets is being raised by the EU.

Within ASEAN, ASEAN economic ministers in March 2020 issued a statement calling for collective action in containing the virus, with a focus on keeping regional markets open and leveraging digital technology to sustain trade activity.

In June 2020, ASEAN economic ministers adopted the Hanoi Plan of Action on Strengthening ASEAN Economic Cooperation and Supply Chain Connectivity in Response to the COVID-19 pandemic.

The Plan of Action aims to ensure smooth flow of essential goods and other supplies critical to combating the pandemic, facilitate information sharing on trade-related issues and exchange on best practices of member states in handling COVID-19.

The South Asian Association for Regional Cooperation (SAARC) held its first high-level meeting since 2014 following Indian Prime Minister Narendra Modi's proposal for a SAARC Emergency Fund to combat the pandemic in South Asia, with an initial contribution of US$10 million.[14]

The majority of the other SAARC countries added to the fund in the proceeding weeks and India's initial financial offering has allowed for the supply of medical supplies and testing equipment to the member states of Maldives, Sri Lanka, Afghanistan, Nepal and Bangladesh.

Specific

First, regions need to uphold transparency in sharing information on the impact of the pandemic, through providing accurate and up-to-date case numbers and fatalities. Open and transparent exchange on each member's experience with COVID-19 will allow for enhanced tracking of case transmissions and facilitate contingency plans.

Second, regional blocs need to pursue multilateralism, not unilateralism, in the face of a global public health emergency. Should member states act independently, collective responses will be fractured and impeded.

Third, disparity within regions needs to be addressed. In a given regional area, there will be countries both better and worse off. Wealthier economies need to aid members where help is needed, be that through shipment of critical medical equipment or funding.

Fourth, regions should leverage upon past lessons derived from surprise events that have necessitated intensified cooperation.

The limited effectiveness of the ASEAN Agreement on Transboundary Haze Pollution (AATHP), which has not prevented the annual recurrence of haze, presents an example of where ASEAN should reflect on disunited action to inform cooperation in the coronavirus pandemic.

Lastly, members in a regional organisation should translate discussion and meetings into tangible intervention-led action. Coordinating policy, intensifying information exchange, establishing frameworks and guidelines to take actionable steps toward containing COVID-19 should be swift and concerted.

RECOMMENDATIONS AT THE NATIONAL LEVEL

This section provides specific recommendations to governments at the national level. Key economic and public health suggestions have been synthesised with the view that COVID-19 has irrevocably changed life as we know it.

Overall, the quality of governance needs to be questioned through the identification of existing loopholes in internal systems, which have been laid bare in the course of COVID-19.

While country-to-country experiences differ, targeted overall recommendations in this section allow a broad diagnosis on common issue areas and related remedy options.

Economic

The more severe a country's coronavirus outbreak and the less a government's ability to control it, the more muted consumer demand will be, particularly in the restaurant, retail, accommodation and tourism sectors.

A weak government response to a severe outbreak results in an extended time period of social distancing measures, which inevitably slows the resumption of economic activity. On the other hand, the stronger a government's response to the economic disruption caused by the pandemic, the less economic hardship its people will face, and the faster its economy can bounce back after the pandemic.

A country's economic condition will also depend on other factors, including (but not limited to) the size of its economy and its dependence on global exports. Its pre-COVID-19 economic conditions and growth trajectory; the degree to which it is dependent on hard-hit sectors such as tourism; and the extent to which its neighbours and close trading partners have managed to contain the virus themselves.

For the first time, the United Kingdom issued sovereign bonds at a negative interest rate. In the United States, federal funds rates were reduced to 0 percent. In Singapore, headline inflation fell to -0.7 percent in April 2020, a result of a decline in the cost of transport, petrol prices, retail goods and utilities, amongst others.

With interest rates incapable of going materially beyond the zero-lower bound, governments have limited monetary policy space to stimulate economic activity.

Countries with remaining public high debt loads, incurred during and after the 2008-2009 Global Financial Crisis, will have limited space for fiscal policy action. Such governments would be in a weak position to reignite economic activity in a post-COVID-19 world, even if they are today nominally considered advanced economies.

General

Short-term

Direct cash aid to individuals and households, as well as increases in unemployment benefits and subsidising wages, will help to prevent economic hardship and a rise in poverty.

The United States is instructive in this regard – despite record levels of unemployment, poverty had only grown from 12.5 percent to 12.7 percent by June 2020, as a result of direct cash aid to households and expansion in unemployment insurance benefits.[15]

The subsidising of wages for employees that firms would otherwise lay off, meanwhile, prevents mass unemployment.

Singapore's use of such a scheme has meant that a rise in unemployment will be contained to between 4 and 5 percent by the end of 2020, from 2.3 percent at the start of the year.[119]

This compares favourably to countries like the United States, where the unemployment rate rose sharply by 9.2 percent in the space of three months, from 3.8 percent in February 2020 to 13 percent in May 2020,[120] and where unemployment claims in March 2020 alone jumped to 6.6 million people.[121]

Medium-term

To ensure a speedy economic recovery, direct bridging loans from the government should be made to firms to tide them over for the duration of the pandemic. These firms would otherwise go under, which would depress investment and – by hindering the ability of unemployed individuals to return to work after the pandemic – undermines growth.

It is also important that these bridging loans be forgiven after the pandemic; the debt burden would otherwise risk causing the collapse of these businesses anyway, or otherwise limit their investment and hiring – all of which delay the recovery of the job market and hence growth.

Meanwhile, lending in support of growth can also be encouraged by extending public guarantees to banks that limit their downside exposure when extending loans to cash-strapped borrowers.

Central banks can also recommend to commercial banks that they draw down the capital buffers they are required to maintain by the Basel III international regulatory accords. This increases lending and boosts economic growth, while not affecting the banks' capital positions, as higher GDP growth minimises credit losses and increases bank profits.

A critical criterion is the provision of central bank reassurances that replenishment of capital buffers will be measured, rather than accelerated, once the crisis is over.

Governments can also invest, increasing aggregate demand but also setting a foundation for the future, with funding directed towards improving health systems, infrastructure, green technology and education.

Long-term

Beyond mere economic recovery, policymakers are faced with the challenge of building an economy that is not merely prosperous, but also resilient and ready to weather the next economic shock, whether that manifests as a financial, political or public health crisis.

Digitalisation: By moving towards a digital economy, governments and enterprises will be able to function more smoothly in a future pandemic.

Telehealth will allow doctors to have consultations with their patients remotely and health monitoring can occur in real time, with machine learning supporting clinical analysis and flagging at risk cases for quick intervention. This will make public health management more targeted and cost efficient.

Remote learning permits teachers to hold classes and impart knowledge without compromising quality or putting faculty and students at risk. Students will not be required to sacrifice their learning opportunities. Virtual reality will bring the online and offline experiences closer together in effects.

Online banking allows consumers to pay bills, check their accounts and apply for loans from the comfort of their home. Block chain technology and digital tokens will provide greater security and more flexibility in individual, household and enterprise financing.

A digital economy is also, by necessity, more resilient to other sorts of crises. Restrictions on the cross-border flow of people, arising from diplomatic crises – as in the blockage of Qatar by the Kingdom of Saudi Arabia, the United Arab Emirates and Bahrain – will be more manageable if a digital economy and flexible employment rules permit offshore hiring and provision of services through purely digital channels.

Knowledge-based economy: Knowledge-based professional services – in consulting, law, finance, insurance, accounting and economics – have so far proved relatively resilient to the pandemic, accounting for only 5 percent of the job losses during the first wave of pandemic-induced cuts in the United States.[122]

The same pattern holds in the United Kingdom, with the early stages of the pandemic seeing primarily blue-collar workers in retail and hospitality being retrenched.

This is a result of workers in knowledge-based professional services tending to do their work using digital devices.

Telecommuting is hence not such a problem for their companies. If an economy moves towards becoming a knowledge-based one, and grows its numbers in the professional services industry, it can increase its resilience to any future pandemics.

Diversification: Certain sectors, such as the tourism industry, are particularly vulnerable to pandemics, and it would be wise for governments to diversify their economies and reduce such risk.

Generally, diversification helps insulate a country's economy from downturns in one particular sector, like oil, which could otherwise cause deep recessions and severe shortfalls in the government budget.

Individual companies, too, might look to diversify their supply chains, so that the manufacture and distribution of goods – particularly essential ones related to food and medicine – are not badly disrupted by disease outbreaks in any one particular country.

Enhanced automatic fiscal stabiliser: The pandemic, if nothing else, has shown the need for swift and decisive counter-cyclical fiscal policy in response to imminent recessions.

However, such action is not always forthcoming, not just because of ordinary governmental inertia, but because of political gridlock.

In Presidential-style democracies, for instance, different political parties might control the presidency and the legislature, and because the president tends to be blamed by the public for poor economic conditions, an opposition-controlled legislature has the political incentive to sabotage effective policymaking and to refuse to pass an appropriate counter-cyclical budget.

As the IMF notes, improving unemployment benefit systems and social safety nets can protect household incomes from adverse shocks and strengthen resilience against future epidemics.

To circumvent this problem, governments could implement enhanced automatic fiscal stabilisers. Beyond the ordinary increase in unemployment benefits and fall in tax revenues that occur during recessions, government expenditures, such as in the form of direct cash to households, could be explicitly designed to increase in times when the unemployment rate rises beyond a pre-determined threshold.

Averting climate change: The deeper, more crucial, lesson to be learnt from the COVID-19 pandemic is that governments need to be organised and prepared for crises before they happen and that scrambling for a response after the fact is unlikely to be effective.

Experts had been concerned for years over governments' lack of funding for pandemic research and preparation, and their worries have been demonstrated to be justified in the most catastrophic manner.

It is therefore critical that this mistake of unpreparedness is not repeated for climate change, the other global threat facing humanity.

Urgent and drastic steps need to be taken to limit global warming by curbing the emission of greenhouse gases. The pandemic is a wake-up call to humanity that existential crises are not theoretical but real. Similarly, climate change is not fanciful but is reaching the point of no return. Conspiracy theorists, encouraged by populist right wing leaders such as Donald Trump, Jair Bolsonaro and Australia's Prime Minister Scott Morrison, will continue to inhibit progress on tackling climate change.

However, the pandemic has made populations more alert and sentient of the need to pay heed to global threats. Many of the responses to the pandemic, such as public-private partnerships, self-organising research sharing and consortiums and philanthropic support for research – not to mention a reduced dependency on the United States and a more muscular leadership by China – are a combination which could work in favour of a more focused, sustainable and scaled-up response to climate change.

City governments, led by Mayors, are also becoming more empowered to take action independent of their federal governments. This is particularly evident in the United States and Australia. One area they can work quickly to put into effect with policy action is encouraging the wider use of public transport and discouraging the use of cars through the use of congestion charges in cities going forward.

COVID-19 has made people feel less certain about the safety of public transport, and it would set back efforts to protect the environment if such sentiment persists.

As Marion Terrill, director of the transport and cities programme at the Grattan Institute notes, "The case is strong now in the light of COVID-19. Cities are repurposing their streets, and people don't feel safe in public transit, so if governments do nothing to manage traffic, it would be a disaster."

> *If we learn the lessons of COVID-19, we can approach climate change more informed about the consequences of inaction.*

Bill Gates
Co-Chair, Bill & Melinda Gates Foundation

> *COVID-19 is the toughest practical challenge to government I have ever seen.*

Tony Blair
former Prime Minister of the United Kingdom

Specific

National governments can also do more on the economic front.

First, they can support growth and avoid deflation by: (i) engaging in robust expansionary fiscal policy to the best of a government's fiscal abilities; (ii) using aggressive and creative monetary policy; and (iii) coordinating between the two.

Second, they can engage with experts with knowledge of and experience in monetary and fiscal policy as well as in crisis management.

Third, they can avoid making long-tail commitments hastily, without the proper cost-benefit analysis.

Fourth, if international financial aid is required and unavoidable, they ought to request it earlier rather than later. This is for two reasons:

- Several countries will be in similar straits, and an early request can mean the difference between getting sufficient aid in time to head off the worst of a crisis, or instead accepting additional debt burden while being too late to avert economic damage. As IMF Chief Economist Gita Gopinath noted, "We've had a hundred countries approach us for emergency financing. It's never happened before. That tells you the gravity of this crisis."
- Putting in an early request can trigger speculative currency attacks and raise premiums on international money markets; such costs are inevitable regardless – it is only a question of whether this cost is incurred early or late.

Fifth, they can treat money market debt with the appropriate concern; while the most accessible form of funding, they come with the most risks and constraints.

Sixth, they need to also understand that there is no perfect cocktail of prescriptions that will work for every country; judgement and an understanding of local conditions are required to navigate a country out of its crisis.

Public Health and Governance

The viral outbreak has delivered an extraordinary test to global governments, exposing the preparedness – or lack thereof – of public health systems and requiring clarity in communication under emergency circumstances, both within the government administration itself and toward citizens.

Success in reacting to a rapidly-evolving viral situation is contingent on a multitude of factors within the wide spheres of public health and governance, and range from rooted structural factors to action-oriented responses.

General

Travel Bans

Despite early policy recommendations from the WHO against the institution of travel bans, there is strong scientific evidence that travel bans do help to delay – though not stop – the spread of the coronavirus.

Dr Matteo Chinazzi of Northeastern University and his team of international researchers from the United States, Italy and China used the Global Epidemic and Mobility Model (GLEAM) to show that the internal lockdown of Wuhan by the Chinese government delayed the overall progression of the then-epidemic by three to five days within China itself.[123]

International travel restrictions on China then helped to slow the spread of the virus to the rest of the world until the middle of February 2020.

An important caveat to this finding is that travel restrictions alone only modestly affect the overall trajectory of the epidemic unless in-country community transmission is itself limited by other pandemic control policies.

Fundamentally, the world is highly globalised and interconnected – which is a risk factor, for better or for worse. As WHO Director-General Tedros has come to admit: "And in our situation now with more technology, and of course with more connectiveness, the virus has a better chance of spreading, it can move fast because we are more connected now".[124]

Lockdowns

Evidence suggests that lockdowns – variously known as mandatory stay-at-home orders, or shelter-in-place regulations – help reduce the spread of COVID-19.

Admittedly, such evidence can be difficult to tease out. This is because in a direct method of investigation – such as looking across various countries and seeing whether places with strict lockdowns have less severe outbreaks – the direction of causality is hard to identify.

For example, if a country with strict lockdowns nonetheless has a bad outbreak, would that be evidence that lockdowns do not work, or that places with worse outbreaks are forced into harsher lockdowns in the first place?

That said, one creative proxy is 'rainfall'. When there is the threat of heavy rains, people are more likely to choose to stay at home – producing the same effect as a lockdown. With this in mind, researcher Rolly Kapoor and her team at the University of California show that rainfall in a region – and by logical extension, lockdowns – do lead to people staying home more, and to lower infection rates further down the line.[125]

Beyond mandatory lockdowns, however, it important to pre-emptively cue the population to self-isolate as a precautionary measure until more is known about the virus.

> *No country can just pretend the pandemic is over. The reality is this virus spreads easily. Opening up without control is a recipe for disaster. Decisions about how and when to allow gatherings of people must be taken with a risk-based approach, in the local context.*

Dr Tedros Adhanom Ghebreyesus
Director-General of the WHO
31st August 2020

Quarantine and Contact Tracing

The backbone of any COVID-19 control policy will be isolating symptomatic individuals and then tracing, testing and further isolating those who have been in contact with the initial patient.

Dr Adam Kucharski of the London School of Hygiene and Tropical Medicine finds that a test-trace-isolate regime works. Using data on transmission rates within and outside households, as well as survey data on whom people interact with on a daily basis, Dr Kucharski and his team build a model that shows that isolation of the symptomatic individual and their household can cut the virus's effective reproduction rate by 37 percent. Engaging in tracing, testing and quarantine of contacts can then further cut the virus's effective reproduction rate by anything from 47 percent to 66 percent.[126]

Mask-Wearing and Other Measures

A meta-analysis, by a COVID-19 Systematic Urgent Review Group Effort study, of cross-country observational studies on viral transmission shows that control measures such as mask-wearing, physical distancing and eye protection all help to reduce the rate at which a virus is transmitted.[127]

Mask-wearing is especially important given the new and unexpected ways in which the coronavirus can be spread. Public restrooms are one such vector, as flushing releases clouds of virus-laden aerosols that others can then inhale. Airborne dust is another such vector, with influenza viruses being capable of spreading through microscopic particles like dust and fibres – not just through respiratory droplets produced by coughing, sneezing or talking.

Ventilator and ECMO Machine Production

Beyond measures to control the spread of the infection, there are also policies available to control the fatality rate amongst the COVID-19-infected population, such as the compulsion of private industry to switch to the production of ventilators and extracorporeal membrane oxygenation (ECMO) machines, as is possible under legislation such as the Defence Production Act in the United States.

Ventilators can improve the survival chances of sufferers of severe acute respiratory failure,[128] of the sort COVID-19 patients can develop.[129] Meanwhile, ECMO machines have proven to increase survival rates and quality-adjusted-life-years in patients suffering from severe acute respiratory failure, beyond what is achievable via ventilator usage.[130]

"We've always had emerging infectious diseases. We will continue to have them in the future. Just as emerging infections provide for us a perpetual challenge, we need to be perpetually prepared.

Dr Anthony Fauci
Director of United States National Institute of Allergy and Infectious Diseases
20th July 2020

Specific

Healthcare System Readiness

The pandemic has highlighted the immediate need for revision of healthcare systems worldwide and to equip health infrastructure and workers for a possible future pandemic or epidemic. For example, elective surgeries going forward will require surgeons to have sufficient personal protective equipment.

Meanwhile, dental procedures – which can be especially high risk, given the nature of dental procedures producing aerosol – such as teeth cleaning via dental air/water sprays – will require not just dentists to be equipped with PPEs but also adequate ventilation to reduce the risk of aerosol-based virus spread.

WHO infection prevention and control minimum standards are categorised into national and facility levels and should compel countries to improve healthcare workforce staffing, the sufficiency of bed occupancy and equipment levels and sound intra-facility coordination.

Preparing for an emergency involves public health measures set up to prevent, detect and then respond, requiring too the ability to manage emergency logistics and scale-up healthcare capacity in short periods.

Equipping health systems comprehensively will enable government response to be expedited and proactive in a public health emergency. Viral testing, contact tracing, and advanced care for ill patients must all proceed with immediacy to contain an outbreak.

Intergovernmental Coordination

Countries that have mounted successful reactions to the COVID-19 pandemic demonstrated high levels of inter-ministerial coordination in the early stages of the outbreak.

Close coordination between tiers of government at the national and local spheres enabled the dissemination of important directives and communication of information and updates.

Coordinated, top-down approaches serve to bolster the allocation and management of critical resources. This allows an administration to categorise the severity of the outbreak in specific regions and provinces, which enables the preparation of informed and guided plans in an evolving viral situation.

Where governance is highly decentralised, delineating responsibilities and roles of federal and provincial governments help to effect complex decision-making and reduce the likelihood of blind-spots, such as the existence of vulnerable communities.

Directing national response via coordination with public health and medical professionals, who provide expertise according to a consistent and scientifically-backed approach, will facilitate success.

Risk Communication

COVID-19 has challenged the ability of public health and government systems to communicate effectively with populations, which directly impacts the trust of citizens in leadership and the chances of success of the coordinated national effort.

Transparently disclosing critical information provides clarity and encourages voluntary citizenry participation in mitigation measures, reducing the threat of misinformation and the related risks it poses to public health.

Countries where the government has been a reliable source of guidance during the crisis provide up-to-date statistics on infection spread and regular notifications of new viral cases via technology-supported platforms, integrating accessibility to information and time-sensitive messaging to populations.

Integrating Technology

Application of digital technology in policy and healthcare is beneficial to pandemic management. This can be seen in measures of surveillance, contact tracing, quarantine, testing and healthcare – far exceeding what can be achieved when using manual tools in normal operations.

Contact tracing mobile applications that alert users on proximity to diagnosed COVID-19 patients, remote health monitoring systems for patients under home care, and use of new technologies to track the viral spread and identify high-risk patients, are among a variety of technologically-motivated solutions to containing the spread of COVID-19.

The pandemic has revealed the potential of digital technologies – including AI, big data, machine learning, blockchain technology and the Internet of Things – in enabling public health systems to viably collect data, model risks and implement public measures in public health crises.

Technology also has the potential to directly aid diagnosis, with AI systems like the convolutional neural network-based, COVID-Net, possibly being able to identify signs of COVID-19 via chest x-rays.

Active Learning

China, Singapore, Hong Kong, Taiwan and Vietnam all learned from SARS in 2002-2003, just as South Korea did from MERS in 2012. These lessons for preparedness primed them for responding to COVID-19 in 2020.

Despite differences when comparing COVID-19 to past crises – whether that is SARS, Zika or Ebola– it will serve countries well to extrapolate lessons from these experiences to bolster domestic health system preparedness and forward adaptive policy plans in readiness for the next unprecedented public health situation.

"The pandemic is a once-in-a-century health crisis, the effects of which will be felt for decades to come."

Dr Tedros Adhanom Ghebreyesus
Director-General of the WHO
2nd August 2020

CONSOLIDATED INSIGHTS AND RECOMMENDATIONS

Theme	Insight
Governance	(1) Quality of governance is what ultimately determines success or failure in handling COVID-19 and its consequences. (2) COVID-19 has nonetheless had severe political consequences: • General instability • Intensified US-China geopolitical rivalry • Possible ebbing of the hard-right populist surge
Public Health	(1) Beyond direct deaths, COVID-19 is a threat to public health by: • Impeding routine vaccination • Deterring regular visits to the doctor • Delaying crucial surgeries • Undermining food access for vulnerable people in war zones • Accelerating antibiotic misuse and development of antibiotic resistant bacteria • Diverting resources away from research in other diseases • Increasing domestic abuse (2) As seen in countries ranging from New Zealand to the United States, it is quality of governance, more than other factors like wealth or health system capacity, that determines the severity of a pandemic within a country. (3) Going forward, the toll from COVID-19 can be more or less severe, depending on the level of international cooperation, evidence-based policies and public-private partnerships.

Recommendation	Relevant Part of Book
(i) Evidence-based policies	Part A
(ii) Greater cooperation and leadership	Part B
(i) Evidence-based policies such as: • Travel bans • Test, tracing and isolating people at high-risk of infection • Mask-wearing mandates. • Lockdowns • Coordinated production of ventilators and other vital medical equipment (ii) Greater regional cooperation • Identification of common goals • Sharing of information and public health expertise • Helping less affluent neighbours • Learning from past failures in handling transnational crises (iii) Greater international cooperation between governments, business and academia, as focused on: • Supporting scientific research • Protecting the global medicine and medical equipment supply chain from disruption • Ensuring equitable public health funding globally (iv) The WHO must protect its credibility by: • Ensuring clear communication and explaining policy shifts • Avoiding politicisation and resisting unwarranted political pressure from the great powers	Part B Part E Part H

Theme	**Insight**
COVID-Testing and Vaccination Management	(1) A test-trace-isolate regime is necessary (2) A vaccine is not a silver bullet – deployment will come at substantial cost and face significant logistical and political challenges
Fiscal Policy	(1) COVID-19 has brought a deep recession and financial instability, while also deepening inequality.
Monetary Policy	

Recommendation	**Relevant Part of Book**
(i) Quarantining asymptomatic individuals or those tested positive for COVID-19, and proceeding to trace, test and quarantine the patient's contacts. (ii) International cooperation to: • Ensure all countries have the funding to purchase and deploy an eventual vaccine • Avoid counter-productive tariffs or non-tariff restrictions on vaccines or vaccine components	Part D
(i) Expansionary fiscal policy • Expansionary discretionary budgets • Setting up enhanced automatic fiscal stabilisers (ii) At the national level: • Short-term measures to alleviate suffering – Direct cash aid to households – Increases in unemployment benefits – Wage subsidies • Medium-term measures to ensure a speedy economic recovery – Forgivable bridging loans to firms – Public guarantees over bank lending – Expanded government investment in infrastructure, health and education • Long-term measures to build a more resilient economy, with spending and tax policy directed towards: – Digitalisation – Building a knowledge economy – Diversification – Averting climate change (iii) Regional action to stimulate joint economic recovery (iv) Global coordination by the G7 and other major economies on fiscal stimulus	Part C
(1) Accommodating and dovish monetary policy: • Low to zero interest rates • Quantitative easing • Helicopter money • Securing of hard currency • Temporary loosening of macroprudential policy • Avoiding procyclical monetary policy	Part C

Theme	Insight
Technology and Innovation	(1) The pandemic has accelerated trends towards: • Telecommuting • Automation • Contactless delivery • Digitalized services • Open data • Decreased competition in the technology (2) Technology has also been used to combat COVID-19 through: • Innovative testing methods • App-based contact tracing • Digitalized quarantine enforcement (3) This has been supported by radical changes in human habits, including: • Greater hand-washing • Mask-wearing • Social distancing (4) The scientific research process itself has undergone changes, with: • Expedited grant-making • Greater use of pre-print servers • Reforms to the sclerotic peer review process
Public-Private Partnership	(1) Private organisations have stepped up to help governments combat the pandemic: • Universities and pharmaceutical multinationals are racing to develop a vaccine • Firms completely unrelated to healthcare are trying to do their part (e.g. alcohol distilleries switching to disinfection production) (2) GAVI and WHO have set up COVAX, a program meant to ensure that any eventual vaccine is equitably shared and effectively deployed.

Recommendation	Relevant Part of Book
(i) Accelerating digitalisation and use of technology to: • Improve productivity • Ensure greater resilience to future pandemics and the need for social distancing (ii) Ensuring that workers have the skills and capabilities required for a digital economy, so no one gets left behind	Part C
(i) Businesses should continue using technology and innovation to help combat the pandemic (ii) Governments should join COVAX and ensure that the global population is vaccinated in a fair and effective way. • This is a moral imperative. • This is also a matter of national self-interest, for no man is an island – global demand and international supply chains will not recover until even less developed countries are able to vaccinate their populations	Part A Part G

SECTION IV: THE POST-COVID WORLD

I conclude this book with a forward-looking view of the future beyond COVID-19 – what I will call the 'post-Covid world'. There are many points which could be made on the issue, some indisputable, others debatable, most minor and some major. My focus is on structural changes that will permanently alter geopolitics, societal norms, international relations and the need for new mindsets.

Part I: The World after the Pandemic

Global Governance Under Threat

The first point concerns the validation of the crucial importance of international intuitions such as the UN, the World Bank, the IMF, the Bank of International Settlements and the WHO.

These are all products of the aftermath of the bitter and calamitous experience of two consecutive World Wars in the first half of the twentieth century. Other international frameworks or organisations, such as the WTO, are also under threat from the unilateralism and antagonism of the United States.

The heroic irony of this is that every single one of these institutions were conceived, promoted, rooted and sustained by the United States over a period of nearly 70 years until the advent of the Presidency of Donald Trump.

However, the amount of damage he has done in four years has created path dependency which sets a negative and corrosive trajectory that will require the collective willpower of leading and smaller nations to countervail.

Health for and of Humanity

In the context of COVID-19, I will focus on one key international institution which has been a central player in the global response to the pandemic and the need to reform it. This is the WHO.

The WHO was founded in 1948, on the principle that health is a human right that should be enjoyed by all. Over the years, the WHO has helped advise countries on the responsible use of antibodies, facilitated the deployment of vaccines for polio and measles, and monitored and controlled serious infectious diseases like cholera, plague, yellow fever, smallpox, relapsing fever and typhus – with smallpox finally being eliminated in 1979.

WHO has also helped research and promote sexual and reproductive health and rights, tackle tropical diseases, and developed the directly observed treatment strategy to save 37 million lives from tuberculosis.

In the new millennium, WHO has also helped push for tobacco control, produced regulations for responding to public health threats, and collaborated with countries in their fight against viruses like the H1N1 influenza, Ebola and Zika.

As a specialised agency of the UN, the WHO has 194 member states, with a World Health Assembly serving as its legislative body, and with a Director-General leading the agency itself.

The organisation has six regional offices spread throughout the six continents and has 7000 people from more than 150 countries working for it.

In terms of its staff, it is not merely doctors, scientists or epidemiologists that help the WHO fulfil its purpose; experts in economics and emergency relief, as well as corporate staff managing administration, finances and information systems, are key as well.

WHO obtains its funding from two main sources – member countries paying their dues, as well as voluntary contributions made either by member countries above and beyond their compulsory dues, or by other partners.

The United States has historically been the biggest contributing country to WHO; other big donors include the United Kingdom, Germany, Japan and Sweden. Meanwhile, private entities such as the Bill & Melinda Gates Foundation and the GAVI Alliance also provide substantial funding.

The WHO has taken the initiative to launch the Access to COVID-19 Tools (ACT) accelerator in April 2020, which brings governments, health organisations, scientists, businesses, civil society and philanthropy together to support the development and fair distribution of the resources needed in diagnostics, vaccines and treatments to combat the pandemic.

Fully costed plans have been developed in the areas of diagnostics (i.e. to expand testing), therapeutics (i.e. to develop treatments that can reduce morbidity and mortality from COVID-19) and vaccines (i.e. to develop and distribute a safe and effective vaccine).

More generally, WHO has pushed to ensure equitable access for all countries to vital personal protective equipment; it has opposed export restrictions that undermine supply chains and prevent masks, gloves, respirators and the like from going to the countries that need them the most.

WHO has also attempted to ensure equitable international access to controlled medicine (e.g. sedatives and analgesics), by proposing the relaxing of control procedures for the export, transportation and supply of such controlled medicine for the duration of the pandemic.

Further, WHO has worked with governments, international and nongovernmental organisations, as well as research institutes and businesses, with the goals of ensuring international coordination on operations and logistics, to accelerate research, and to scale up country preparedness and response operations

However, the WHO relies on the cooperation of its member nations, and has no authority to compel vital information sharing, or to enforce compliance with recommended paths of action. This reliance on cooperation gives rise to three problems.

First, the WHO cannot ensure that countries adopt a coordinated, evidence-based approach to combating public health problems.

Second, because it cannot afford to offend major countries whose cooperation it relies upon to address medical emergencies, the WHO is susceptible to political pressure and can be manipulated into policies and announcements that do not serve the cause of global health.

For example, early on in the COVID-19 pandemic, the WHO parroted China's talking points – namely that the coronavirus was not a serious threat, or that China had already quickly brought it under control, or that travel restrictions were unnecessary – and evinced reluctance to take strong early measures; all of which led to member countries underestimating the threat of the virus and failing to prepare for the pandemic.

Third, because the WHO relies on funding from its member nations, its operations can be disrupted by countries refusing to pay dues or even leaving the organisation, as recently happened when Donald Trump initiated withdrawal proceedings to take the United States out of WHO, as a protest over its perceived pro-Chinese bias. This withdrawal has also been accompanied by a refusal to pay existing dues.

Given the vital role that WHO plays in combating COVID-19 and other global health threats, countries should seek to support, rather than undermine the organisation.

The WHO should ensure that it is more accountable to its members through more rigorous reporting. But it is a fundamental and vital institution in coordination, diagnosing, organising, and responding to national, regional and global threats to public health. It is a global merit good.

Member countries should tighten ties between their public and private health systems and bio-medical research institutions and the WHO to increase the pool of data and promote cross-fertilisation of learning and application of knowledge.

It is also in the interest of member countries to increase their contributions to the WHO to strengthen it in readiness for future threats to public health. Even if when the threat itself is not global, no country can live on the pretence that they are not susceptible to local outbreaks of contagious diseases.

Beyond increasing annual financial contributions, member countries should commit to a pandemic contingency fund that the WHO can tap on to boost their capacity to respond to any future pandemic rapidly and at an early stage.

The COVID-19 pandemic has validated the need for a respected and well resourced, competently staffed and confidently led global institution to promote and safeguard public health both in the contemporary context and in anticipation of future threats.

Disease X

A crucial reason to validate and reinforce the WHO is that scientists are increasingly raising alarm over the prospect of 'Disease X'. This would be a virus so complex, contagious, fatal and drug resistant than it would defeat most attempts to counter it. As with the Black Death of the Middle Ages, it would have to 'burn itself out', but in doing so, hundreds of millions of lives may be lost.

Such a disease may result from a combination of factors.

First, the reduced effectiveness of antibiotics due to over-prescription over the past 70 years.

Second, the expansion of the human habitation to the exclusion of space for wildlife, which can lead not only to their extinction but increase the risk of animal to human transmission due to proximity.

Third, the growing population of refugees escaping war and persecution, who are often doing so in poor health and while living in unsanitary conditions; they too can become hosts to viruses and bacteria that mutate over time.

Fourth, the pandemic will meet weakened public health systems in developing countries and in some developed countries, making surveillance and early detection of new pathogens less likely. These then can have time to mutate, strengthen and emerge explosively with little notice.

COVID-19 has taught us two valuable lessons. The first is that a global pandemic requires a global response. Second, we cannot fight the next pandemic with the same protocols, prescriptions and procedures used for the previous one.

That is tantamount to always being prepared to fight the last, not the next, war. Thus, investments into bio-medical research, global surveillance of public health and pooling together of public and private knowledge in a coordinated and directed manner are essential to being ready for 'Disease X' when, not if, it comes.

End of Pax Americana

The age of respected American leadership of the global community is over. In 1962, during the Cuban Missile Crisis, before confronting the Soviets with the evidence at the UN, President Kennedy sent delegations to key US allies with secret photographic proof of the presence of missiles in Cuba. When President Charles de Gaulle was shown the photos and a given a personal letter from President Kennedy, he was asked if he would like to speak with the President to confirm their veracity, he simply replied that the word of the President of the United States was sufficient proof.

This is far from the case today. The Presidency of George W. Bush with its waging of endless war on 'global terrorism' and invasion of Iraq on a false premise, severely eroded American credibility internationally.

But President Trump, whose treatment of long-standing US allies and embrace of autocratic leaders, his compulsive lying and erratic and unorthodox policymaking via Twitter, have reduced respect for American leadership to a new low.

His lack of concern for this effect is explained by his complete lack of interest and trust in international frameworks, global cooperation or partnerships. His approach is purely transactional and self-interested. "America First" is actually "America Only".

The induced frictions in trade between the United States and China have expanded into the security sphere, heightening the risks of conflict. This serves no other nation's interests – not even those of the US or China themselves – but it does serve the personal interest of President Trump, who sees himself as the Great Crusader of American interests and is well aware that, historically, Americans always grant a President-at-War a second term.

The abdication of global leadership is compounded by active efforts to undermine global institutions and to disrupt international efforts to work around American obstructionism on trade, diplomacy, geo-politics and even COVID-19 responses.

Hence, in the post-Covid world, nations will no longer look towards the United States for leadership, reversing a dynamic that has been in place for more than a century. Indeed, they are likely to consider the United States as a threat, or at least a risk, they have to consider when deciding how best to respond to any regional or global threat of any nature.

Growing Inequality

Regardless of which scenario or forecast eventuates, what is certain is that the post-Covid world will be far more unequal.

The recovery will be "K-Shaped". The rich with access to capital will be able to access the best medical care, 'jump the queue' for an eventual vaccine and remove themselves from dense cities to country retreats to reduce their vulnerability.

With access to capital they can also take advantage of negative movements in equity, property and other asset classes. The rich also depend more on investment returns than on salaries for their wealth accumulation and so are insulated from economic shocks.

The middle class will bear the brunt of the economic and financial shocks of COVID-19. Many will lose their jobs, cannibalise their savings and have a difficult time refitting into the workforce during an anaemic economic recovery. The lower middle class will also be vulnerable to falling into poverty.

The poor will get poorer and a large proportion will become permanently dependent on state support for subsistence. They are the most vulnerable in all dimensions, from health, to finance and to the social. The children of the poor will constitute a 'lost generation' as they will lack the means or the social support to escape the poverty trap.

Epochal Shifts in Geo-Politics

From a global perspective, most Asian nations, tested and prepared by the Asian Financial Crisis in 1997, SARS in 2003 and the Global Financial Crisis in 2008 will emerge in the post-Covid world in much better economic and financial shape than Western economies.

The centre of gravity for global economic power, which was already shifting East, will accelerate on that path. The principle 'winner' will be China, whose economy will almost certainly be considered the world's largest, overtaking a contracting United States economy increasingly disrupted, dislocated and destroyed by poor federal and state level management of the COVID-19 situation.

The effects of growing inequality will be intergenerational where it comes to people. The effects where it comes to regions will be epochal and also raise the propensity for the activation of the Thucydides Trap – with the United States reluctant and resistant to cede pole position to China and willing to resort to economic, financial and potentially military means to frustrate the expansion of China's sphere of influence.

There is a certain irony in this development given the inward, America-centric policy of the Trump Administration that explicitly does not concern itself with the needs or welfare of the rest of the world.

In the case of the fight against COVID-19, Trump has not only withdrawn the United States as a treaty member of the WHO and withheld its mandated funding to the WHO, but in September 2020 issued directives to its diplomats, health officials and other agencies to withdraw engagements with the WHO at any level and on any issue. This while the death toll in the United States was on track to pass 200,000 by the end of the same month and its number of infections surging towards 7 million in the same period.

Inequality will not only be in terms of wealth but also in terms of international reputation and geo-political capital. The United States has expended their 'Bank of Trust' and is seriously overdrawn on their 'Reputational Account'. It remains to be seen if China's capital stock in both categories will conversely rise to a point that it becomes the new vector for global leadership.

Public Debt Bubbles Bursting

Western and middle-income economies borrowed heavily from international capital markets to cope with the Global Financial Crisis. They have again resorted to massive borrowing to raise funds to finance fiscal expenditures to respond to the COVID-19 pandemic.

These huge debt overhangs will be a fiscal drag on their public finances for generations, limiting their ability to invest in productive public infrastructure. So once dominant Western economies are now on a path dependent trajectory of 'failing fast and to last'.

Their best human capital, facing a lack of opportunities and bearing a lack of trust in their institutions, the political processes and the leaders it produces, will embark on a capital flight to seek better prospects in the East.

This will further inhibit the prospects of recovery and in the longer term will see these economies not only financially, but socially, compromised.

Many of the economies with the largest debt-to-GDP ratios are likely to come under severe stress from international creditors. This will force them to sell national assets in fire sales to raise the capital for repayments. We have seen this happen before when the prized Port of Piraeus was sold by Greece to China in the wake of the Global Financial Crisis.

There is the potential for several advanced economies to default on their sovereign debt. This will reduce their international standing and raise the risk premium for doing business or investing in their economies.

The Post-Democratic World

These same economies are likely to experience the widest wealth inequality spread. The dire future confronting their populations will create the conditions for extremist politics to become mainstream, both from the Left and the Right of the spectrum.

Even as present-day populist politicians lose credibility, they have set the stage for a new generation of extremists who look to place the blame for their national failures and struggles on the 'Other'– be they migrants, Jews or China.

Populations in democratic countries may also perceive that their governments did not respond as effectively as those of authoritarian or more centrally governed countries. This can lead to a ground swell for political reform, which opportunists will take advantage of to install themselves as 'Strong Man' authority figures.

Their impact will be to erode democratic institutions and traditions. The United States is already experiencing this under the leadership of President Donald Trump, abetted by the Republican-controlled Senate led by Senator Mitch McConnell.

Thus, the post-Covid world could easily turn into a post-Democratic world, reversing the Francis Fukuyama argument of the 'End of History', which postulated that with the end of the Cold War, Democracy had been proven supreme as a political ideology and would inevitably be adopted by all nations as a result of the convincing proof of the triumph of the Democratic West over the Communist East.

Towards a Blade Runner World

The movie Blade Runner portrays a world where technology and those who control it have authority over everyone else.

COVID-19 has made us intensely more dependent on technology and ready to embrace its potential. Digitalisation, urbanisation, quality of governance and the capacity for new thinking is going to frame the longer-term future. We are headed to a hybrid experience where the socio-technological interface increasingly becomes fused.

But different countries are going to fall along a spectrum which will lead to very different experiences for their populations.

In a speech delivered on 10 September 2020, Ms Christine Lagarde, President of the European Central Bank and former Managing Director of the IMF, commented, "The digital revolution is transforming our lives in fundamental ways. More than four in five Europeans regularly use the internet, up from one in five two decades ago. This has had a profound impact on how we communicate, how we spend and how we work.

"The COVID-19 pandemic has accelerated this trend towards digitalisation. E-commerce, which has grown steadily in recent years, increased by almost a fifth in terms of volume of sales between February and June 2020, while in-store sales declined.

"As our lives have suddenly gone digital, so have our payments: there has been a surge in online payments and a shift towards contactless payments in shops.

"So it is natural for people to expect and embrace changes in the way they pay. According to the ECB's new payments survey, cash remains the most common way of making small retail payments, with cash payments accounting for 73 percent of all physical retail payments in 2019. But almost half of consumers said they prefer to pay digitally, and this has increased further during the pandemic.

"This trend is unlikely to be reversed once the pandemic is over. A survey conducted by a consulting firm in 17 European countries shows that a vast majority of consumers expect to continue to use digital services as often as they do now or even more often. In other words, the pandemic has served as a catalyst, accelerating the transition towards a digital new normal."

Effective Governance

Governance is generally assumed to be the specific and limited responsibility of the state apparatus. However, when we deal at the level of entire societies and even more broadly, at the level of the general course of humanity, this very limited scope of meaning is clearly inadequate.

The future is a course for which the determination has multiple streams of contribution. Governance must have a broader application, which calls for the contributions of civic, academic, and corporate leaders.

The critical uncertainty of greatest consequence is whether and how effective governance can be achieved and thereby arrive at credible institutional frameworks.

Future Frameworks

Future economies will be defined by their level of digital advances, and digital advances will be overwhelmingly concentrated in select frontier economies, while the vast majority of laggards falls behind. There are two frameworks that will assist the understanding of the new world: (i) the Digital Cities Framework will distinguish economies by their digital development; and (ii) the Digital Population Framework will segment the population by their constituencies.

Under the Digital Cities Framework, three categories of economies may emerge: the digital havens, the digital middle spaces, and the digital deserts.

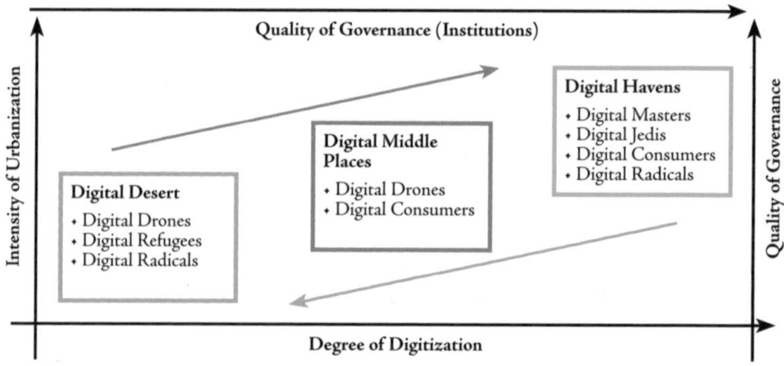

Figure 80: Future Frameworks

Digital Havens

Digital havens have undergone extensive digitisation. These are the economies that are at the frontier and pushing the boundaries of innovation. They have world-class infrastructure, both physical and digital, to facilitate digital interactions, which are the main activities of the global economy.

The governance space has evolved with reinvigorated institutions and policy solutions to ensure that side impacts from digitisation are moderated through social support and skill development programs.

Havens have moderated the curse of consumption through changed social norms, emphasising the economics of "enough." This change is further buttressed by the systemic adoption of energy efficiency, alternative energy, and recycling practices.

The mystery of productivity has been partially resolved through a mix of improved measurement methodologies including hybrid productivity measures and a better, more relevant understanding of the nature of digitisation.

The vast quantities of data generated are kept securely in data centres defended by advanced cybersecurity systems. There are also established public databases with a high quality and quantity of data available to businesses and individuals. Access to high-speed Internet is available throughout the havens.

The adaptation of regulations has maintained a healthy ecosystem in which digital businesses can thrive; regulatory sandboxes are readily introduced to ensure that enterprises are able to experiment with the latest technology. Key digital industries and digital frontier firms thrive in the haven cities and are significant contributors to the economy in terms of productivity, employment, and economic growth.

There are digital identities for all citizens. All personal data are completely digitised onto microchips, and citizens are able to conduct complex transactions securely. Furthermore, the high levels of cybersecurity provide individuals with the confidence to participate fully in the digital economy. The opportunities in these havens are abundant and there is a concentration of wealth, talent, and ideas. Some examples of such cities could be London, New York, Paris, Tokyo, Hong Kong, Singapore, Chicago, Shenzhen, Guangzhou, Shanghai, Los Angeles, Tel Aviv, San Francisco, Tallinn, and Dubai.

Digital Middle Spaces

Middle spaces share the characteristics of havens but not to the same degree. While physical infrastructure is adequate, digital infrastructure remains lagging behind the havens.

There are insufficient data centres in the cities and they rent data centres from digital havens to store the data generated. There is a significant lag before new technologies are adopted.

Digital identities remain under development. Moreover, cybersecurity has vast room for improvement, and these middle spaces become major targets for cybercrimes.

Their governance models also remain under development and are inadequate to cope with the side impacts of digitisation. Middle spaces are at perennial risk of brain drain as their best and brightest leave for the opportunities that can only be found in havens.

Digital Deserts

Digital deserts have struggled to keep up with the digital revolution. Digitisation has seemingly skipped these cities. Physical and digital infrastructures are in tatters. Significant investment is needed to upgrade the existing infrastructure to meet the needs of citizens. Furthermore, the cities are constricted by conflicts and tension at the structural, social, and political levels.

There is a dearth of innovative enterprises. Unemployment rates are high, and the digital deserts remain at the bottom of the GDP-per-capita table.

Governance models are poorly developed. There is low trust in institutions, and a general malaise pervades society. Many digital deserts continue to be extraction economies feeding the demand of havens and middle spaces.

Digital Stratification

The Digital Population Framework stratifies the population into five main groups indexed by their relationship to digitisation.

The digital masters are the owners of digital frontier firms that have become natural monopolies. These include current digital giants, like Facebook, Apple, Amazon, Netflix, Google, Baidu, Alibaba, Tencent, and their future iterations or successors. Digital masters are concentrated in the digital havens.

The digital jedis are individuals who possess high levels of digital skills and the tacit knowledge that are highly valued in this era. They are among the top 1 percent of the population. Most developed their skills within the digital havens; others who had the resources to pick up skills in other worlds eventually gravitated toward the digital havens.

The digital drones are individuals with mediocre digital skills. With AI and machine learning taking up most of the high-value-added activities, they are left with low-value-added jobs and are poorly remunerated. This group is crowded into the digital middle spaces and digital deserts.

There will also be those whose skills or inclinations are incongruent with the worlds they live in. The first group, which are more moderate, can be broadly termed digital refugees. They could be individuals with or who aspire to gain high levels of digital skills but are geographically located outside havens and need to find ways to migrate. Conversely, they could also be individuals in the digital havens who seek a less digitised experience and desire to move to middle spaces.

Digital radicals attempt to disrupt their respective worlds through extreme ends. Digital radicals in the digital havens have high levels of digital skills, but use their capabilities to gain undue power through cyber-manipulation. Radicals in the digital deserts are individuals with high levels of digital skills but have ideological agendas that drive them to infiltrate havens and middle spaces.

The Future of the Quality of Growth

The imperative for strong institutions is indisputable if we are to cram more of the future population into haven- and middle space-like worlds. The response to these challenges must be found in the realm of ideas, in the domain of social attitudes, and through the prism of leadership.

We need new thinking. And time is pressing, as the side impacts of eroding institutions, resource depletion through relentless consumption, and low productivity bleed into each other, creating social and political forces that are upsetting long-held norms at the structural level.

The challenges are profound and broad. Robert Skidelsky held that, "The truth is that we cannot go on successfully automating our production without rethinking our attitudes toward consumption, work, leisure, and the distribution of income."

Policymakers, economists, and the business community need to be cognizant that we are moving toward a situation of hybrid productivity, where both humans and algorithms are responsible for directing and creating output. Our efforts in increasing productivity can no longer be solely focused on extending just labour and capital productivity.

Research efforts are needed to better understand this new digital phenomenon that we are facing to guide the formulation of measurement frameworks that will allow us to assess our productivity better.

Governments, not companies, are at the crux of the change – and the response to this change. Nouriel Roubini captured this neatly when he observed that, "Advanced economies have a large stake in addressing the causes of the productivity slowdown before it jeopardises social and political stability."

The phenomena of Trump, Brexit, and the rise of western populist parties such as the Alternative for Germany (AfD) speak to the prescience of Roubini's warning. The rising tide of protectionism, anti-immigration, mainstreaming of racism, and surge of nationalism are eroding institutional strengths within and between countries.

Governments can take the lead in encouraging social resilience through a combination of policy action and vision in leadership. We are now in imminent danger of actualising a vision Maynard Keynes articulated in a 1930 publication called *Economic Possibilities for Our Grandchildren*, where he warned of the prospect of "technological unemployment" – defined as "unemployment due to the discovery of means of economising the use of labour outrunning the pace at which we can find new uses for labour."

Governments need to step in to provide targeted support to aid those experiencing difficulties in making the change. They must make substantial and sustained public investments in merit goods of education, especially lifelong learning, skills development, and transition support for workers who fall out of employment due to digitisation. We need more digital jedis, fewer drones and refugees, and certainly no radicals.

It is also governments who must forge a concordat with digital masters, the owners of natural monopolies in the digital economies, to better regulate, shape, and police the digital space to protect the interests of their citizens as well as ensure social and political stability.

As in all profound challenges, what needs doing is simple enough to state. But none of what is stated is simple to do. Nonetheless, a way must be found if we are to enlarge the space of digital havens and middle spaces and constrict the space of digital deserts.

Building A Better Future

We need new thinking, greater social resilience, and more relevant leadership across political, civic, corporate, and academic spaces. Generating these much-needed virtues begins by recognising and accepting two fundamental truths.

The first is that governance is a distributed responsibility. The second is that resolving the imperative of institutions, the curse of consumption, and the mystery of productivity is a profound challenge needing urgent attention and imminent action across broad fronts.

Taking the initiative to build a better future rather than relying on past models, or even transient solutions to present challenges, is necessary if we are to confront and overcome the more fundamental imperatives that challenge not only the growth story – but as COVID-19 is instructing us daily – also the continuity of humanity.

Our choice of future depends on it.

POSTSCRIPT

We live in times where fundamental shifts are occurring in multiple dimensions. COVID-19 has become a vector which concentrates changes in geopolitics, economics, finance, social norms, the nature of modern capitalism and technology. Old alliances, structures and institutions are under threat or crumbling. Some will be beyond repair, others still remain capable of restoration.

Whatever the equation of change, it is a formula for a new and different world. The journey of discovery and adventure of this new and still evolving condition will be fraught with danger, but also with excitement and opportunities.

I trust that this book, despite its prognosis of warnings and projections of gloom, will not be interpreted as a tale of pessimism, but instead be read as a call to arms to fight back against divisive, destructive and decaying forces.

As individuals, societies and nations, we should seek collaboration not confrontation; coordination not contention; struggle for consistency, not induce calamity; and collaborate to overcome global challenges, not seek conflict as a premise for ephemeral national triumphs – especially when the stakes are as high as existential peril for humanity.

APPENDICES & ENDNOTES

Appendix I: Methodology used in Part D

This is a country-level analysis conducted on 143 countries worldwide. Data was obtained on the following variables:

- Number of deaths of COVID-19 as at 20 July 2020
- Number of cases of COVID-19 as at 20 July 2020
- GDP per capita
- Worldwide Governance Indicators
- Stringency Indexes

Only countries without missing data were included in the analysis. Correlation and regression analyses were performed. GDP showed a statistically significant correlation with prevalence ratios and Case Fatality Ratios (CFRs). These two ratios are calculated as follows:

- Population Prevalence ratios are calculated based on the standard measure of dividing the total number of cases in a country by the total population.
- Case Fatality Ratios are calculated based on dividing the total number of deaths by the total number of cases in the population.

GDP per capita showed a positive correlation with Prevalence ratios, indicating that richer countries have a higher population Prevalence of COVID-19. The reverse can be said for CFR – countries with a higher GDP per capita showed a lower CFR. To control for the effects of governmental intervention, the University of Oxford Stringency Index measure was used to account primarily for containment and closure policies.[131]

There was no clear statistical relationship between the Stringency Index and either Prevalence ratios or CFRs, although some countries which scored well on Stringency, such as the UAE, France and New Zealand, saw Prevalence ratios that are lower than expected relative to their GDP, assuming a linear relationship between Prevalence and GDP.

Preliminary exploration of the data also indicates that Stringency index measures have a non-uniform effect across countries of different size, urban concentration and wealth. Countries with a lower GDP per capita are expected to have lower Prevalence ratios and higher CFRs in general, likely attributed to the lack of testing and medical infrastructure which understate prevalence ratios and negatively impact CFR.

Countries were also clustered into seven groups, taking into account their geographical region and stage of economic development. Countries in Western Europe are expected to be hardest-hit by the crisis, with the highest CFRs due to their ageing population.

On the other hand, regions like Northern Africa are expected to see a disproportionately high CFR due to the lack of testing and poorer medical infrastructure.

Surprisingly, Asian countries have the lowest CFR in general and this could be down to a variety of reasons, including strict stringency measures and a relatively younger population (with exceptions such as Japan).

Two of the groups consist of predominantly Asian countries, and these two groups have the highest Stringency Indexes, as well as the lowest CFRs, among the seven groups studied.

While it appears that there is no clear statistical relationship between stringent policy and CFR it would be premature to conclude from this that stringent policy does not help reduce infections and fatalities from COVID-19.

The lack of a clear inverse relationship between stringent policy and CFR might not necessarily be due to the ineffectiveness of the former; it might also be due to countries and regions with worse outbreaks being forced to impose more stringent policy – causality might run in the opposite direction.

Hence, it will be more useful to examine policies at the individual level, using instrumental variables where possible to control for endogeneity issues.

Appendix II: Index of Figures

ENDNOTES

1. The World Bank. (2020, June). *Global Economic Prospects*. Retrieved September 3, 2020, from the World Bank website: https://www.worldbank.org/en/publication/global-economic-prospects
2. CNBC. (2020, June). *IMF slashes its forecasts for the global economy and warns of soaring debt levels.* Retrieved September 3, 2020, from CNBC website: https://www.cnbc.com/2020/06/24/imf-global-economy-to-contract-with-coronavirus-recovery-slow.html
3. Our World in Data (2020). *COVID-19 Cases*. Retrieved September 3, 2020, from Our World in Data website: https://ourworldindata.org/covid-cases
4. Our World in Data (2020). *COVID-19 Deaths*. Retrieved September 3, 2020, from Our World in Data website: https://ourworldindata.org/covid-deaths
5. CNA. (2020, August 5). *Global COVID-19 deaths exceed 700,000, one person dies every 15 seconds on average*. Retrieved September 3, 2020, from CNA website: https://www.channelnewsasia.com/news/world/global-covid-19-deaths-one-person-dies-every-15-seconds-12991910
6. CNBC. (2020, July 29). *WHO warns that waiting to achieve herd immunity to the coronavirus will kill a lot of people*. Retrieved September 3, 2020 from CNBC website: https://www.cnbc.com/2020/07/29/who-warns-that-waiting-to-achieve-herd-immunity-to-the-coronavirus-will-kill-a-lot-of-people.html
7. World Health Organization. (2020, August 4). *Estimating mortality from COVID-19*. Retrieved September 3, 2020 from WHO website: https://www.who.int/news-room/commentaries/detail/estimating-mortality-from-covid-19
8. Reuters. (2020, May 21). *Swedish antibody study shows long road to immunity as COVID-19 toll mounts*. Retrieved. September 3, 2020 from Reuters website: https://www.reuters.com/article/us-health-coronavirus-sweden-strategy/swedish-antibody-study-shows-long-road-to-immunity-as-covid-19-toll-mounts-idUSKBN22W2YC
9. CNA. (2020, September 4). *Commentary: When COVID-19 symptoms last for months, recovery feels slow and strained*. Retrieved September 3, 2020, from CNA website: https://www.channelnewsasia.com/news/commentary/covid-19-coronavirus-symptoms-last-for-months-pain-headaches-13078824?
10. Puntmann, V. O. et al. (2020, July 27). Outcomes of Cardiovascular Magnetic Resonance Imaging in Patients Recently Recovered From Coronavirus Disease 2019 (COVID-19). *JAMA Cardiol*. Retrieved September 3, 2020, from jamanetwork website: https://jamanetwork.com/journals/jamacardiology/fullarticle/2768916
11. Shi, S. et al. (2020, March 25). Association of Cardiac Injury With Mortality in Hospitalized Patients With COVID-19 in Wuhan, China. *JAMA Cardiol*. Retrieved September 3, 2020, from jamanetwork website: https://jamanetwork.com/journals/jamacardiology/fullarticle/2763524
12. Roy Morgan. (2020, June 1). *PM Jacinda Ardern ascendant as Labour support (56.5%) is now more than double National (26.5%) three months from NZ Election*. Retrieved September 3, 2020, from Roy Morgan website: http://www.roymorgan.com/findings/8429-nz-national%20-voting-intention-may-2020-202006010651
13. Ibid.
14. Korber, B. et al. (2020, August 20). Tracking Changes in SARS-CoV-2 Spike: Evidence that D614G Increases Infectivity of the COVID-19 Virus. *Cell Press*. Retrieved from Cell Press website: https://www.cell.com/cell/fulltext/S0092-8674(20)30820-5

15. Zhang, L. et al. (2020, June 12). The D614G mutation in the SARS-CoV-2 spike protein reduces S1 shedding and increases infectivity. *bioRxiv*. Retrieved from bioRxiv website: https://www.biorxiv.org/content/10.1101/2020.06.12.148726v1

16. Daniloski, Z. et al. (2020, June 14). The Spike D614G mutation increases SARS-CoV-2 infection of multiple human cell types. *bioRxiv*. Retried from bioRxiv website: https://www.biorxiv.org/content/10.1101/2020.06.14.151357v2

17. Live Science. (2020, July 10). *A new coronavirus mutation is taking over the world. Here's what that means*. Retrieved September 3, 2020, from Live Science website: https://www.livescience.com/new-coronavirus-mutation-explained.html

18. Grubaugh, N. D. et al. (2020, August 20). Making Sense of Mutation: What D614G Means for the COVID-19 Pandemic Remains Unclear. *Cell*. Retrieved from sciencedirect website: https://www.sciencedirect.com/science/article/pii/S0092867420308175

19. Ibid.

20. Healthline. (2020, June 15). *COVID-19 Will Mutate — What That Means for a Vaccine*. Retrieved September 3, 2020 from healthline website: https://www.healthline.com/health-news/what-to-know-about-mutation-and-covid-19

21. The Washington Post. (2020, July 2). *This coronavirus mutation has taken over the world. Scientists are trying to understand why*. Retrieved September 3, 2020, from The Washington Post website: https://www.washingtonpost.com/science/2020/06/29/coronavirus-mutation-science

22. New York Times. (2020, July 31). *Scared That Covid-19 Immunity Won't Last? Don't Be*. Retrieved September 4, 2020 from the New York Times website: https://www.nytimes.com/2020/07/31/opinion/coronavirus-antibodies-immunity.html

23. Prem, K. et al. (2020, May 4). The effect of control strategies to reduce social mixing on outcomes of the COVID-19 epidemic in Wuhan, China: a modelling study. *Lancet*. Retrieved from Lancet website: https://www.thelancet.com/action/showPdf?pii=S2468-2667%2820%2930073-6

24. The Conversation. (2020, September 1). *Will the new 15-minute COVID-19 test solve US testing problems?* Retrieved September 4, 2020 from The Conversation website: https://theconversation.com/will-the-new-15-minute-covid-19-test-solve-us-testing-problems-145285

25. The Washington Post. (2020, May 22). *Antimalarial drug touted by President Trump is linked to increased risk of death in coronavirus patients, study says*. Retrieved September 3, 2020, from The Washington Post website: https://www.washingtonpost.com/health/2020/05/22/hydroxychloroquine-coronavirus-study/

26. Our World in Data. (2020). *Total confirmed COVID-19 deaths per million people*. Retrieved September 3, 2020, from Our World in Data website: https://ourworldindata.org/grapher/total-COVID-deaths-per-million?tab=chart&country=SWE+NOR+DNK+FIN

27. City A.M. (2020, August 18). *London coronavirus cases: How many infections are in your London borough?*. Retrieved September 3, 2020, from City A.M. website: https://www.cityam.com/coronavirus-worst-affected-london-boroughs/

28. The Guardian. (2020, March 31). *England: more than third of hospital Covid-19 deaths in London*. Retrieved September 3, 2020 from The Guardian website: https://www.theguardian.com/world/2020/mar/31/england-more-than-third-of-hospital-COVID-19-deaths-in-london

29. Vox. (2020, May 11). *Covid-19 could reverse decades of global progress*. Retrieved September 3, 2020 from Vox website: https://www.vox.com/future-perfect/2020/5/11/21246992/coronavirus-pandemic-collateral-damage-hunger-poverty

30. World Health Organization. (2017). *The power of vaccines: still not fully utilized. Ten years in public health 2007–2017*. Retrieved September 3, 2020 from WHO website: https://www.who.int/publications/10-year-review/vaccines/en/

31. Vox. (2019, November 19). *The post-antibiotic era is here*. Retrieved September 3, 2020 from Vox website: https://www.vox.com/future-perfect/2019/11/14/20963824/drug-resistance-antibiotics-cdc-report

32. World Health Organization. (2017, October). *Multidrug-Resistant Tuberculosis (MDR-TB)*. Retrieved September 3, 2020, from WHO website: https://www.who.int/tb/challenges/mdr/MDR-RR_TB_factsheet_2017.pdf

33. World Health Organization. *Drug-resistant TB: XDR-TB FAQ*. Retrieved September 3, 2020, from WHO website: https://www.who.int/tb/areas-of-work/drug-resistant-tb/xdr-tb-faq/en/

34. The World Bank. (2020, June). *Lasting Scars of the COVID-19 Pandemic*. Retrieved September 4, 2020, from the World Bank website: http://pubdocs.worldbank.org/en/112641588788257004/Global-Economic-Prospects-June-2020-Topical-Issue-1.pdf

35. International Monetary Fund. (2020, June). *World Economic Outlook Update, June 2020*. Retrieved September 3, 2020 from the IMF website: https://www.imf.org/en/Publications/WEO/Issues/2020/06/24/WEOUpdateJune2020

36. International Monetary Fund. (2020, June). *Global Financial Stability Report June 2020*. Retrieved September 3, 2020 from the IMF website: https://www.imf.org/en/Publications/GFSR/Issues/2020/06/25/global-financial-stability-report-june-2020-update

37. Reuters. (2020, April 1). *Zoom takes lead over Microsoft Teams as virus keeps Americans at home: Apptopia*. Retrieved September 3, 2020 from Reuters website: https://www.reuters.com/article/us-health-coronavirus-zoom/zoom-takes-lead-over-microsoft-teams-as-coronavirus-keeps-americans-at-home-idUSKBN21I3AB

38. Business Insider. (2020, March 19). *Microsoft Teams added 12 million daily active users in a single week amid the coronavirus crisis, bringing it up to 44 million total*. Retrieved September 3, 2020 from Business Insider website: https://www.businessinsider.sg/microsoft-teams-coronavirus-daily-active-users-2020-3?_ga=2.237012807.674604748.1585725311-764543661.1581499728&r=US&IR=T

39. CNBC. (2020, March 31). *Peloton could emerge 'much stronger' after coronavirus shutdowns end, analysts say*. Retrieved September 3, 2020 from CNBC website: https://www.cnbc.com/2020/03/31/peloton-much-stronger-after-coronavirus-analysts-say.html

40. TODAY. (2020, March 8). *Food delivery companies see more orders as Covid-19 outbreak forces some to stay home*. Retrieved September 3, 2020 from TODAYonline website: https://www.todayonline.com/singapore/food-delivery-companies-see-more-orders-COVID-19-outbreak-forces-some-stay-home

41. CNA. (2020, August 17). *Commentary: E-commerce is set to boom, driven by COVID-19*. Retrieved September 3, 2020, from CNA website: https://www.channelnewsasia.com/news/commentary/e-commerce-boom-covid-19-online-shopping-sales-retail-13025254

42. NBC News. (2020, April 2). *YouTube thrives as a window for those isolated by coronavirus*. Retrieved September 3, 2020, from NBC News website: https://www.nbcnews.com/tech/social-media/youtube-thrives-window-those-isolated-coronavirus-n1173651

43. The Edge Singapore. (2020, September 4). *Airlines can't afford to wait for Covid vaccine, says IATA's chief medical adviser*. Retrieved September 4, 2020, from The Edge Singapore website: https://www-theedgesingapore-com.cdn.ampproject.org/c/s/www.theedgesingapore.com/amp/news/aviation/airlines-cant-afford-wait-covid-vaccine-says-iatas-chief-medical-adviser

44. Bloomberg. (2020, August 27). *Virus Threatens to Set Back Poor Nations by 10 Years, IMF Says*. Retrieved September 4, 2020, from Bloomberg website: https://www.bloomberg.com/amp/news/articles/2020-08-27/virus-threatens-to-set-back-poor-nations-by-10-years-imf-says

45. Hirtle, B. & Kellerher, J. (1990). *Financial market evolution and the interest sensitivity of output. Quarterly Review, Federal Reserve Bank of New York*. Retrieved September 3, 2020 from RePEc website: https://ideas.repec.org/a/fip/fednqr/y1990isump56-70nv.15no.2.html

46. Chung, H. et al. (2012, February 3). Have We Underestimated the Likelihood and Severity of Zero Lower Bound Events?. *Journal of Money, Credit and Banking*. Retrieved from Wiley Online Library website: https://onlinelibrary.wiley.com/doi/abs/10.1111/j.1538-4616.2011.00478.x

47. Bank of England. (2011, September 19). *The United Kingdom's quantitative easing policy: design, operation and impact*. Retrieved September 4, 2020, from BoE website: https://www.bankofengland.co.uk/quarterly-bulletin/2011/q3/the-uk-quantitative-easing-policy-design-operation-and-impact

48. Kapetanios, G. et al. (2012, October 29). *Assessing the Economy-wide Effects of Quantitative Easing. The Economic Journal*. Retrieved from Wiley Online Library website: https://onlinelibrary.wiley.com/doi/abs/10.1111/j.1468-0297.2012.02555.x

49. International Monetary Fund. (2012, October). *World Economic Outlook October 2012.* Retrieved September 3, 2020 from the IMF website: http://www.imf.org/external/pubs/ft/weo/2012/02/pdf/c1.pdf

50. Reinhart, C. M. & Rogoff, K. S. (2010, January). Growth in a Time of Debt. *The National Bureau of Economic Research.* Retrieved from the NBER website: https://www.nber.org/papers/w15639

51. Herndon, T. et al. (2013, April 15). Does High Public Debt Consistently Stifle Economic Growth? A Critique of Reinhart and Rogof. *PERI.* Retrieved from PERI website: https://www.peri.umass.edu/images/WP322.pdf

52. Economic Policy Institute. (2010, July 16). *Government Debt and Economic Growth.* Retrieved September 3, 2020 from EPI website: https://www.epi.org/publication/bp271/

53. Shental, N. (2020, August 21). *Efficient high-throughput SARS-CoV-2 testing to detect asymptomatic carriers. Science Advances.* Retrieved from sciencemag website: https://advances.sciencemag.org/content/early/2020/08/20/sciadv.abc5961

54. Lally, P. et al. (2020, July 16). How are habits formed: Modelling habit formation in the real world. *European Journal of Social Psychology.* Retrieved from wiley website: https://onlinelibrary.wiley.com/doi/abs/10.1002/ejsp.674

55. Brookings. (2020, April 6). *Telecommuting will likely continue long after the pandemic.* Retrieved September 4, 2020 from brookings website: https://www.brookings.edu/blog/up-front/2020/04/06/telecommuting-will-likely-continue-long-after-the-pandemic/

56. The Business Times. (2020, August 26). *Share of accounting tasks done by machines to surge by 80%: study.* Retrieved September 4, 2020 from The Business Times website: https://www.businesstimes.com.sg/banking-finance/share-of-accounting-tasks-done-by-machines-to-surge-by-80-study

57. The Economist. (2020, July 4). *The pandemic is giving unmanned deliveries a fillip.* Retrieved September 4, 2020 from The Economist website: https://www.economist.com/business/2020/07/04/the-pandemic-is-giving-unmanned-deliveries-a-fillip

58. Bloomberg. (2020, May 20). *World's Greenest Coronavirus Recovery Package Arriving in Europe.* Retrieved September 4, 2020 from Bloomberg website: https://www.bloomberg.com/news/articles/2020-05-20/eu-to-unveil-world-s-greenest-virus-recovery-package

59. University of Oxford. (2020). *Oxford COVID-19 Government Response Tracker.* Retrieved September 3, 2020 from BSG website: https://www.bsg.ox.ac.uk/research/research-projects/coronavirus-government-response-tracker

60. TODAY. (2020, March 8). *10 countries account for 80% of Africa COVID-19 testing - Africa CDC.* Retrieved September 3, 2020 from TODAYonline website: https://www.todayonline.com/world/10-countries-account-80-africa-covid-19-testing-africa-cdc

61. TODAY. (2020, March 8). Exclusive: *Vaccine alliance eyes range of prices for COVID shots, says $40 would be maximum.* Retrieved September 3, 2020 from TODAYonline website: https://www.todayonline.com/world/exclusive-vaccine-alliance-eyes-range-prices-COVID-shots-says-40-would-be-maximum

62. Asian Development Bank. (2020). *Multimedia Features| Asian Development Bank.* Retrieved September 3, 2020, from ADB website: https://www.adb.org/news/multimedia

63. The World Bank. (2020). *World Bank Open Data.* Retrieved September 4, 2020 from The World Bank website: https://data.worldbank.org/

64. Our World in Data. (2020). *Our World in Data.* Retrieved September 4, 2020 from Our World in Data website: https://ourworldindata.org/

65. World Health Organization. (2020). *Coronavirus disease (COVID-19), Situation Report – 194.* Retrieved September 4, 2020, from WHO website: https://www.who.int/docs/default-source/coronaviruse/situation-reports/20200801-covid-19-sitrep-194.pdf?sfvrsn=401287f3_2

66. The Regulatory Review. (2020, June 9). *Lessons from New Zealand's COVID-19 Success.* Retrieved September 4, 2020 from The Regulatory Review website: https://www.theregreview.org/2020/06/09/parker-lessons-new-zealand-COVID-19-success/

67. CNN. (2020, April 27). *April 27 coronavirus news.* Retrieved September 4, 2020 from CNN website: https://edition.cnn.com/world/live-news/coronavirus-pandemic-04-27-20-intl/h_a1fbf0be9a0242e71cc8e155261ce07b

68. Nikkei Asian Review. (2020, June 18). *New Zealand GDP takes its biggest slide in three decades.* Retrieved September 4, 2020, from NAR website: https://asia.nikkei.com/Economy/New-Zealand-GDP-takes-its-biggest-slide-in-three-decades

69. INTHEBLACK. (2020, May 15). *New Zealand Budget highlights 'Rebuilding Together'.* Retrieved September 4, 2020, from INTHEBLACK website: https://www.intheblack.com/articles/2020/05/15/new-zealand-budget-highlights-rebuilding-together

70. Time. (2020, April 20). *Why Singapore, Once a Model for Coronavirus Response, Lost Control of Its Outbreak.* Retrieved September 4, 2020, from Time website: https://time.com/5824039/singapore-outbreak-migrant-workers/

71. Ministry of Health. (2020, April 28). *28 April 2020 Daily Report on COVID-19* [Press release]. Retrieved from MOH website: https://www.moh.gov.sg/docs/librariesprovider5/2019-ncov/situation-report---28-apr-2020.pdf

72. Reuters. (2020, May 22). *How migrant worker outbreaks supercharged coronavirus spread in Singapore.* Retrieved September 4, 2020 from Reuters website: https://www.reuters.com/article/us-health-coronavirus-singapore-clusters/how-migrant-worker-outbreaks-supercharged-coronavirus-spread-in-singapore-idUSKBN22Y29U

73. Foreign Policy. (2020, April 21). *Singapore's Coronavirus Success Story Hits a Snag.* Retrieved September 4, 2020, from Foreign Policy website: https://foreignpolicy.com/2020/04/21/singapore-coronavirus-response-snag/

74. Business Insider. (2020, June 4). *China hid crucial information about the coronavirus early on. Here's what was really happening while Chinese authorities stayed silent.* Retrieved September 4, 2020 from Business Insider website: https://www.businessinsider.com/china-coronavirus-hid-information-delayed-response-who-2020-6#the-who-first-learned-about-the-virus-through-an-open-source-platform-on-december-31-the-ap-reported-4

75. S&P Global Ratings. (2020, April 16). *China Banks After COVID-19: Big Get Bigger, Weak Get Weaker.* Retrieved September 4, 2020 from spglobal website: https://www.spglobal.com/ratings/en/research/articles/200416-china-banks-after-COVID-19-big-get-bigger-weak-get-weaker-11439811

76. World Economic Forum. (2020, April 27). *Managing COVID-19: How the pandemic disrupts global value chains.* Retrieved September 4, 2020 from the World Economic Forum website: https://www.weforum.org/agenda/2020/04/COVID-19-pandemic-disrupts-global-value-chains/

77. The Straits Times. (2020, July 21). *Covid-19 cases cross 2,000 mark in Hong Kong, crucial week for public health system.* Retrieved September 4, 2020 from The Straits Times website: https://www.straitstimes.com/asia/east-asia/COVID-19-cases-cross-2000-mark-in-hong-kong-crucial-week-for-public-health-system

78. CNN. (2020, March 13). *What the US can learn from Singapore's coronavirus strategy.* Retrieved September 4, 2020 from CNN website: https://edition.cnn.com/2020/03/13/opinions/coronavirus-what-the-us-can-learn-from-singapore-hk-bociurkiw/index.html

79. South China Morning Post (2020, February 3). *Coronavirus: Hong Kong's economy slumps 8.9 per cent in worst contraction on record.* Retrieved September 4, 2020, from SCMP website: https://www.scmp.com/news/hong-kong/hong-kong-economy/article/3082769/coronavirus-hong-kongs-economy-slumps-89-cent

80. Ibid.

81. Macrotrends. (n.d.). *Hong Kong Trade to GDP Ratio 1960-2020.* Retrieved from Macrotrends website: https://www.macrotrends.net/countries/HKG/hong-kong/trade-gdp-ratio

82. South China Morning Post (2020, February 3). *Coronavirus: Hong Kong's economy slumps 8.9 per cent in worst contraction on record.* Retrieved September 4, 2020, from SCMP website: https://www.scmp.com/news/hong-kong/hong-kong-economy/article/3082769/coronavirus-hong-kongs-economy-slumps-89-cent

83. International Monetary Fund. (2020). *POLICY RESPONSES TO COVID-19.* Retrieved September 4, 2020 from the IMF website: https://www.imf.org/en/Topics/imf-and-COVID19/Policy-Responses-to-COVID-19

84. World Health Organization. (2020). *Sweden: WHO Coronavirus Disease (COVID-19) dashboard.* Retrieved September 4, 2020, from the WHO website: https://COVID19.who.int/region/euro/country/se/

85. The Washington Post. (2020, June 5). *Scientist behind Sweden's covid-19 strategy suggests it allowed too many deaths.* Retrieved September 4, 2020, from The Washington Post website: https://www.washingtonpost.com/world/europe/sweden-epidemiologist-anders-tegnell/2020/06/03/063b20e4-a5a0-11ea-b619-3f9133bbb482_story.html

86. Bloomberg. (2019, September 26). *Swedish Confidence Drops for a Fifth Month on Consumer Gloom.* Retrieved September 4, 2020, from Bloomberg website: https://www.bloomberg.com/news/articles/2019-09-26/swedish-confidence-declines-for-fifth-month-on-consumer-gloom

87. FocusEconomics. (2020, September 1). *Sweden Economy – GDP, Inflation and Interest Rate.* Retrieved September 4, 2020, from FocusEconomics website: https://www.focus-economics.com/countries/sweden

88. Government Offices of Sweden. (2020, June 18). *Some signs of recovery in the economy – but situation still very serious* [Press release]. Retrieved from Government Offices of Sweden website: https://www.government.se/press-releases/2020/06/some-signs-of-recovery-in-the-economy--but-situation-still-very-serious/

89. Financial Times. (2020, May 10). *Sweden unlikely to feel economic benefit of no-lockdown approach.* Retrieved September 4, 2020 from FT website: https://www.ft.com/content/93105160-dcb4-4721-9e58-a7b262cd4b6e

90. CNBC. (2020, April 30). *Sweden had no lockdown but its economy is expected to suffer just as badly as its European neighbors.* Retrieved September 4, 2020, from CNBC website: https://www.cnbc.com/2020/04/30/coronavirus-sweden-economy-to-contract-as-severely-as-the-rest-of-europe.html

91. CNBC. (2020, April 30). *WHO says record number of coronavirus cases isn't just because of more testing.* Retrieved September 4, 2020, from CNBC website: https://www.cnbc.com/2020/06/22/who-says-record-coronavirus-numbers-is-not-just-because-of-more-testing.html

92. Our World in Data (2020). *COVID-19 Deaths.* Retrieved September 4, 2020 from Our World in Data website: https://ourworldindata.org/covid-deaths

93. New York Times. (2020, July 22). *Spike in U.S. Cases Far Outpaces Testing Expansion.* Retrieved September 4, 2020 from the New York Times website: https://www.nytimes.com/2020/07/22/world/coronavirus-covid-19.html

94. Financial Times. (2020, April 29). *How coronavirus broke America's healthcare system.* Retrieved September 4, 2020 from FT website: https://www.ft.com/content/3bbb4f7c-890e-11ea-a01c-a28a3e3fbd33

95. John Hopkins Coronavirus Research Center. (September 3, 2020). *Mortality Analysis.* Retrieved September 4, 2020 from JHU website: https://coronavirus.jhu.edu/data/mortality

96. Our World in Data (2020). *COVID-19 Deaths.* Retrieved September 4, 2020, from Our World in Data website: https://ourworldindata.org/covid-deaths

97. The World Bank. (2020, June). *Global Economic Prospects.* Retrieved September 4, 2020, from the World Bank website: https://www.worldbank.org/en/publication/global-economic-prospects

98. The Washington Post. (2020, March 26). *Senate approves $2.2 trillion coronavirus bill aimed at slowing economic free fall.* Retrieved September 4, 2020, from The Washington Post website: https://www.washingtonpost.com/business/2020/03/25/trump-senate-coronavirus-economic-stimulus-2-trillion/

99. Economic Policy Institute. (2020, June 26). *Cutting off the $600 boost to unemployment benefits would be both cruel and bad economics.* Retrieved September 4, 2020 from EPI website: https://www.epi.org/blog/cutting-off-the-600-boost-to-unemployment-benefits-would-be-both-cruel-and-bad-economics-new-personal-income-data-show-just-how-steep-the-coming-fiscal-cliff-will-be/

100. The Washington Post. (2020, July 15). *Canada's coronavirus performance hasn't been perfect. But it's done far better than the U.S.* Retrieved September 4, 2020, from The Washington Post website: https://www.washingtonpost.com/business/2020/03/25/trump-senate-coronavirus-economic-stimulus-2-trillion/

101. Kaiser Family Foundation. (2020, December 13). *Key Facts about the Uninsured Population.* Retrieved September 4, 2020 from KFF website: https://www.kff.org/uninsured/issue-brief/key-facts-about-the-uninsured-population/

102. Open Democracy. (2020, April 11). *Why is the Canadian healthcare system faring better than its counterpart in the US?*. Retrieved September 4, 2020 from opendemocracy website: https://www.opendemocracy.net/en/oureconomy/why-canadian-healthcare-system-faring-better-its-counterpart-us/

103. The Conversation. (2020, July 22). *How Canada compares to other countries on COVID-19 cases and deaths.* Retrieved September 4, 2020 from The Conversation website: https://theconversation.com/how-canada-compares-to-other-countries-on-COVID-19-cases-and-deaths-142632

104. Global News. (2020, May 29). *Canadian GDP dropped 8% in the first quarter, StatCan says.* Retrieved September 4, 2020 from Global News website: https://globalnews.ca/news/7001702/canadian-gdp-dropped-8-in-the-first-quarter-statcan-says/

105. Global News. (2020, June 5). *Canada's unemployment rate reaches record 13.7%.* Retrieved September 4, 2020 from Global News website: https://globalnews.ca/news/7029601/canada-may-unemployment-rate/

106. International Monetary Fund. (2020). *POLICY RESPONSES TO COVID-19.* Retrieved September 4, 2020 from the IMF website: https://www.imf.org/en/Topics/imf-and-COVID19/Policy-Responses-to-COVID-19

107. Bartsch, S. M. et al. (2020, July 15). Vaccine Efficacy Needed for a COVID-19 Coronavirus Vaccine to Prevent or Stop an Epidemic as the Sole Intervention. *American Journal of Preventive Medicine.* Retrieved from AJPM website: https://www.ajpmonline.org/article/S0749-3797(20)30284-1/fulltext

108. The Straits Times. (2020, August 16). *44% of people in Singapore tired of rules to limit Covid-19 spread: Survey.* Retrieved September 4, 2020 from The Straits Times website: https://www.straitstimes.com/singapore/health/44-of-people-here-tired-of-rules-to-limit-virus-spread-survey

109. Scientific American. (2020, July 16). *Second Coronavirus Strain May Be More Infectious—but Some Scientists Are Skeptical.* Retrieved September 4, 2020 from Scientific American website: https://www.scientificamerican.com/article/second-coronavirus-strain-may-be-more-infectious-but-some-scientists-are-skeptical/

110. Live Science. (2020, July 10). *A new coronavirus mutation is taking over the world. Here's what that means.* Retrieved September 4, 2020, from Live Science website: https://www.livescience.com/new-coronavirus-mutation-explained.html

111. MIT Technology Review. (2020, June 15). *What's a coronavirus superspreader?*. Retrieved September 4, 2020, from MIT Technology Review website: https://www.technologyreview.com/2020/06/15/1003576/whats-a-coronavirus-superspreader/

112. The Washington Post. (2020, July 2). *This coronavirus mutation has taken over the world. Scientists are trying to understand why.* Retrieved September 4, 2020, from The Washington Post website: https://www.washingtonpost.com/science/2020/06/29/coronavirus-mutation-science

113. World Economic Forum. (2020, August 28). *80% of economists see a chance of a double-dip recession, survey finds.* Retrieved September 4, 2020 from the World Economic Forum website: https://www.weforum.org/agenda/2020/08/80-of-economists-see-a-chance-of-a-double-dip-recession-survey-finds

114. BBC. (2020, July 7). *Coronavirus: Trump moves to pull US out of World Health Organization.* Retrieved September 4, 2020 from BBC website: https://www.bbc.com/news/world-us-canada-53327906

115. United Nations. (2020, April 12). *COVID-19: Major airlift operation, part of wider UN supply chain effort, reaches 'most vulnerable' African nations.* Retrieved September 4, 2020 from UN website: https://news.un.org/en/story/2020/04/1061662

116. International Monetary Fund. (2020, September). *COVID-19 Financial Assistance and Debt Service Relief.* Retrieved September 4, 2020 from the IMF website: https://www.imf.org/en/Topics/imf-and-COVID19/COVID-Lending-Tracker

117. The Diplomat. (2020, March 23). *Can a Global Pandemic Resuscitate SAARC?.* Retrieved September 4, 2020 from The Diplomat website: https://thediplomat.com/2020/03/can-a-global-pandemic-resuscitate-saarc/

118. New York Times. (2020, April 23). *Vast Federal Aid Has Capped Rise in Poverty, Studies Find.* Retrieved September 4, 2020 from the New York Times website: https://www.nytimes.com/2020/06/21/us/politics/coronavirus-poverty.html

119. The Straits Times. (2020, June 15). *Singapore's total employment sees biggest decline ever in first quarter.* Retrieved September 4, 2020 from The Straits Times website: https://www.straitstimes.com/singapore/manpower/singapores-total-employment-sees-biggest-decline-ever-in-first-quarter

120. Pew Research Center. (2020, June 11). *Unemployment rose higher in three months of COVID-19 than it did in two years of the Great Recession.* Retrieved September 4, 2020 from Pew Research Center website: https://www.pewresearch.org/fact-tank/2020/06/11/unemployment-rose-higher-in-three-months-of-COVID-19-than-it-did-in-two-years-of-the-great-recession/

121. The Washington Post. (2020, July 2). *Over 10 million Americans applied for unemployment benefits in March as economy collapsed.* Retrieved September 4, 2020, from The Washington Post website: https://www.washingtonpost.com/business/2020/04/02/jobless-march-coronavirus/

122. McKinsey & Company. (2020, April 2). *Lives and livelihoods: Assessing the near-term impact of COVID-19 on US workers.* Retrieved September 4, 2020 from Mckinsey website: https://www.mckinsey.com/industries/public-and-social-sector/our-insights/lives-and-livelihoods-assessing-the-near-term-impact-of-covid-19-on-us-workers

123. Chinazzi, M. et al. (2020, April 24). *The effect of travel restrictions on the spread of the 2019 novel coronavirus (COVID-19) outbreak. Science.* Retrieved from sciencemag website: https://science.sciencemag.org/content/368/6489/395

124. CNA. (2020, August 22). *WHO chief hopes coronavirus pandemic will last less than two years.* Retrieved September 4, 2020, from CNA website: https://www.channelnewsasia.com/news/world/covid-19-who-hopes-over-two-years-tedros-13042962

125. https://papers.ssrn.com/sol3/papers.cfm?abstract_id=3605549

126. Kucharski, A. J. et al. (2020, June 16). Effectiveness of isolation, testing, contact tracing, and physical distancing on reducing transmission of SARS-CoV-2 in different settings: a mathematical modelling study. *Lancet.* Retrieved from Lancet website: https://www.thelancet.com/journals/laninf/article/PIIS1473-3099(20)30457-6/fulltext#

127. Chu, D. K. (2020, June 1). Physical distancing, face masks, and eye protection to prevent person-to-person transmission of SARS-CoV-2 and COVID-19: a systematic review and meta-analysis. *Lancet.* Retrieved from Lancet website: https://www.thelancet.com/journals/lancet/article/PIIS0140-6736(20)31142-9/fulltext

128. Nava, S. & Hill, N. (2009, July 16). Non-invasive ventilation in acute respiratory failure. *Lancet.* Retrieved from NCBI website: https://www.ncbi.nlm.nih.gov/pmc/articles/PMC7138083

129. Ye, Q. et al. (2020, June). The pathogenesis and treatment of the `Cytokine Storm' in COVID-19. *J Infect.* Retrieved from NCBI website: https://www.ncbi.nlm.nih.gov/pmc/articles/PMC7194613/

130. Peek, G. J. et al. (2009, October 17) Efficacy and economic assessment of conventional ventilatory support versus extracorporeal membrane oxygenation for severe adult respiratory failure (CESAR): a multicentre randomised controlled trial. *Lancet.* Retrieved from NCBI website: https://pubmed.ncbi.nlm.nih.gov/19762075/

131. University of Oxford. (2020). *Oxford COVID-19 Government Response Tracker.* Retrieved September 4, 2020 from BSG website: https://www.bsg.ox.ac.uk/research/research-projects/coronavirus-government-response-tracker

ACKNOWLEDGEMENTS

This book is the work of many minds and hands. It would not even have been possible, much less reached the quality it has, without the contributions of Ms Eunice Leong, Ms Annalise Foong, Ms Farah Fami, Dr Li Bo, Ms Isabel Chew, Mr Joel Tan, Ms Rachel Phang, Mr Edward Neo, Ms Yap Qi and Dr Ryan Chow. Their individual thinking, skills and collective commitment to support me in the research, analysis, writing and preparation of the book cannot be understated. This book is as much theirs as it is mine.

I would also like to thank Mr Glenn Wray and the team at Marshall Cavendish International for their professionalism and support. This is my fourth book published in association with them and I am pleased with the long-term relationship shared between writer, editor and publisher.

ABOUT THE AUTHOR

Devadas Krishnadas is the founder and CEO of Future-Moves Group, a boutique consultancy focused on public policy and corporate strategy. Prior to founding Future-Moves Group, Devadas played a leading role in developing Singapore's fiscal and social policy where he led efforts in long-term planning and strategic thinking. He served two and half years in the Singapore Infantry and ten years as a Senior Police Officer, including as Commanding Officer and a Head of Operations. He served for three years as Honourary Aide-de-Camp to the President of Singapore, the late President S. R. Nathan. He also served five years in public policy in multiple Ministries, including the Ministry of Finance.

Devadas is the author of *Sensing Singapore: Reflections in a Time of Change* (2014), *FUSE: Foresight-Driven Understanding, Strategy and Execution* (2015), and *The Seduction of the Simple* (2016). His work is often cited and published in international publications on foresight and strategy.

ABOUT FUTURE-MOVES GROUP

Headquartered in Singapore, Future-Moves Group (FMG) is a strategy and management consultancy firm with a focus in public policy and has an international and multi-sectoral practice.

We develop and deploy our proprietary foresight-driven strategic management framework FUSE®, to help our clients stay ahead of the curve by understanding trends, identifying emerging risks, and anticipating change to make practical decisions and deliver tangible outcomes.

Since our beginnings in 2012, we have grown to offer expertise and bespoke services in advisory, consulting and executive training in strategy, public policy, data analysis and economic analysis.

If you are interested in engaging our services or would like to find out more about us, please visit our website at future-moves.com and reach out to us at *contactus@future-moves.com*